Instructor's Annotated Edition

THE WORLD OF WORDS

Instructor's Annotated Edition

THE World OF Words

Vocabulary for College Students

SIXTH EDITION

Margaret Ann Richek
Northeastern Illinois University

HOUGHTON MIFFLIN COMPANY Boston New York

Dedicated to the memories of my father, Seymour Richek, and my stepfather, Milton Markman; and to my husband, Perry Goldberg

Publisher: Patricia A. Coryell
Senior Sponsoring Editor: Lisa Kimball
Development Editor: Kellie Cardone
Editorial Assistant: Peter Mooney
Senior Project Editor: Margaret Park Bridges
Manufacturing Coordinator: Carrie Wagner
Senior Marketing Manager: Annamarie Rice
Marketing Associate: Laura Hemrika

Cover illustration © Jane Sterrett / Stock Illustration Source

Definitions throughout: Copyright © 2000 by Houghton Mifflin Company. Reproduced by permission from *The American Heritage Dictionary of the English Language,* Fourth Edition.

Art and Photo Credits

Library of Congress Control Number: 2004103828

Student Text ISBN: 0-618-26178-8
Instructor's Annotated Edition ISBN: 0-618-43289-2

123456789-MP-08 07 06 05 04

Contents

Chapter 7   Word Elements: Movement   *210*

Chapter 8   Word Elements: Together and Apart   *244*

Chapter 9   Word Elements:
Numbers and Measures   *280*

Chapter 10   Word Elements: Thought and Belief   *314*

Chapter 11   Word Elements: The Body and Health   *344*

Chapter 12   Word Elements: Speech and Writing   *375*

Preface

The World of Words, Sixth Edition, will help students master strategies for becoming independent learners of vocabulary, learn specific words that will be useful in their academic work, and develop a lifelong interest in words. Through a series of carefully paced lessons, students learn several hundred words directly. In addition, they master three vocabulary development strategies: using the dictionary, using context clues, and using ancient Greek and Latin word elements.

The Sixth Edition of **The World of Words** continues to link students' general knowledge to vocabulary, covering such topics as food, popular music, sports, and the origins of names. I find that students enjoy these features and begin to see that learning vocabulary *is* relevant to their lives. While reinforcing these links, the text also supplies information that will help students acquire a firmer base for college academic work. Thus, as the book progresses, students read about science, art, and classic literature.

The word lists and the ancient Greek and Latin word elements have both been carefully selected on the basis of their appropriate level and usefulness in students' academic work. Word elements are presented so that students can easily recognize and use them in modern English words. Avoiding complex discussions of infinitive, participle, and stem forms, the text nevertheless provides the spellings of word elements most commonly found in English.

Feedback from students and instructors has enabled me to adapt this book to the needs of today's diverse student population. Instructors will find **The World of Words,** Sixth Edition, suitable for students of many cultural and linguistic backgrounds, including those for whom English is a nonnative language.

Organization

Part 1 concentrates on dictionary skills and context clues; Part 2 stresses word elements (ancient Greek and Latin prefixes, roots, and suffixes). A theme for each chapter (for instance, Words About People, Chapter 1) helps make vocabulary study more cohesive.

Each chapter of **The World of Words** contains these features:

- *Quiz Yourself* is a four-item true-false test by which students can determine their prior knowledge of four chapter words.

- *Did You Know?* presents interesting word facts to help spark students' interest in vocabulary.
- *Learning Strategy* provides instruction to help students independently learn new words.
- *Words to Learn* presents twenty-four vocabulary words with pronunciations, definitions, and example sentences. Related Words allows students to see how one base word can be adapted for use in several different ways, and usage notes help students use their new vocabulary words correctly. The Words to Learn are divided into two parts containing twelve words each. Word facts, etymologies, and trivia quizzes provide a context for the words and help students internalize the definitions.
- *Exercises* follow each set of Words to Learn; additional exercises are included at the end of each chapter. A wide variety of carefully scaffolded exercises, including Matching Definitions, Words in Context, Related Words, Companion Words, Writing with Your Words, and Practicing Strategies, provide thorough practice in both the Words to Learn and the Learning Strategy. Enriching factual and cultural information has been extensively used in these exercises.
- A new *Making Connections* feature helps students practice vocabulary words in an extended writing format.
- The *Passage* for each chapter uses many of the chapter words in context and gives students practice reading short essays. Each passage is followed by a brief exercise and three discussion questions.
- *Idioms* present the meanings of several widely used English expressions centered around a theme related to the chapter.

New to This Edition

Having used this text for twenty-one years at Northeastern Illinois University and having reviewed constructive comments on the Fifth Edition from users across the country, I have been able to refine those features students found most useful and add the following new features to the Sixth Edition:

- Review and revision of the word list to reflect changes in word frequency and use.
- A new feature, entitled *Making Connections*, which facilitates use of chapter words in an extended writing format.
- Two additional pieces of art for each chapter to help students visualize and extend word meanings. Cartoons are new to this edition.
- Revision and updating of contents to reflect contemporary developments. Changes include substantially revised example sentences, refreshed exercises, and four new passages.

- A student website containing additional exercises to reinforce learning.

Support for Instructors

An *Instructor's Annotated Edition* provides answers to exercises. In addition, an *Instructor's Resource Manual with Test Bank* contains teaching suggestions, supplementary exercises, and a complete test bank. Finally there is a self-correcting website for students that includes supplementary exercises. To obtain these resources, contact your local representative at *http://college.hmco.com/instructors*, call Faculty Services at 800-733-1717 ext. 4015, or fax your request to 800-733-1810. The student website may be accessed at *http://college.hmco/devenglish/students/dev_reading.html*.

Acknowledgments

I wish to thank the many people who have contributed ideas, inspiration, and support for this book. These include the editorial staff of Houghton Mifflin Company. Editor Ann Marie Radaskiewicz provided invaluable assistance in shaping the manuscript. Nancy Benjamin of Books By Design provided outstanding editorial and design aid. B. J. Carrick of Books By Design did an extremely effective job of selecting art. Gabrielle Naue, Rachel Hogan, and Mary Carvlin provided superb manuscript preparation and editorial assistance. Thanks are also due to Perry Goldberg, Sandra Goldberg, Irene Nowicki, Stephen Richek, Jean Richek Markman, Milton Markman, Anne Feuerstein, Jai Kim, Marina Ulanovskaya, Julia Ulanovskaya, Phyllis Glorioso, Eleanor Zeff, Daniel Zeff, Iris Cosnow, Kate Feinstein, David Lang, Neil Adelman, and Bill Zwecker. Special acknowledgment is reserved for Sophia Ruiz, Rocio Ruiz, Semir Mohammed, William Mojica, and Viem Nguyen, whose writing exercises appear in the review sections. The following reviewers helped to formulate the shape and direction of the manuscript: Dr. Barbara Boyd of California State University, Northridge; Patricia Brennecke of Massachusetts Institute of Technology; Thomas Butler of Paradise Valley Community College; Lisa Redson Cook of Laney College; and Clifford M. Davis of Cerro Coso Community College.

P A R T

1

Dictionary Skills and Context Clues

Did you know that the size of your vocabulary predicts how well you will do in school? This book will improve your vocabulary so that you become a better reader, writer, listener, and speaker. As you master more words, you will improve your performance in all subjects—from astronomy to electronics to marketing to zoology. A larger vocabulary will also help you make a good impression in a job interview. People judge others by the way they communicate, and vocabulary is a key to communication.

This book will help you use words more precisely and vividly. Instead of describing a *friendly* gathering, you will be able to distinguish between a *convivial* party and an *amicable* meeting. Instead of saying that someone gave money to a charity, you may call that person a *philanthropist* or a *benefactor*. Your reading comprehension will also improve when you know more words.

Working through this book will help your vocabulary in two ways. First, you will learn the words presented in each chapter. Second, you will master learning strategies that enable you to learn words on your own. Chapters 1 through 4 will teach you the strategies of using the dictionary and of understanding context clues. In Chapters 5 through 12, you will learn how to use word elements such as prefixes, roots, and suffixes. Each chapter contains several sections:

Quiz Yourself allows you to check your knowledge of chapter words before you study.
Did You Know? highlights interesting facts about English words.
Learning Strategy provides methods that will enable you to learn words independently.

Words to Learn presents twenty-four words that appear frequently in college texts, books, magazines, and newspapers. Every Words to Learn section is divided into two parts containing twelve words each.

The *Exercises* give you practice with the words and strategies. One set of exercises follows the first part of the Words to Learn section, another set follows the second part, and a final set appears at the end of the chapter. A new "Making Connections" exercise helps you use writing to connect the words you have learned to your own life.

The *Passage* presents a reading selection that includes several "Words to Learn" from the chapter. It is followed by an exercise that tests your understanding of words used in context and discussion questions that check your comprehension of the passage.

Finally, the *English Idioms* section discusses several phrases that have special meanings.

Parts of Speech

Parts of speech are essential to the definition and use of words. In order to master the vocabulary words in this book, you will need to know the part of speech for each word. In addition, if you understand how words can be changed to form different parts of speech, you can expand your vocabulary by using one word in many different ways.

Nouns, adjectives, verbs, and adverbs are presented in this book.

A **noun** is a person, place, thing, or idea.

> *Paul* is a *student.*
> *San Diego* is a beautiful *city.*
> *Snow* covered the *road.*
> *Liberty* and *justice* are precious.

An **adjective** describes, or modifies, a noun.

> The *busy* mother cleaned the kitchen. (*Busy* modifies *mother.*)
> The dog was *wet.* (*Wet* modifies *dog.*)

A **verb** expresses an action or a state of being.

> I *study* vocabulary.
> The class *is* interesting.

Verbs may be divided into two categories: transitive and intransitive. A **transitive verb** has an action that is directed toward someone or something. A transitive verb cannot stand alone in a sentence; it needs a direct object to make the sentence complete. In contrast, an **intransitive verb** does not need a direct object.

> Transitive verb: Delphine *bought* a computer. (*Computer* is the direct object.)

> Intransitive verb: The skunk *smelled*. (No direct object is needed.)

Verbs may express past, future, or present action. Past-tense verbs are usually formed by adding the ending *-ed*.

> Armando *rented* an apartment last year.

Not all verbs are regular. For example, the past tense form of the verb *ride* is actually *rode*.

The future tense of a verb is often expressed through the use of the helping verb *will*. This is often shortened to *'ll*.

> I *will shop* in the mall tomorrow. *I'll* shop tomorrow

When we use the present tense, we add an *s* to third-person singular verbs, that is, verbs that have any one person as the subject except *I* or *you*. (Examples of subjects that require third-person singular verbs are *she, Joe,* and *the door.*)

> The musician *plays* the piano and the violin.

> Tucson *grows* rapidly each year.

We often express actions that started in the past and are still taking place by using a form of the helping verb *to be* and adding *-ing* to the end of the main verb. This is called the present progressive tense, and the *-ing* form is called a **present participle.**

> I *am waiting* for a reply to my e-mail.

> The sun *is shining*.

The *-ing* and *-ed* forms of verbs are also used to form other parts of speech. The *-ing* forms of verbs are called **gerunds** when they are used as nouns.

> *Smoking* is forbidden in the restaurant.

> Ashanti went *dancing* at the club.

The *-ing* and *-ed* forms of verbs are called **participles** when they are used as adjectives.

> The *insulting* man made others feel terrible. (In this sentence, the man insults other people.)

> The *insulted* man felt terrible. (In this sentence, other people insult the man.)

An **adverb** modifies a verb, an adjective, or another adverb. Many adverbs end in *-ly*.

The athlete ran *quickly*. (*Quickly* modifies *ran*, a verb.)

We admired the *brightly* colored mural. (*Brightly* modifies *colored*, an adjective.)

The disease spread *more rapidly* than we had expected. (*More*, an adverb, modifies *rapidly*, another adverb. *Rapidly*, in turn, modifies *spread*, a verb.)

In addition to nouns, adjectives, verbs, and adverbs, parts of speech include pronouns, conjunctions, interjections, and prepositions.

A **pronoun** replaces a noun.

Wallace locked the door when *he* left.

We will meet *her* at the airport.

A **conjunction** connects words, phrases, or clauses.

Andrew ate bean sprouts *and* tofu.

Will Mercedes go out with friends, *or* will she stay at home?

An **interjection** is an exclamatory word that may appear by itself or in a sentence.

Great!

Oh, look at that!

A **preposition** joins a noun or pronoun with another word in a sentence. Prepositions appear at the beginning of prepositional phrases, which usually function as adjectives and adverbs.

I have a love *of* books.

In this sentence, the preposition *of* joins the noun *books* to another noun in the sentence, *love. Of* is the first word in the prepositional phrase *of books*. The entire prepositional phrase functions as an adjective because it modifies the noun *love*.

This sentence shows a prepositional phrase used as an adverb:

Carmen ran *across* the street.

Here, the preposition *across* connects the noun *street* to the verb *ran*. The prepositional phrase *across the street* functions as an adverb that modifies the verb *ran*.

Words and phrases commonly used as prepositions include *about, above, according to, across, after, against, before, below, beside, by, during, for, from, in, inside, into, like, of, off, on, out, over, through, to, toward, under, until, up,* and *with*.

It is often difficult to know which preposition to use in a sentence. Mastery of these small words comes only with practice. Therefore, one exercise in this book, "Companion Words," provides practice in using prepositions with the words you will learn.

Word Endings and Parts of Speech

One word can often be changed to form several different related words. These related words have similar meanings, but they usually function as different parts of speech. For example, as shown in the illustration, the word *nation* (a noun) can form *national* (an adjective), *nationally* (an adverb), *nationalize* (a verb), and *nationality* (another noun).

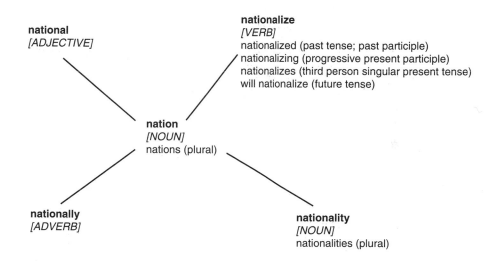

national
[ADJECTIVE]

nationalize
[VERB]
nationalized (past tense; past participle)
nationalizing (progressive present participle)
nationalizes (third person singular present tense)
will nationalize (future tense)

nation
[NOUN]
nations (plural)

nationally
[ADVERB]

nationality
[NOUN]
nationalities (plural)

Related words are formed by adding *suffixes*—word parts attached to the ends of words—to change the part of speech. The following table shows a list of suffixes and examples of words they form.

Suffix	*Base word*	*Suffixed word*
Suffixes that form nouns		
-ance, -ancy	insure, truant	insurance, truancy
-ence	differ	difference
-er	teach	teacher
-ion, -tion	confuse, compete	confusion, competition
-ism	real	realism
-ity	reliable	reliability
-ment	require	requirement
-ness	happy	happiness
-ure	fail	failure
Suffixes that form adjectives		
-able, -ible	wash, reverse	washable, reversible
-al	season	seasonal

-ful	watch	watchful
-ic	angel	angelic
-ous, -ious	fame, space	famous, spacious
-ive	react	reactive
-y	stick	sticky

Suffixes that form verbs

-ate	valid	validate
-ify	simple	simplify
-ize	idol	idolize

Suffix that forms adverbs

| -ly | rapid | rapidly |

Some suffixes change the syllable of the word that we stress in speech. A dark accent mark (′) shows which syllable of a word receives the main stress. A light accent mark (′) shows that another syllable is also stressed, but not as strongly as the syllable with the darker accent mark. The following examples show the pronunciation changes in a word when these suffixes are added.

When -*ic* or -*tic* is added to a word, the stress moves to the syllable before the -*ic* or -*tic*. The stress remains on the syllable before the -*ic* or -*tic*, even if another suffix is added.

| cha′ os | cha′ ot′ ic | cha′ ot′ i cal ly |
| dip′ lo mat | dip′ lo mat′ ic | dip′ lo mat′ i cal ly |

When -*ion* or -*tion* is added to a word, the main stress falls on the syllable before the suffix. Sometimes an *a* is added before the -*ion* or -*tion*. Note the light and heavy stresses in these words.

| pro hib′ it | pro′ hi bi′ tion | |
| con demn′ | con′ dem na′ tion | (Note the added *a*.) |

When -*ity* is added to a word, the main stress again falls on the syllable before the suffix.

| gul′ li ble | gul′ li bil′ i ty |
| am′ i ca ble | am′ i ca bil′ i ty |

When you learn a new word, you will often be able to form a number of related words simply by adding suffixes. The related words formed in this way are listed with many of the words you will be studying.

As you work through this book, refer to the table of suffixes and the explanation of pronunciation changes in this introduction when you meet words ending in -*ic*, -*ion*, (-*tion*), and -*ity*.

1

Words About People

The earth is home to more than six billion people, and each of us is different in personality, lifestyle, and interests. It is no wonder that we have so many words to describe people! The words in this chapter will expand your ability to describe yourself and others. You can use these words in school, on the job, in your social life, and at home.

Chapter Strategy: Using the Dictionary

Chapter Words:

Part 1

adroit	capricious	gullible
aficionado	cosmopolitan	hypocritical
altruistic	disdain	intrepid
ascetic	fraternal	venerable

Part 2

affluent	candid	gauche
alien	dogmatic	novice
amicable	exuberant	renegade
astute	frugal	stoic

Quiz Yourself

To check your knowledge of some chapter words before you begin to study, identify these statements as true or false. Answers are on page 409.

Altruistic people are selfish.	True	False
A **novice** has lots of experience.	True	False
A **frugal** person likes to save money.	True	False
An **intrepid** person is brave.	True	False

You will learn the answers as you study this chapter.

Did You Know?

What's in a Name?

Did you know that many first names have meanings? Parents often research names before they select one for their baby. Here are the names most commonly chosen in the United States in 2002. Each is listed with its meaning.

For Boys

1. Jacob—replacer
2. Michael—God-like
3. Joshua—God saves us
4. Matthew—God's gift
5. Ethan—firm
6. Joseph—God's addition
7. Andrew—manly
8. Christopher—carrier of Christ
9. Daniel—God is judge
10. Nicholas—victory of the people

For Girls

1. Emily—hard-working, striving
2. Madison—an English last name
3. Hannah—blessed by God
4. Emma—nurse
5. Alexis—helper of mankind
6. Ashley—ash tree grove
7. Abigail—my father is joy
8. Sarah—princess
9. Samantha—God heard us
10. Olivia—symbol of peace

You may have noticed some differences between the boys' and girls' lists. Six of the frequently chosen boys' names have roots in religion; in contrast, popular girls' names tend to have broader origins. Popular girls' names also seem to change more frequently than boys' names. Only four of the ten most popular names for girls in 2002 were on the list for the 1990s. In contrast, nine of the ten most popular boys' names for the 1990s appear on the 2002 list.

Names come from many different languages. Several, including Jacob, Michael, Joshua, Abigail, and Hannah, come from Hebrew. Alexis and Nicholas come from Ancient Greek. Olivia comes from Latin, the language of the ancient Romans. Madison originated as an English last name. Over the years, it has changed into a popular first name for girls.

Common names have many associations. The name *George*, for example, brings to mind a variety of people and places.

1. *Saint George*, the patron saint of England, probably lived around the year 300. According to legend, an evil dragon threatened to destroy a town with its poisonous breath unless it was given a princess. George rescued the town, and the princess, by slaying the dragon. In return for his services, he asked the townspeople to convert to Christianity. Saint George is said to have baptized 15,000 people.

2. England has had six kings named *George*. George I, who ruled from 1714 to 1727, came from Germany and spoke no English.

3. *Georgia*, a state in the United States, was named for the English king George II. It was founded as a colony where poor people who had been thrown in prison for their debts could start a new life.

4. *Georgia* is also a country near Russia. It is famous for claims that Georgians have often lived to the age of 120!

5. Did you think all Georges were male? *George Sand* was the pen name of Amandine Lucie Aurore Dudevant, a nineteenth-century French novelist. She took a man's name so that the public would accept her work. She also adopted the free lifestyle generally reserved for men; she is famous for her many love affairs.

Learning Strategy

Using the Dictionary

The Learning Strategies presented in this book will teach you how to figure out the meanings of unknown words on your own. This book presents about 500 words that you will learn directly from the Words to Learn sections. However, by using techniques from the Learning Strategy sections, you will be able to expand your vocabulary to include thousands of other words.

This chapter's Learning Strategy concentrates on the effective use of the dictionary. The dictionary is the best source for finding the precise meaning of a word.

There are many different types of dictionaries. The smallest is the pocket or abridged dictionary, usually a paperback, which gives short definitions. The college-level dictionary includes just enough detail for most college students. The most complete kind is the unabridged dictionary, which includes many unusual words, long definitions, and full word histories. You may have used an unabridged dictionary in the library or referred to an unabridged dictionary on CD-ROM or on the Internet. Some popular dictionary sites are **www.dictionary.com** and **www.onelook.com**. Dictionaries for people who are not native speakers of English include *The American Heritage English as a Second Language Dictionary.*

Because a dictionary gives a considerable amount of information in a small space, learning to use this important tool takes practice. A skillful dictionary user can find not only the meaning of a word but also its pronunciation, its history, and other words related to it.

Here is an entry from a college-level dictionary, the *American Heritage Dictionary, Fourth College Edition.* Each part is labeled.

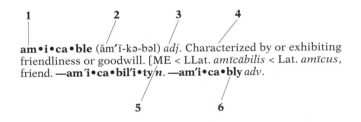

A standard dictionary entry contains the following parts:

1. **The word.** The entry word is printed in boldface type and divided into syllables.

2. **The pronunciation.** A key in the border of each fully opened page of a dictionary shows you how to interpret the pronunciation symbols. (You can also find a key to these symbols on the inside front cover of this textbook.) The key gives a common word that contains the sound represented by each symbol. For example, the symbol ă (which represents the first sound in *amicable*) should be pronounced like the sound of *a* in the word *păt.*

   An accent mark (´) follows the syllable that should be stressed when you pronounce a word. In *amicable*, only the first syllable is stressed. If two syllables have accent marks, the syllable with the darker accent mark receives more stress.

   At times, an entry will give two pronunciations for a word. The pronunciation that appears first is the preferred one.

3. **The part of speech.** The parts of speech you will most often encounter are commonly abbreviated as follows.

n.—noun   *tr. v.*—transitive verb
adj.—adjective   *intr. v.*—intransitive verb
adv.—adverb

These parts of speech and their functions are described in the Introduction to Part One.

4. **The definition.** Since some words have more than one definition, you must choose the one that best fits the sentence you are reading. Choosing the best definition often requires some thought. Be sure to read all of the definitions before you select one.

Dictionary definitions usually state only the precise, or *denotative,* meanings of words. But words also have implied, or *connotative,* meanings, which are suggested by the images, ideas, and emotions that we associate with them. For example, the words *skinny* and *slender* have the same denotative meaning, "thin," but they differ in connotative meaning. *Skinny* has negative associations, or connotations, and is an uncomplimentary word; *slender* has positive connotations and is a complimentary word. In the same way, *car* has a neutral connotation; *limousine* connotes an expensive, luxurious automobile; and *wreck* connotes an automobile that is worthless. Although dictionaries give some hints about connotative meanings, most information is learned simply by observing the ways people use words when they write and speak.

5. **The etymology.** In this section, the history of a word is traced to its origin. The word *amicable* comes from Middle English. Before this, the word appeared in Late Latin as *amicabilis,* which can be followed back still further to the Latin word *amicus,* meaning "friend." Note that the most modern form is listed first and the oldest form is listed last. The dictionary includes a complete list of the abbreviations for languages used in etymologies. The most common abbreviations follow.

ME—Middle English, spoken in England from 1100 to 1500 CE (AD 1100 to 1500)
OE—Old English, spoken in England before 1100 CE
Fr.—French, spoken in France today
OFr.—Old French, spoken in France from 800 to 1200 CE
Lat.—Latin, spoken by the Romans in Italy about 2,000 years ago (LLat., Late Latin, was spoken at a later time.)
Gk.—Ancient Greek, spoken in Greece about 2,500 years ago

Etymologies are usually enclosed in square brackets ([ ]) in a dictionary entry.

6. **Related words.** Sometimes several forms of a word are listed under one dictionary entry. Related words usually contain *suffixes,* or word endings that make them into different parts of speech. For instance,

under the main entry *amicable* (an adjective), a noun (*amicability*) and an adverb (*amicably*) are also listed. A discussion of suffixes and how they change the part of speech can be found in the Introduction to Part One.

The dictionary entry for *amicable* is relatively simple; however, some entries are more complex. In the entry below, the word *rule* has many definitions, which are separated according to different parts of speech.

(1) **rule** (ro͞ol) *n.* **1a.** Governing power or its possession or use; authority.   **b.** The duration of such power.   **2a.** An authoritative prescribed direction for conduct.   **b.** The body of regulations prescribed by the founder of a religious order for governing
(5) the conduct of its members.   **3.** A usual, customary, or generalized course of action or behavior.   **4.** A generalized statement that describes what is true in most or all cases.   **5.** *Mathematics* A standard method or procedure for solving a class of problems.   **6.** *Law*   **a.** A court order limited in application to a specific case.
(10) **b.** A subordinate regulation governing a particular matter.   **7.** See **ruler** 2.   **8.** *Printing* A thin metal strip of various widths and designs, used to print borders or lines, as between columns.   ❖ *v.* **ruled, rul•ing, rules** —*tr.*   **1.** To exercise control, dominion, or direction over; govern.   **2.** To dominate by powerful
(15) influence.   **3.** To decide or declare authoritatively or judicially; decree. See Syns at **decide.**   **4a.** To mark with straight parallel lines.   **b.** To mark (a straight line), as with a ruler. —*intr.*   **1.** To be in total control or command; exercise supreme authority.   **2.** To formulate and issue a decree or decision.   **3.** To prevail at
(20) a particular level or rate. **4.** *Slang* To be excellent or superior: *That new movie rules!* —***phrasal verb:*** **rule out**   **1.** To prevent; preclude.   **2.** To remove from consideration; exclude. —***idiom:*** **as a rule** In general; for the most part. [ME *reule* < OFr. < VLat. **regula* < Lat. *rēgula*, rod, principle. See **reg-** in App.] —**rul′a•ble** *adj.*

This entry shows that *rule* can be used as either a noun (line 1) or a verb (line 13). Notice, too, that it can be used as either an intransitive (—*intr.*) (line 17) verb or a transitive (—*tr.*) (line 13) verb. *Rule* has different forms when it is used as a verb. These forms are (1) *ruled,* (2) *ruling,* and (3) *rules* (line 13), and they show (1) the past participle, (2) the present participle, and (3) the third-person singular verb form.

If the entry had been for a verb of more than one syllable, these forms might have been listed without the first syllable. For example, the forms for the verb *answer* are listed in the dictionary as *-swered, -swering, -swers,* with *an-* simply left out. Entries for nouns list the spelling of irregular plural forms. Entries for adjectives like *pretty* list spellings for comparative forms, such as *prettier* and *prettiest.*

As you look at the definitions within each part-of-speech category of *rule,* you will notice three other features of the dictionary entry. First, two or more closely related definitions may be listed under one number. This is true for several definitions of *rule.* Definitions 1, 2, and 6 of *rule* as a noun each have parts a and b (lines 1–5 and 9–10). Definition 4 of *rule* as a transitive verb also has two parts (lines 16–17).

Next you may notice that a word in italics (such as *Mathematics, Law,* or *Printing*) is included in some definitions. This word, which is called a *label*, indicates that a definition is used in a special manner. For example, the fifth definition of *rule* (line 7) as a noun is used mainly in math. Definition 6 is used in law, and 8 is used in printing.

Other labels give information about the style or use of a definition. For instance, the labels *Obs.* (for *obsolete*) and *Archaic* indicate that this meaning of a word is no longer used. The label *Informal* shows that this use of the word is acceptable only in informal speech. *Nonstandard* indicates a usage that is not commonly accepted.

The fourth definition of *rule* as an intransitive verb is used as *slang* (line 20). Note that a sentence illustrates the definition: "That new movie *rules!*" In some cases, sentences written by well-known authors are quoted in dictionary entries. In other cases, a phrase is used to illustrate a meaning.

Toward the end of the entry for *rule* some phrases using the word are shown. A phrasal verb is a phrase that functions as a verb. In the entry for *rule*, the phrasal verb *rule out* is defined (line 21). An idiom is a common phrase. In this entry, the idiom *as a rule* is included (lines 22–23).

The last part of the entry shows the etymology of *rule*. It was first used in Latin, then made its way to old French, and finally entered Middle English. The English we speak is a descendant of Middle English.

A dictionary can also help you find other words that have the same meaning, or *synonyms*. Synonyms for the third meaning of *rule* as a transitive verb (line 16) are listed at the entry for *decide*.

To check your knowledge of the dictionary, read the following dictionary entry and then answer the questions below.

> **paw** (pô) *n.* **1.** The foot of an animal, esp. a quadruped, that has claws or nails.   **2.** *Informal* A human hand, esp. a large clumsy one: *"Lennie dabbled his big paw in the water"* (John Steinbeck). ❖ *v.* **pawed, paw•ing, paw** —*tr.*   **1.** To strike with the paw or paws.   **2.** To strike or scrape with a beating motion.   **3.** To handle clumsily, rudely, or with too much familiarity. —*intr.* **1.** To scrape the ground with the forefeet.   **2.** To paw someone or something as in rudeness. [ME *pawe* < OFr. *powe*.] —**paw′er** *n.*

1. What three part-of-speech functions does *paw* have? **noun, transitive verb, intransitive verb**

2. Which definition (including part of speech) is acceptable only in informal speech? **2, as a noun**

3. In which language was *paw* first recorded? **Old French**

Answers are on page 409.

Words to Learn

Part 1

1. **adroit** (adjective)   ə-droit′

    skillful; clever

    > Celebrities like Madonna are **adroit** at changing their images to keep the public interested.

    > The **adroit** knitter moved her needles so rapidly that we could hardly see them.

    NOTE: The word *adroit* can refer to quickness of body or mind.

2. **aficionado** (noun, person)   ə-fĭsh′ē-ə-nä′dō

    fan; admirer; follower

    > **Aficionados** of comic books spent their Saturdays looking for rare items in local shops.

    > Sports **aficionados** can watch many different games on the split screen of one television.

Many stamp collectors are *aficionados* who do careful research.

3. **altruistic** (adjective)   ăl′trōo-ĭs′tĭk

dedicated to the good of others; unselfish

> The **altruistic** man donated his kidney to save the life of a sick child.

> An **altruistic** one-hundred-year-old woman in Chicago distributes free food to poor people.

▶ *Related Word*
altruism (noun) (ăl′trōo-ĭz′əm)   The minister's *altruism* inspired him to run a shelter for abused children.

Famous sports figures Roberto Clemente, Dikembe Mutombo, and Sammy Sosa have displayed great *altruism*. Puerto Rican baseball legend Clemente died in a plane crash in 1972 on his way to help earthquake victims in Nicaragua. All-star basketball center Mutombo gave $2 million for construction of a hospital in his hometown of Kinshasa in the Congo. As a child, star professional baseball player Sosa begged a peso to buy his mother a gift. Now he has given her three homes. He has sponsored baseball training and purchased computers for his native town in the Dominican Republic. After a terrible hurricane Sosa led the effort to aid his native land.

---

4. **ascetic** (noun, adjective)   ə-sĕt′ĭk

a person who gives up pleasures and practices self-denial (noun)

> Saint Augustine, a leader of the early Christian Church, gave up his wealth to live as an **ascetic.**

avoiding or giving up pleasures (adjective)

> Sophia's **ascetic** diet included only vegetables, bread, and water.

NOTES: (1) *Ascetics* are often religious people who feel that self-denial and social isolation will bring them closer to God. (2) Do not confuse *ascetic* with *aesthetic,* which means "beautiful" or "appealing to the senses." The two words sound almost the same.

An *ascetic* existence can be a source of great moral authority, as the life of the fourteenth Dalai Lama shows. Born into a poor family, Gyalwa Tenzin Gyatso was chosen when he was two years old to be the Dalai Lama, or reincarnation of the Buddha. He studied religion and philosophy until he assumed leadership of the Tibetan people at sixteen. In 1959, during the invasion of Tibet by China, he was forced to flee to India. There, living in a small cottage, he rises at 4 a.m. every day to meditate and ends each day with prayer. In 1989, he was awarded the Nobel Peace Prize for his efforts to liberate Tibet without using violence. He often says, "I am a simple Buddhist monk, no more, no less."

5. **capricious** (adjective)   kə-prĭsh′əs

unpredictable; changeable; not based on reason or judgment; fickle

> Students could never predict whether the **capricious** assistant principal would punish them for skipping class.

> The teenager's **capricious** behavior was the first sign of her drug addiction.

▶ *Related Word*
capriciousness (noun) The *capriciousness* of a hurricane's path prevents weather forecasters from knowing exactly where it will hit.

Caligula, emperor of the Roman Empire in 37–41 CE, was known for his *capriciousness*. He provided his favorite horse with a marble stall and a jeweled collar. When his sister died, he declared her a goddess and built a shrine to her. Yet he treated advisers like slaves and, with no explanation, removed awnings that protected people from the hot sun during public gatherings. His *capricious* nature could be combined with great cruelty: he sentenced people to death for no apparent reason. This puzzling behavior came to an end when he was killed by some of his own guards.

6. **cosmopolitan** (adjective)   kŏz′mə-pŏl′ĭ-tn

from several parts of the world; international

> Los Angeles has a **cosmopolitan** population.

having a worldview; free from local bias

> Travel throughout Europe and Asia gave the flight attendant a **cosmopolitan** view of the world.

7. **disdain** (verb, noun)   dĭs-dān′

to scorn; to treat as unworthy (verb)

> The rich businessman **disdained** the poor beggar.
> The politician **disdained** to respond to the insult.

scorn (noun)

> The opera critic treated rock music with **disdain.**
> Teenagers often show **disdain** for their parents' advice.

▶ *Common Phrase*
  disdain for

8. **fraternal** (adjective)   frə-tûr′nəl

referring to brothers

> My loyal older brother taught me much about **fraternal** love.

like a brother; very friendly

> Clarence had **fraternal** feelings for the men he had served with in the navy.

▶ *Related Word*
  fraternize (verb) (frăt′ər-nīz′) The supervisor did not **fraternize** with his employees. (*Fraternize* means "to socialize.")

The word *fraternity* comes from *frater,* the Latin word for "brother." College *fraternities* are meant to foster brotherly relationships. Other *fraternal* organizations, such as the Fraternal Order of Police, foster friendships or associations in a community or profession.

NOTE: Fraternal twins are twins who do not share identical genes. In contrast, *identical* twins have the exact same genes.

9. **gullible** (adjective)   gŭl′ə-bəl

easily deceived; easily cheated

> The **gullible** child believed the story that the moon was made out of cheese.
> The **gullible** man lost all the money he invested in the phony retirement plan.

▶ *Related Word*
gullibility (noun)   Marsha's *gullibility* allowed the crook to convince her that the brass ring was really gold.

10. **hypocritical** (adjective)   (hĭp′ə-krĭt′ĭ-kəl)

giving a false appearance of virtue; saying one thing while doing another

The **hypocritical** governor spoke against public waste while using state employees to mow her lawn.

▶ *Related Words*
hypocrisy (noun)   (hĭ-pŏk′rĭ-sē)   We were shocked at the *hypocrisy* of the minister who robbed a bank.

hypocrite (noun, person)   (hĭp′ə-krĭt′)   That *hypocrite* told us not to smoke, but we knew he smoked himself.

NOTE: The word *hypocrite* comes from an ancient Greek word meaning "actor."

11. **intrepid** (adjective)   ĭn-trĕp′-ĭd

fearless; brave

The **intrepid** explorer traveled alone through the dangerous jungle.

12. **venerable** (adjective)   vĕn′ər-ə-bəl

worthy of great respect because of dignity or age

The new instructor sought advice from the **venerable** professor.

The **venerable** Notre Dame cathedral has stood in Paris since 1189.

NOTES: 1. *Venerable* often refers to people or things of great age. 2. Do not confuse *venerable* with *vulnerable*. (*Vulnerable* means "easily injured or hurt.")

▶ *Related Words*
venerate (verb)   (vĕn′ə-rāt′)   We *venerate* the founders of our country.

veneration (noun)   Countries show *veneration* of great leaders by putting their pictures on currency.

Exercises

Part 1

■ *Who's Who?*

The sentences below begin by naming a type of person. For each example, choose the letter of the word or phrase on the right that defines the type most accurately. Use each choice only once.

1. An adroit person ____**i**____.

2. A person who shows disdain

    ____**h**____.

3. A venerable person ____**l**____.

4. An intrepid person ____**b**____.

5. A cosmopolitan person

    ____**a**____.

6. An aficionado ____**d**____.

7. An ascetic ____**f**____.

8. Capricious people ____**k**____.

9. A gullible person ____**g**____.

10. A hypocritical person

    ____**c**____.

a. has a worldview

b. is brave

c. gives a false appearance of virtue

d. is a fan

e. are brothers or close friends

f. gives up pleasures

g. is easily fooled

h. is scornful

i. is skillful

j. is unselfish

k. change their minds often

l. is worthy of respect

■ *Words in Context*

Complete each sentence with the word that fits best. Use each choice only once.

a. adroit
b. aficionado
c. altruistic
d. ascetic

e. capricious
f. cosmopolitan
g. disdain
h. fraternal

i. gullible
j. hypocritical
k. intrepid
l. venerable

1. The **j, hypocritical** _____ boss took two-hour lunches, but complained if his workers took more than thirty minutes.

2. The chef showed her **g, disdain** _____ for the poorly cooked meal.

3. The cat is a(n) **a, adroit** _____ animal who can easily walk on top of narrow fences.

4. The **k, intrepid** _____ soldier led his men into battle.

5. Military service in many different countries can make a person more

   f, cosmopolitan _____.

6. Younger family members often asked for advice from their

   l, venerable _____ grandfather.

7. The **d, ascetic** _____ lived alone in the mountains and prayed most of the day.

8. The **i, gullible** _____ man believed that streets in the United States were paved with gold.

9. Billionaire Li Ka-Shing showed his **c, altruistic** _____ nature by giving money to build roads in his native town of Shantou.

10. Writers and actors Damon Wayans and Keenan Ivory Wayans have

    a(n) **h, fraternal** _____ relationship.

■ *Using Related Words*

Complete each sentence by using a word from the pair of related words above it. Use each choice only once.

THOMAS JEFFERSON (1743–1826): THIRD U.S. PRESIDENT

1. venerate, venerable

   People of the United States **venerate** _____ their Founding

   Fathers. Among the most **venerable** _____ is Thomas

Jefferson, chief author of the Declaration of Independence and third President of the United States. Under his guidance, the Louisiana Purchase more than doubled the land of the United States. He was a talented architect and spoke seven languages.

2. hypocrite, hypocritical

Despite these achievements, Jefferson was a **hypocrite** in some ways. In the Declaration of Independence, he wrote that

people have a right to liberty, yet the **hypocritical** Jefferson kept slaves. In fact, recent genetic testing shows that he probably fathered a son by one slave, Sally Hemmings.

3. capriciousness, capricious

Jefferson was also **capricious** in his spending habits. Born a wealthy plantation owner, at times he simply ignored his finances, importing expensive items from England and France regardless of whether he could afford them. Perhaps because of

this **capriciousness** in spending, he died in debt, and his family was forced to auction off his estate and possessions.

4. fraternized, fraternal

For years he **fraternized** with another founding father, John Adams. Their friendship ended in a political fight. Yet, toward the end of their lives, their letters show that they once again established a

fraternal relationship.

5. altruistic, altruism

Jefferson's belief in working for the public good made him a great

patriot and president. One example of his **altruism** is that he founded the University of Virginia. He was

altruistic enough to design all of its buildings without pay. He also served as the university's first director. Jefferson worked four hours per day just assembling a catalog for the university's library.

■ *Which Should It Be?*

To complete the following sentences, choose the letter of the word that makes better sense.

1. A man who wrestled crocodiles with his bare hands would be ____**b**____.
   a. adroit   b. intrepid

2. A good minister would be ____**b**____.
   a. intrepid   b. altruistic

3. A person who believes a card trick is magic would be ____**a**____.
   a. gullible   b. ascetic

4. A person who has lived in many different countries is probably ____**a**____.
   a. cosmopolitan   b. capricious

5. The wise and experienced newscaster was considered ____**a**____.
   a. venerable   b. gullible

Words to Learn

Part 2

13. **affluent** (adjective)   ăf′lo͞o-ənt

    wealthy; prosperous

    > People who earn college degrees often become **affluent.**
    > Bill Gates is one of the most **affluent** people in the United States.
    > Enormous oil reserves have made Kuwait an **affluent** country.

    ▶ *Related Word*
    affluence (noun) The hard-working immigrant rose from poverty to *affluence*.

14. **alien** (adjective, noun)   ā′lē-ən

    strange; foreign (adjective)

    > The custom of bowing to others is **alien** to most Americans.

    a foreigner; a person who is not a citizen (noun)

    > After the September 11 terrorist attacks, **aliens** found it harder to enter the United States.

a being from outer space (noun); coming from outer space (adjective)

It is not likely that **aliens** will land on Earth. (noun)

Scientists study **alien** rocks from the moon. (adjective)

© 1984 Jim Unger

**"Lily, see if there's anything on
the 6 o'clock news about it."**

NOTE: All three meanings connote (or hint at) being unknown or strange.

▶ *Related Words*

alienate (verb)   The man's selfishness *alienated* his friends. (*Alienate* means "to make hostile or unfriendly.")

alienation (noun)   A fight about a friend led to Jamal's *alienation* from his father. (*Alienation* means "psychological isolation.")

Customs of public affection differ across cultures. In Brazil, meetings with government ministers commonly end with hugs, and guests at parties kiss everyone. These practices would be quite *alien* in Japan, where many gatherings begin with bows. Romantically involved couples in Japan are now kissing in public, which many Japanese feel is disgusting.

---

15. **amicable** (adjective)   ăm′ĭ-kə-bəl

friendly; peaceful

> Despite being enemies in World War II, the United States and Japan now enjoy an **amicable** relationship.
>
> The divorced mother had an **amicable** relationship with her ex-husband.

NOTE: Amicable indicates a friendly, but not very close, relationship.

▶ *Related Word*
> **amicability** (noun)   *Amicability* between the United States and Russia has existed only since the end of the Cold War.

16. **astute** (adjective)   ə-st$\overline{oo}$t′

having excellent judgment; shrewd

> The **astute** reporter could sense that, despite their friendly words, the two politicians were enemies.
>
> **Astute** politicians know that a good economy is key to public satisfaction.

▶ *Related Word*
> **astuteness** (noun) The worker's *astuteness* helped him to get a promotion .

NOTE: An *astute* person will know what is really important, rather than what people *say* is important.

Behind her public image of a loving and warm woman, Oprah Winfrey is one of the most *astute* business people in the United States. Raised in poverty, she is the first African-American woman to become a billionaire. Her empire includes the hit *Oprah Winfrey Show*, a television show with more than 26 million viewers each week. She owns the powerful Harpo Productions, and publishes *O Magazine. Time* magazine rated Oprah as one of the one hundred most influential people of the twentieth century.

---

17. **candid** (adjective)   kăn′dĭd

truthful; frank; honest in giving opinions

> In the TV interview, the movie star was **candid** about her former drug addiction.

not rehearsed or posed

> The **candid** photograph caught me with my mouth open and my eyes shut.

▶ *Related Word*
> **candor** (noun)   Joshua's *candor* about his girlfriend's dress hurt her feelings.

18. **dogmatic** (adjective)   dôg-măt′ĭk

arrogant in belief; opinionated

> **Dogmatic** thinkers seldom question their own beliefs.
>
> Workers found it hard to suggest new ideas to their **dogmatic** boss.

▶ *Related Word*
> **dogma** (noun)   (dôg′mə)   The leader of the cult set forth a *dogma* for all to follow. (A *dogma* is a system of beliefs.)

19. **exuberant** (adjective)   ĭg-zoo′bər-ənt

very enthusiastic; joyfully energetic

> **Exuberant** at seeing his mother after ten years, Sean grabbed her and lifted her into the air.
>
> The crowd applauded the **exuberant** cheerleaders.

▶ *Related Word*
> **exuberance**   (noun)   In their *exuberance,* audience members ran onto the stage and began dancing.

20. **frugal** (adjective)   froo′gəl

thrifty; economical; attempting to save money; sparing

> **Frugal** grocery shoppers use coupons, compare prices, and hunt for bargains.
>
> Unfortunately, my husband is **frugal** with compliments.

▶ *Related Word*
> **frugality** (noun)   The parents' *frugality* enabled them to save thousands of dollars for their son's college education.

21. **gauche** (adjective)   gōsh

awkward; lacking in social graces

> The **gauche** bride complained about her gifts at the wedding.
>
> Our cousin was so **gauche** that he wiped his mouth on his sleeve.

In many languages, words that refer to the right side are positive and words that refer to the left side are negative. Two words in this chapter have roots in the concepts of "right" or "left." In French, *à droit* means "to the right," and in both French and English *adroit* is a positive word meaning "skillful." *Gauche,* French for "left," means "socially awkward" or "clumsy" in English.

22. **novice** (noun, person)   nŏv′ĭs

beginner; person in a new situation

> The expert chef patiently taught the **novice** how to make sauces.
>
> Since the city council member was a political **novice,** he often said foolish things to the press.

NOTE: Novice can also be used as an adjective: *Novice* skaters often fall on the ice.

23. **renegade** (noun, person)   rĕn′ĭ-gād′

traitor; deserter; outlaw

> According to legend, Robin Hood was a **renegade** who stole from the rich and gave to the poor.
>
> The president of the country was a **renegade** who refused to follow international guidelines on nuclear weapons.

For centuries, Spain ruled over much of Mexico, Central America, South America, and what became the southwestern United States. As a result, most countries south of the United States are Spanish speaking. In addition, millions of people within the United States speak Spanish. Not surprisingly, many Spanish words have entered American English. Two such words, *aficionado* and *renegade,* are introduced in this chapter. In Spanish, *aficionado* means "fan," in particular, a follower of the popular sport of bullfighting; and *renegado* means "deserter." Other examples of Spanish words found in American English are *corral, desperado, fiesta, patio,* and *rodeo.*

NOTE: Like *novice, renegade* can be used as an adjective: The *renegade* soldier fired on his commander.

24. **stoic** (adjective)   stô′ĭk

not affected by pain or pleasure (adjective)

> Soldiers are trained to be **stoic** if they are injured or captured.

▶ *Related Word*
    stoicism (noun) (stō′ĭ-sĭz′əm) Workers accepted the late pay and harsh working conditions with *stoicism*.

NOTE: In modern English usage, *stoic* is usually associated with pain, bad luck, or misfortune.

The word *stoic* refers to an ancient Greek school of philosophical thought that originated in 308 BCE. The philosopher Zeno taught that because gods had made the world, it was perfect. Therefore, human beings must accept their fates without expressing sorrow or joy. The word *stoic* is taken from the covered porch (*stoa* in Greek) where Zeno taught.

Exercises

Part 2

■ Who's Who

The following sentences begin by naming a type of person. For each example, choose the letter of the word or phrase on the right that defines the type most accurately. Use each choice only once.

1. An astute person is ___**l**___.

2. An affluent person is ___**j**___.

3. A novice is ___**c**___.

4. A candid person is ___**a**___.

5. A stoic is ___**f**___.

6. A dogmatic person is ___**d**___.

7. A frugal person is ___**g**___.

8. A renegade is ___**k**___.

9. A gauche person is ___**h**___.

10. An amicable person is ___**e**___.

a. honest in giving opinions
b. a foreigner
c. a beginner
d. arrogant in belief
e. friendly
f. not affected by pain
g. thrifty, economical
h. awkward, lacking social graces
i. enthusiastic
j. wealthy
k. a rebel
l. a person with excellent judgment

■ *Words in Context*

Complete each sentence with the word that fits best. Use each choice only
once.

a. affluent	e. candid	i. gauche
b. alien	f. dogmatic	j. novice
c. amicable	g. exuberant	k. renegade
d. astute	h. frugal	l. stoic

1. Race car fans were amazed when the **j, novice** won the
   championship.

2. The **l, stoic** farmer did not complain when cold
   weather killed his orange trees.

3. The **a, affluent** couple can afford many vacations.

4. The doctor was **e, candid** with the patient about the
   seriousness of her illness.

5. John was **g, exuberant** when he found out he had won a
   million-dollar lottery.

6. Discount stores appeal to **h, frugal** people.

7. Her date was so **i, gauche** that he talked to other
   women on his cell phone during dinner.

8. Although I am now a(n) **b, alien** living in Canada, I
   soon hope to be a Canadian citizen.

9. The **k, renegade** refused to obey orders.

10. My **f, dogmatic** aunt insisted that there was only one
    right way to train a dog.

■ *Using Related Words*

Complete each sentence by using a word from the pair of related words
above it. Use each choice only once.

ABRAHAM LINCOLN (1809–1865):
SIXTEENTH U.S. PRESIDENT

1. affluent, affluence

   Although many U.S. presidents come from **affluent** families, Abraham Lincoln was born in relative poverty. He lost his mother when he was a small child. His family moved several times, often making hard journeys through wilderness. He attended school for only a few years. But through self-education, he was able to become a lawyer. In this profession, he rose to **affluence** .

2. frugal, frugality

   Nevertheless, Lincoln remained quite **frugal** . His lack of luxury was a habit from his childhood. His wife, however, did not enjoy **frugality** . She liked parties and fine clothes.

3. amicable, amicability

   In the small towns of Illinois, Lincoln developed a reputation for **amicability** . As an **amicable** lawyer, he spent many hours telling stories to others.

4. astute, astuteness

   This proved to be an **astute** courtroom strategy, for other lawyers often underestimated him. Behind his friendliness lay much **astuteness** and sophistication in legal matters.

5. candor, candid

   As president of the United States during the Civil War, Lincoln had to make many difficult decisions. At times, he was considered less than **candid** with his advisers. But Lincoln had to please many people. If he used **candor** with all of them, they would have been quite unhappy. So, as he did in the law, he entertained them with stories and put off decisions. Lincoln led the North to victory in the Civil War, but shortly afterward, he was assassinated.

■ *Which Should It Be?*

To complete the following sentences, choose the letter of the word that makes better sense.

1. A person who refuses to change his mind is ___**a**___.
   a. dogmatic   b. alien

2. Friendly neighbors are ___**b**___.
   a. alien   b. amicable

3. People who like to save money are ___**b**___.
   a. exuberant   b. frugal

4. Her quiet acceptance of her illness made her seem ___**b**___.
   a. exuberant   b. stoic

5. A person who talks loudly in a quiet library is ___**b**___.
   a. amicable   b. gauche

Chapter Exercises

■ *Practicing Strategies: Using the Dictionary*

Read the definitions, and answer the questions that follow.

> **or•nate** (ôr-nāt′) *adj.* **1.** Elaborately, heavily, and often excessively ornamented. **2.** Flashy, showy, or florid in style or manner; flowery. [ME < Lat. *ōrnātus*, p. part. of *ōrnāre*, to embellish.] **—or•nate′ly** *adv.* **—or•nate′ness** *n.*

1. What part of speech is *ornate*? **adjective** _____

2. Which syllable of *ornate* is stressed in pronunciation?

   second _____

3. What noun is related to *ornate*? **ornateness** _____

4. In which language did *ornate* originate? **Latin** _____

> **eb•on•y** (ĕb′ə-nē) *n.*, *pl.* **-ies** **1.** Any of various tropical Asian or African trees of the genus *Diospyros*. **2.** The wood of such a tree, esp. the hard black heartwood of *D. ebenum* used in cabinetwork and for piano keys. **3.** The hard dark wood of various other trees. **4.** The color black; ebon. ❖ *adj.* **1.** Made of or suggesting ebony. **2.** Black in color. [Prob. < ME *hebenyf*, ebony wood < alteration of LLat. *hebeninus*, of ebony < Gk. *ebeninos* < *ebenos*, ebony tree < Egypt. *hbny*.]

5. Which two parts of speech can *ebony* be? **noun, adjective** _____

6. How is the plural of *ebony* spelled? **ebonies** _____

7. In which language did *ebony* originate? **Egyptian** _____

> **max•i•mum** (măk′sə-məm) *n.*, *pl.* **-mums** or **-ma** (-mə) **1a.** The greatest possible quantity or degree. **b.** The greatest quantity or degree reached or recorded; the upper limit of variation. **c.** The time or period during which the highest point or degree is attained. **2.** An upper limit permitted by law or other authority. **3.** *Astronomy* **a.** The moment when a variable star is most brilliant. **b.** The magnitude of the star at such a moment. **4.** *Mathematics* **a.** The greatest value assumed by a function over a given interval. **b.** The largest number in a set. ❖ *adj.* **1.** Having or being the maximum reached or attainable: *maximum temperature*. **2.** Of, relating to, or making up a maximum: *the maximum number in a series*. [Lat. < neut. of *maximus*, greatest. See **meg-** in App.]

8. What are the two full plural spellings of *maximum*? **maximums,** _____

maxima _____

9. What two parts of speech can *maximum* be? **noun, adjective** _____

10. What is the number and the part of speech of the definition of *maximum* most often used in mathematics? **4, noun** _____

■ *Practicing Strategies: Using a Dictionary Pronunciation Key*

It takes practice to use a pronunciation key efficiently. For each of the following words, use the key on the inside front cover of this book to figure out the pronunciation. Try saying each word out loud several times.

1. accolade   ăk′ə-lād
2. pseudonym   soo̅′də-nĭm′
3. cuisine   kwĭ-zēn′
4. epitome   ĭ-pĭt′ə-mē
5. cliché   klē-shā′

■ *Practicing Strategies: Using the Dictionary Independently*

Use a college or unabridged dictionary to research the answers to the following questions. Be sure to consult a recently published dictionary.

1. What is a *mallemuck*? **a seabird** _____

   _____

2. In what language was the word *sheriff* first recorded? **Old English** _____

   _____

3. Which syllable of the word *plasmagene* receives most stress? _____

   the first _____

4. If you do something *gingerly*, how do you do it? _____

   with great care; carefully _____

5. What is a *tupelo*? **a tree** _____

   _____

■ *Companion Words*

Complete each sentence with the word that fits best. Look back at the "Words to Learn" for help. Choose your answers from the words below. You may use words more than once.

Choices: for, of, with, about

1. The student was candid **about** _____ the fact that he hadn't studied.

2. My friend is an aficionado **of** _____ mystery novels.

3. I have fraternal feelings **for** _____ my best friend.

4. Eugenio has amicable relationships **with** his cousins.

5. The renegade had disdain **for** the government.

■ *Writing with Your Words*

This exercise will give you practice in writing effective sentences that use the vocabulary words. Each sentence is started for you. Complete it with an interesting phrase that also indicates the meaning of the italicized word.

1. I knew she was a *hypocrite* because _____

_____ .

2. The sports *aficionado* _____

_____ .

3. In a *cosmopolitan* society, _____

_____ .

4. I knew a person so *gauche* that _____

_____ .

5. I have *disdain* for people who _____

_____ .

6. A *novice* at dating might _____

_____ .

7. When I gave my *candid* opinion, _____

_____ .

8. If I were as *affluent* as Bill Gates, _____

_____ .

9. I would feel *exuberant* if _____

_____ .

10. The *renegade* shouted _____

_____ .

■ *Making Connections*

These questions will help you relate the words you have learned in this chapter to your own life. Answer each question by writing a paragraph or more on a separate sheet of paper.

1. Have you ever felt gauche? Describe the situation.

2. Who is the most hypocritical person you know? Why?

3. Have you found that immigrants are more cosmopolitan than people born in this country? Why?

Passage

Two Real Guys: The Story of Ben & Jerry's Ice Cream

Their $8,000 investment grew to a business worth $100 million. Along the way, they became known for their sense of humor and their commitment to social concerns. This is the story of Ben Cohen and Jerry Greenfield, the two real guys behind Ben & Jerry's ice cream.

Ben Cohen and Jerry Greenfield met in junior high school and soon **(1)** developed a relationship so close that it was almost **fraternal.** Both **candidly** describe themselves as fat "nerds" who hated sports but loved to eat ice cream. **(2)** Ben, who left college without graduating, was a **renegade.** Once, when he was working in a kitchen, his boss ordered him to get rid of his beard. Instead, he simply shaved a thin line down the middle of his chin and declared that he now had sideburns! Not surprisingly, Ben was fired from a series of jobs, although he did do well at mopping floors. His partner, Jerry, managed to complete college, but was rejected by forty medical schools.

In 1978, Ben and Jerry decided to start an ice-cream shop in Burlington, Vermont, one of the coldest towns in the United States. **(3)** They completed a mail-order course in ice-cream making for **novices** and applied for a loan from the Merchant's Bank. **(4)** Hoping to impress

Ben and Jerry are the two real guys behind a large ice-cream company.

the **venerable** bankers, they dressed in suits for the first time in years. Their strategy must have worked, for the loan was granted. Ben and Jerry were in business.

For the next several months they worked day and night converting an abandoned gas station that lacked heating or adequate plumbing into an ice-cream shop. To save money, they lived in a trailer and existed on an **ascetic** diet of sardines and crackers. **(5)** In their desire to be **frugal,** Ben and Jerry paid construction workers with promises of free ice cream for life, instead of with money.

From the moment the shop opened, customers knew the ice cream was special. Ben, who lacked a strong sense of taste, had to approve each flavor. Because he could not taste mild things, he insisted that the flavors be rich and have lots of crunchy additions. *Time* magazine reported that Ben and Jerry's ice cream was among the best in the world.

(6) Customers also loved the shop's **amicable** atmosphere, which featured personal service, games, and live piano music. In keeping with the company motto "If it's not fun, why do it?" Ben and Jerry threw a public party that included an ice-cream-eating contest and an award for the longest unbroken apple peel. An **exuberant** Jerry demonstrated his fire-eating abilities and smashed a cinder block on Ben's stomach.

Sales were great, but there was not much profit. Since Ben and Jerry **disdained** standard business practices, they failed to keep track of their costs. Often they supplied too much ice cream on their cones, and lack of **adroit** scooping meant that they did not serve people quickly enough to make money. **(7)** Their accounting practices were so **capricious** that they often crumpled up checks, put them in their pockets, and forgot them. To help produce a profit, Ben and Jerry hired professional management staff and started to sell ice cream to grocery stores.

Despite their need to focus on profits the fun continued as they created many imaginative and delicious flavors. **(8)** Two **aficionados** of the Grateful Dead rock group suggested the flavor Cherry Garcia, a combination of chocolate and cherry named after the group's leader, Jerry Garcia. Ben and Jerry's rich-tasting New York Super Fudge Chunk combined white and dark chocolate chunks with three kinds of nuts. Best-selling Chocolate Chip Cookie Dough contained raw cookie dough. Publicity also continued to ignore the **dogma** of conventional advertising. In the summer of 1986 Ben and Jerry crossed the United States in a "Cowmobile," giving away free ice-cream samples. In 1994, they hired Spike Lee to direct a humorous ad campaign for a new "smooth" ice cream, without chunks.

Ben & Jerry's Homemade, Inc. continued to grow in size and profits. Despite their new **affluence,** however, Ben and Jerry remained true to their original values. **(9)** Formality continued to be **alien** to the company style, for everyone from factory workers to bosses wore jeans, participated in Elvis Presley look-alike contests, and received three pints of ice cream per day. As another worker benefit, 5 percent of company profits were distributed to all employees. Since recycling was important to Ben and Jerry, the company bought 200 pigs—one of them named after Ben and another after Jerry—to eat ice-cream waste. (Unfortunately, the pigs refused to eat mint ice cream.)

Ben and Jerry also became famous for their **altruism.** When they sold their first public stock, they announced a policy of "linked prosperity," meaning that the company would use profits to support charitable causes. **(10)** The announcement turned out to be **astute,** for it encouraged more people to buy their ice cream. Projects sponsored by Ben & Jerry's have included a New York store that funds a drug counseling center and a homeless shelter, efforts to preserve Brazilian rain forests, and a Mexican cooperative company that supports poor peasants. Ben & Jerry's also give free franchises to "partnershops" that train disadvantaged teenagers.

Although the company was sold to Unilever, it continues to give at least $1 million per year to charity. Ben & Jerry's still creates special flavors, like the one-day "Maple-Powered Howard" special to honor 2004 Democratic presidential candidate Howard Dean. Ben created antiwar ads against the 2003 Iraq war that were so controversial that many networks refused to carry them. In short, despite the company's size and fame, its heart lies in two real guys who remain true to their values.

■ *Exercise*

Each numbered sentence below corresponds to a sentence in the Passage. Fill in the letter of the choice that makes the sentence mean the same thing as its corresponding sentence in the Passage.

1. Ben and Jerry developed a relationship that was almost ___**c**___.
   a. friendly   b. unselfish   c. brotherly   d. brave

2. Ben, who left college without graduating, was a ___**d**___.
   a. fan   b. failure   c. tease   d. rebel

3. They completed a mail-order course in ice-cream making for

   ___**c**___.

   a. foreigners   b. poor people   c. beginners   d. skillful people

4. They hoped to impress the ___**a**___ bankers.
   a. dignified   b. truthful   c. unfeeling   d. shrewd

5. In their desire to be ___**c**___, the partners paid construction workers with promises of free ice cream for life.
   a. friendly   b. scornful   c. thrifty   d. excited

6. Customers loved the shop's ___**a**___ atmosphere.
   a. friendly   b. fooling   c. new   d. rich

7. Their accounting practices were ___**d**___.
   a. careless   b. dishonest   c. bad   d. unpredictable

8. Two ___**d**___ of the Grateful Dead rock group suggested the flavor Cherry Garcia.
   a. singers   b. friends   c. partners   d. fans

9. Formality continued to be ___**a**___ to the company style.
   a. foreign   b. important   c. helpful   d. damaging

10. The announcement turned out to be ___**c**___.
    a. helpful   b. charitable   c. shrewd   d. friendly

■ *Discussion Questions*

1. Give two examples of the informality of Ben & Jerry's Homemade, Inc.

2. Describe three factors that contributed to the success of Ben and Jerry's company. Defend your choices.

3. How do you think the informality of Ben and Jerry's company might have been an astute business practice?

ENGLISH IDIOMS

Color

Each chapter in this book discusses the meaning of some English idioms. Idioms are groups of words that have special meanings, which are different from the usual meanings of the words. Since the Passage in this chapter is about Ben and Jerry, two colorful (or lively and interesting) characters, the idioms for Chapter 1 are about colors.

Some color idioms have negative meanings. *Feeling blue* means feeling depressed or bad, and *yellow-bellied* means cowardly. The words *green* and *rose* are used in idioms that have positive meanings. A person with a *green thumb* has a talent for gardening. People who look at the world *through rose-colored glasses* see things as much better than they really are.

Idioms containing the words *black* and *red* are used in business. A firm that is *in the red* is losing money, but one that is *in the black* is profitable.

During ancient Roman holidays, rival groups of young men would compete to see who could cover the most statues with red wine. Not surprisingly, the statue of Bacchus, god of wine, was particularly popular as a target. Today, when people go out for the evening to have a good time, they *paint the town red*.

Words in the News

Even on a remote mountaintop, we are never more than a few seconds away from the news. With the touch of a button, the radio brings us the latest reports of international events, disasters, sports scores, and gossip about our favorite stars. Television transports images from thousands of miles away into our living rooms. Newspapers bring us in-depth political analysis, advice columns, and tips on living. We can access the Internet through computers and cell phones for instant traffic and weather reports. In a world so small that events in Europe and Asia affect U.S. financial markets within seconds, we need to broaden our understanding of words in the news.

Chapter Strategy: Context Clues of Substitution

Chapter Words:

Part 1

accord	catastrophe	entrepreneur
attrition	consumer	intervene
bureaucracy	corroborate	media
cartel	diplomacy	pacify

Part 2

apprehend	ludicrous	radical
chaos	ominous	liberal
defer	supplant	conservative
epitome	thrive	reactionary

Quiz Yourself

To check your knowledge of some chapter words before you begin to study, identify these statements as true or false. Answers are on page 409.

A **chaotic** room is neat.	True	False
To **thrive** is to live and grow.	True	False
To **supplant** is to replace.	True	False
A **cartel** is a group of animals.	True	False

You will learn the answers as you study this chapter.

Did You Know?

How Many Ways Can a Team Win or Lose?

Many sportswriters are masters of the English language who express game results with drama and humor. Every day, football, basketball, baseball, or hockey games are reported in newspapers; yet day after day, sportswriters make their reports sound fresh and enthusiastic.

How do they do it?

Because sportswriters have had to report wins and losses over and over again, they have developed clever synonyms (words that mean the same thing) for the words *win* and *lose*.

Let's look at some of the many ways to say *win*, with examples taken from newspaper sports pages.

> Marlins *beat* Cubs.
>
> Patriots *top* Panthers.

And here are some examples of ways to say *lose*.

> Cubs *drop* heartbreaker.
>
> Hawks *are doormats* again.

These headlines show big wins.

> Packers *pound* Bears.
>
> Iowa State *rips* number 4 Kansas.

Sportswriters use many synonyms for *win* and *lose*.

On the other hand, the connotations of these words show that the winners barely got by.

> Bengals *struggle past* Rams.
> Chiefs *edge* Redskins.

This headline shows that the game changed in the middle.

> Bears *struggle,* then *cruise.*

Sometimes the name of a team is used in an imaginative way. The headlines that follow are metaphors, whose meanings are suggested by the team names.

> Flyers *soar past* Islanders. (Something that flies can soar.)
> Pirates *slice up* Cubs. (The Pirates take their swords and "slice up" the Cubs.)
> 49ers *shear* Rams. (A ram is a sheep; a sheep's wool gets sheared.)

At other times, sportswriters use rhyme.

Bears *sack the Pack.*

Hoosiers *fake, shake, break* Illini.

A short headline can tell much about a game. What happened in these games?

1. Bruins' rally on ice from 2 down stuns Rangers 4-3.

2. Penn surprises Ohio in overtime.

3. Bulls butcher Bucks, end road slump.

Answers are on page 409.

Learning Strategy

Context Clues of Substitution

Using *context clues* is a powerful strategy that can help you figure out the meaning of unknown words. *Context* refers to the words, sentences, or even paragraphs that surround a word. When you use context clues, you use the words that you know in a sentence to make an intelligent guess about the meaning of an unknown word.

You may think that it is not a good strategy to guess at words. After all, it is better to know the answer on a test than just to guess. However, intelligent guessing is very important in reading. English has so many words that no one can know them all. Good readers often use context clues when they meet unfamiliar words.

Context clues have two important advantages:

1. You do not have to interrupt your reading to go to the dictionary.

2. You can rely on your own common sense. Common sense is your best learning tool.

In fact, you probably use context clues already, although you may not realize it. For example, context clues are the only way to choose the correct meaning for words that have more than one meaning, such as *hot*. You must use context clues to figure out what the word *hot* means in the following sentences.

a. The stove is *hot*.

b. The chili pepper is *hot*.

c. Gregory has a *hot* temper.

In which sentence does *hot* mean

1. spicy?

2. having a high temperature?

3. quick, emotional?

Answers are on page 409.

Let's turn to a more difficult word. What are the meanings of the word *concession* in these sentences?

a. He bought some food at the hot-dog *concession.*

b. Because the country wanted peace, the leaders made a *concession* of land to the enemy.

In which sentence does *concession* mean

1. something that is surrendered or given up?

2. a business that sells things?

Answers are on page 409.

Context clues and the dictionary are natural partners in helping you determine the meaning of unknown words. Context clues usually give you an approximate meaning for a word and allow you to continue your reading without interruption. After you have finished reading, you can look up the word in a dictionary. Why not use the dictionary first? People usually remember words whose meanings they figured out for themselves far better than those they simply looked up in a dictionary.

You may be wondering exactly how to determine the meaning of unknown words that you find in your reading. Many people find the following steps helpful:

1. As you are reading, try to pinpoint words you do not know. This advice sounds almost silly, but it isn't. Many people lose the opportunity to learn words simply because they let unknown words slip by. Don't let this happen to you. Try to capture difficult words!

2. Use context clues to make an intelligent guess about an unknown word's meaning. The strategies you will learn here and in the following chapters will help you do this. Remember that context clues will often give you an approximate—not an exact—meaning.

3. Write down the word and later check it in a dictionary. This step will tell you whether you guessed correctly and will give you a more exact definition of the word.

How does a person learn to make "intelligent guesses"? In this book, we will present three different methods: substitution in context (in this chapter), context clues of definition (in Chapter 3), and context clues of opposition (in Chapter 4).

Substitution in context is perhaps the most useful way to determine a word's meaning. To use this strategy, simply substitute a word or phrase that makes sense in place of an unknown word. The word you substitute will usually be an approximate definition for the unknown word. Here are some examples.

> Ron's two brothers were hitting each other, but Ron would not join the *fray*. (Since people often hit each other in a fight, the word *fight* is a good substitution and provides an approximate meaning.)
>
> The *indigent* student could not afford books or school supplies. (A person who cannot afford things necessary for school is poor, and the word *poor* may substitute for *indigent*.)

Of course, context clues of substitution cannot be used all the time. Some sentences simply do not provide enough context clues. For example, in the sentence "Jane saw the *conger*," it would be impossible to find a good substitution for *conger*. (A *conger* is a type of eel.) However, since many sentences do provide context clues, substitution in context will help you much of the time.

Two additional examples are given below. Try using context clues of substitution to make intelligent guesses about the meanings of the italicized words. To do this, take out the unknown word and substitute a word you know that seems to make sense in the sentence.

1. Your smiling *countenance* suggests that you are happy.

2. A broken traffic light is a *vexation* to a driver.

Answers are on page 409.

Each of the following sentences contains a word that will be presented in the Words to Learn section. Read the sentence and use a context clue of substitution to make an intelligent guess about the meaning of the italicized word.

1. The outdated computer manual was *supplanted* by a new edition.

    Supplanted means **replaced**_____.

2. The two countries reached an *accord* that enabled them to stop fighting.

    Accord means **agreement**_____.

Answers are on page 409.

Words to Learn

Part 1

1. **accord** (noun, verb)   ə-kôrd′

   agreement; harmony (noun)

   > The Kyoto **Accord** limits the amount of carbon dioxide that can be released into the atmosphere.

   > We are in **accord** with your proposal to increase funding for education.

   to give or grant (verb)

   > Iranian lawyer Shirin Ebadi was **accorded** the 2003 Nobel Peace Prize for her fight to protect human rights.

   ▶ *Common Phrases*
   in accord with; in accordance with (in agreement with); reach an accord (reach an agreement)

2. **attrition** (noun)   ə-trĭsh′ən

   slowly wearing down; wearing away

   > Too much fishing and a polluted water supply have caused **attrition** in the salmon population.

   > **Attrition** tends to be high in very difficult college courses.

After the September 11, 2001, terrorist attacks, security at airports was tightened. In one measure, the jobs of U.S. airport screeners came under the control of the federal government. Since then, job turnover has dropped from a very high rate to a record low of 4 percent per year. This extremely low *attrition* rate has surprised federal officials, who believe it is due to better training, salaries, and benefits.

---

3. **bureaucracy** (noun)   byo͝o-rŏk′rə-sē

   administration by employees who follow fixed rules and complex procedures

   > The newly elected mayor promised to reform the inefficient city **bureaucracy.**

   > My health insurance benefit was delayed because it had to be approved by several levels of **bureaucracy.**

NOTE: Bureaucracy is usually a negative word that refers to a government or organization involving too many officials and too much delay. In government, *bureaucrats* are appointed, not elected. Whether a *bureaucracy* is part of a government, business, or other organization, the officials often are more concerned with following rules than with getting things done.

▶ *Related Words*

bureaucratic (adjective) Because of *bureaucratic* problems in the registration office, my transcript was lost.

bureaucrat (noun) For twenty years, the *bureaucrat* made four copies of every letter he received.

Bureaucracy is often associated with the term *red tape* in sentences such as "There is too much bureaucratic red tape." In the 1700s, red tape was used to bind piles of English government documents. Since the government was *bureaucratic* and inefficient, *red tape* came to refer to excessive and silly official routines.

---

4. **cartel** (noun) kär-tĕl′

a combination of independent business organizations formed to control prices

The Organization of Petroleum Exporting Countries (OPEC) is a powerful oil **cartel** made up of twelve nations.

Several illegal drug **cartels** operate throughout the Americas.

In 2002, the world's largest rubber producers—Thailand, Indonesia, and Malaysia—each contributed millions of dollars to form the International Rubber Company. This new *cartel* controls more than 70 percent of the world's rubber trade. The *cartel* agreed to buy rubber if market prices went down from a lack of demand. As this example shows, *cartels* are formed to control world prices—and keep profits high.

---

5. **catastrophe** (noun) kə-tăs′trə-fē

a great disaster

The bubonic plague of the 1400s was a **catastrophe** that killed one-third of all people in Europe.

The computer virus was a **catastrophe** that shut down systems nationwide.

▶ *Related Word*
    catastrophic (adjective)   kăt′ə-strŏf′-ĭk   War has had *catastrophic* effects on the lives of many people in the Middle East.

6. **consumer** (noun)   kən-sōō′mər

a buyer

    Advertising influences a **consumer's** choices.

▶ *Related Words*
    consume (verb) People worldwide *consume* Coca-Cola. (*Consume* usually refers to eating and drinking.)

    consumption (noun) (kən-səmp′shən) The doctor wanted me to limit my *consumption* of fatty foods. Gas *consumption* has risen in the United States. (*Consumption* may refer to eating and drinking, as well as to buying and using.)

7. **corroborate** (verb)   kə-rŏb′ə-rāt′

to confirm; to make more certain

    Five eyewitnesses **corroborated** the police report.

    Newspaper reporters try to **corroborate** the information they get from interviews.

▶ *Related Word*
    corroboration (noun)   The landing of an alien spaceship on Earth has not received scientific *corroboration*.

More than 1,500 years ago, someone walking by the Loch Ness (*loch* means "lake") in Scotland noticed a strange creature coming out of the water. It looked like a combination of a snake and a dinosaur. Since then, there have been thousands of reports of the Loch Ness monster. However, in 2003, the British Broadcasting Company sent a team of researchers to determine whether the legend was true. They used a satellite navigation system and 600 separate sonar beams, but could not *corroborate* the existence of the monster. So it doesn't exist, or does it . . . ?

---

8. **diplomacy** (noun)   dĭ-plō′mə-sē

the process of official international relations

    A failure of **diplomacy** led to the 2003 war in Iraq.

politeness; tact

    It can be difficult to combine honesty and **diplomacy.**

▶ *Related Words*

diplomat (noun, person)   Prudence Bushnell, the *diplomat* serving as U.S. ambassador to Kenya, was injured during a 1998 embassy bombing.

diplomatic (adjective)   In 1993, Israel established *diplomatic* relations with Russia.

The United States has an enormous network of *diplomats* stationed in other countries. These *diplomats* represent U.S. interests, help U.S. citizens who travel abroad, and grant visas to foreigners who wish to visit the United States. *Diplomatic* work is sometimes dangerous. From 1979 to 1980, more than 100 U.S. *diplomatic* employees were held captive in Iran for 444 days.

People in the U.S. *diplomatic* corps work in embassies, which are located in other countries, but considered U.S. land. Foreigners who need protection from their own governments may request asylum in a U.S. embassy, where other governments have no official control.

---

9. **entrepreneur** (noun)   ŏn′trə-prə-nûr′

a person who organizes and runs a business

The Chinese-American **entrepreneur** An Wang built Wang Laboratories into one of the largest computer firms in the United States.

▶ *Related Word*

entrepreneurial (adjective)   Berry Gordy's *entrepreneurial* skills helped make Motown Record Corporation a huge success.

Entrepreneurs have emerged from many backgrounds. African-American John H. Johnson founded the enormous Johnson Publishing Company. William and Ralph Cruz, both talented Hispanic musicians, codirect the Miami-based Omega Research Company. Oprah Winfrey's *entrepreneurial* skills in the entertainment industry have made her one of the wealthiest women in the United States. Elizabeth Arden, Estée Lauder, Madam C. J. Walker, and Mary Kay Ash are legends in the cosmetics business.

---

10. **intervene** (verb)   ĭn′tər-vēn′

to interfere; to act in a matter involving others

The teacher **intervened** to stop the fight between the two fifth graders.

The government of Kenya **intervened** in the illegal hunting of elephants.

▶ *Related Word*

intervention (noun)   In 1953, the United Nations' *intervention* ended North Korea's invasion of South Korea.

NOTE: To *intervene* can also mean to come between points of time, as in "Four years *intervene* between summer Olympics."

11. **media** (plural noun; adjective)   mē′dē-ə

means of communication, especially TV, radio, and newspapers (plural noun)

Criminal trials of famous stars are closely followed by the **media.**

Through the **medium** of television, war is brought into our living rooms. (Here, the singular form, *medium*, is used.)

referring to the media (adjective)

Reporters turned the terrible crime into a **media** event.

NOTE: Media and *medium* can also refer to the tools of artists, as in "The artist's main *medium* was oil, but she also used watercolor."

12. **pacify** (verb)   pas′ə-fī′

to calm; to establish peace

Mothers can often **pacify** crying infants with a bottle.

Political reforms helped to **pacify** the country's angry farmers.

NOTE: Pacify can also mean to establish peace by conquering, as in "The army *pacified* the rebels."

In 1513, after crossing many miles of Central American jungle, the Spanish explorer Vasco Núñez de Balboa found himself facing a large body of calm water. He chose the Spanish word for *peaceful* as a name for his discovery. In English it is now called the *Pacific* Ocean.

Exercises

Part 1

■ *Matching Words and Definitions*

Check your understanding of words in the news by matching each word with the letter of its definition. Use each choice only once.

1. corroborate __k__

2. pacify __d__

3. cartel __b__

4. consumer __j__

5. bureaucracy __g__

6. intervene __c__

7. entrepreneur __e__

8. accord __l__

9. media __i__

10. attrition __a__

a. wearing away

b. a group that agrees to control prices

c. to act in a matter involving others

d. to calm

e. person who starts a business

f. disaster

g. administration by employees who follow fixed rules.

h. the process of official international relations

i. means of communication

j. buyer

k. to confirm; make more certain

l. agreement

■ *Words in Context*

Complete each sentence with the word that fits best. Use each choice only once.

a. accord
b. attrition
c. bureaucracy
d. cartel

e. catastrophe
f. consumer
g. corroborate
h. diplomacy

i. entrepreneur
j. intervene
k. media
l. pacify

1. Businesses can gain more power by joining together in a(n)

   d, cartel   .

2. Workers in a(n) **c, bureaucracy**   often take days to process a
   simple form.

3. A(n) **a, accord**   reached between the workers and owners ended the strike.

4. To **g, corroborate**   the fact I found in one encyclopedia, I
   looked in another.

5. To **l, pacify**   his angry wife, the man washed the
   dishes.

6. Presidential trips outside the United States receive much attention

   from the **k, media**   .

7. World War I (1914–18) was a war of **b, attrition**   in which
   the enemies gradually weakened each other.

8. The United Nations decided to **j, intervene**   to stop the
   fighting in Bosnia.

9. Because of her great skill at **h, diplomacy**   , Jantima was
   able to criticize others without hurting their feelings.

10. The plane crash was a(n) **e, catastrophe**   that killed 300
    people.

■ *Using Related Words*

Complete each sentence by using a word from the group of related words
above it. Use each choice only once.

1. consume, consumption, consumers

   SUVs, or sport utility vehicles, have become increasingly popular

   with **consumers**   . In 1985 they accounted for only
   2 percent of automobile sales; today more than 25 percent of all
   vehicles sold are SUVs. However, many people worry about the gas

consumption of SUVs. They feel that when vehicles

consume one gallon of gas every ten miles, they are wasting energy.

2. diplomatic, diplomacy, diplomat

Benjamin Franklin was an extremely skilled **diplomat**. In 1776, when the U.S. colonies declared independence from England, Franklin was sent to France on a **diplomatic**

mission. His great skill at **diplomacy** convinced France to enter an alliance with the tiny new nation. This partnership gave the colonies a chance to win independence.

3. catastrophe, catastrophic

Scientists are disturbed that a declining frog population may have

catastrophic consequences even for humans. The decreasing number of frogs throughout the world may signal that

the earth is approaching a **catastrophe** for all forms of life. Three suspected causes for frog deaths are infectious disease, a thinning of the ozone layer, and chemical pesticides.

4. bureaucratic, bureaucracy

Texan Calvin Graham won medals for bravery in World War II, but navy officials expelled him and took away his medals when they discovered he was only twelve years old! Graham spent the last

years of his life asking the military **bureaucracy** to

return his medals. But **bureaucratic** agencies move slowly. The last medal, a Purple Heart, was returned only after his death.

5. entrepreneur, entrepreneurial

Reverend Man Singh Das is an **entrepreneur** who makes money while doing good. Owner of a service station and several

apartment buildings, he has used his **entrepreneurial** skills to provide jobs and housing to the needy. Instead of arresting a man who was trying to break into his gas station, Das offered him a job cleaning it.

■ *Reading the Headlines*

This exercise presents five headlines that might appear in newspapers. Read each headline and then answer the questions that follow. (Remember that small words, such as *is, are, a*, and *the*, are often left out of newspaper headlines.)

NEWS REPORT CORROBORATES WEATHER CATASTROPHE

1. Is this the first report? **no**

2. Is the weather terrible? **yes**

BUREAUCRAT BLOCKS RELEASE OF CONSUMER SURVEY

3. Is the person blocking the report an elected official? **no**

4. Is the survey about people who buy? **yes**

DIPLOMATIC ENTREPRENEUR BUYS MEDIA COMPANY

5. Is the entrepreneur polite? **yes**

6. Is the company involved in communications? **yes**

COUNTRIES REACH ACCORD NOT TO INTERVENE IN WAR OF ATTRITION

7. Will the countries interfere? **no**

8. Will the war be over quickly? **no**

OIL CARTEL CANNOT PACIFY ANGRY PUBLIC

9. Can the cartel calm the public? **no**

10. Does the cartel work to control prices? **yes**

Words to Learn

Part 2

13. **apprehend** (verb)   ăp′rĭ-hĕnd′

    to arrest or take a criminal into custody

    > The police **apprehended** the escaped convicts.

    to understand mentally; to grasp

    > Many people find it difficult to **apprehend** the meaning of abstract modern art.

    ▶ *Related Words*

    apprehension (noun)   The *apprehension* of the rapist calmed our fears. I had *apprehensions* about the test. (In the first sentence, *apprehension* means "arrest"; in the second sentence, it means "fear.")

    apprehensive (adjective)   Children are often *apprehensive* about visiting doctors. (*Apprehensive* means "fearful.")

14. **chaos** (noun)   kā′ŏs′

    a state of total disorder or confusion

    > A power failure left the city in **chaos.**

    > In a single afternoon, the five active children reduced the neat room to **chaos.**

    ▶ *Related Word*

    chaotic (adjective)   The nightclub became *chaotic* as people rushed to escape from the fire.

15. **defer** (verb)   dĭ-fûr′

    to delay

    > My college will **defer** my tuition payment until my financial aid check arrives.

    to show respect; to submit to the wishes of another

    > When boarding a bus, you should **defer** to people who are physically disabled by letting them on first.

    > I **deferred** to my father's wishes and attended college.

    ▶ *Common Phrase*
    defer to

► *Related Words*

deference (noun)   (dĕf′ər-əns)   He showed his *deference* to the queen by bowing to her. (*Deference* means "respect.")

deferential (adjective)   The student used a *deferential* tone when talking to his professor.

16. **epitome** (noun)   ĭ-pĭt′ə-mē

a defining example; the best example; a symbol

Many consider Adolf Hitler to be the **epitome** of evil. (In this sentence, *epitome* is used in a negative sense.)

Tiger Woods is the **epitome** of a champion golfer.

▶ *Related Word*

epitomize (verb)   Rising 630 feet into the air, the graceful Gateway Arch has come to *epitomize* the city of St. Louis.

NOTE: The final *e* of *epitome* is pronounced.

17. **ludicrous** (adjective)   lōō′dĭ-krəs

absurd, ridiculous, or outrageous

> It is **ludicrous** to think that an ant could carry an elephant.
>
> The fat, middle-aged singer looked **ludicrous** playing a young lover in the opera.

The popular hip-hop star Ludacris takes his name from the word *ludicrous*. As his name suggests, he exposes the ridiculous by making fun of rap and the "Ghetto Fabulous" lifestyle. His crazy hairdos and the clearly visible logos and slogans on his clothes help him to do this. His videos imitate and exaggerate the style of other rappers. Songs like "Rollout" and "Act a Fool" highlight how silly this lifestyle can become.

18. **ominous** (adjective)   ŏm′ə-nəs

warning of bad things; threatening evil

> The **ominous** black clouds warned us of a thunderstorm.
>
> As I walked through the house, I heard the **ominous** growl of an angry dog.

19. **supplant** (verb)   sə-plănt′

to replace

> No other pet could ever **supplant** the girl's first puppy in her affections.
>
> In the future, plastic "smart cards" may **supplant** cash.
>
> Computers have almost entirely **supplanted** typewriters.

20. **thrive** (verb)   thrīv

to grow vigorously; to do well

> Protected by strong laws, rain forests **thrive** in Costa Rica.
>
> Children **thrive** on praise.

The neglected dog **thrived** after she was adopted by a loving family.

Scientists now think that bacteria may have been the first form of life on Earth. Extremely hardy, some forms of bacteria *thrive* even without sunlight or oxygen. They can survive in boiling water or steaming volcanic vents, in ice, and beneath the ground. So when scientists search for life in places like the frozen moons of Jupiter, they look for bacteria.

The next four words—*radical, liberal, conservative,* and *reactionary*—refer to political opinions that range from left to right. These words can also refer to the people who hold such opinions.

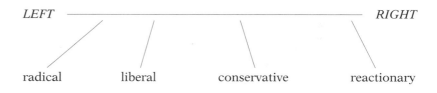

LEFT ———————————————————————— *RIGHT*

radical   liberal   conservative   reactionary

     Radical and liberal politicians are called *left-wing* because they sat on the left side (or wing) of the semicircular seating of the French National Assembly of 1789. Other European assemblies have continued this custom. Radical politicians want swift reforms that will benefit poor people, minorities, and others without political power. Liberal politicians favor the extension of rights and privileges through gradual reform. Between liberals and conservatives, in the middle, are *moderate* politicians.

     Conservatives and reactionaries are called *right-wing* because they sat on the right wing of the French National Assembly. Conservative politicians favor tradition and oppose change. They want to protect business interests, religion, and the traditional family. *Reactionary* politicians oppose change so strongly that they often want to return to the way things used to be. *Radical, liberal,* and *conservative* also have nonpolitical meanings.

---

21. **radical** (adjective)   răd′ĭ-kəl

favoring great change; extreme

> The public demanded **radical** changes in airport safety.
>
> **Radical** politicians wanted to give all the land to the peasants.
>
> Leshan's new business suit was a **radical** departure from the jeans and T-shirt he usually wore.

▶ *Related Word*
> **radical** (noun)   In Iran, some *radicals* have been replaced with moderate leaders. (*Radical* means "a person who holds radical beliefs.")

NOTE: The definition of *radical* often depends on the political situation. In many Muslim countries, for example, *radical* means favoring a return to strict obedience to religion. In Latin American countries, it means favoring an equal distribution of land and wealth. In all countries, however, *radicals* favor great change.

22. **liberal** (adjective)   lĭb′ər-əl

favoring gradual progress and reform

> Many **liberal** politicians in the United States favor providing health care for everyone.

favoring liberty; tolerant

> The college's **liberal** rules allowed all students to live in off-campus apartments.

plentiful; generous in amount

> Employees were pleased when they received **liberal** bonuses.

▶ *Related Words*
> **liberal** (noun)   The *liberal* voted for increased legal aid for the poor. (*Liberal* means "a person who holds liberal beliefs.")
>
> **liberalize** (verb)   When the government *liberalized* rules on censorship, the number of newspapers increased.

23. **conservative** (adjective)   kən-sûr′və-tĭv

favoring traditional beliefs and actions; traditional

> The **conservative** senator favored prayer in schools.
>
> Coming from a **conservative** background, Fay was surprised to see gay couples kissing in the street.
>
> George's nose ring was a strange contrast to his **conservative** business suit.

cautious or moderate

> A **conservative** estimate was that there were 20,000 people at the rally; there may have been more.

▶ *Related Words*
> **conservative** (noun)   Senator Ruggles, a *conservative,* opposed new laws permitting same-sex marriages.

conserve (verb)   People who live in the desert try to *conserve* water. (*Conserve* means "to save.")

24. **reactionary** (adjective)   rē-ăk'shə-nĕr'ē

    opposing progress in an extreme way

    > The **reactionary** educator wanted to use century-old methods to teach reading.

    ▶ *Related Word*
    > **reactionary** (noun)   The *reactionary* wanted to stop all immigration to the United States. (*Reactionary* means a person who holds reactionary beliefs.)

    NOTE: Reactionary usually has a negative connotation.

Exercises

Part 2

■ Matching Words and Definitions

Check your understanding of words in the news by matching each word with the letter of its definition. Use each choice only once.

1. chaos ____**i**____

2. epitome ____**k**____

3. radical ____**l**____

4. ominous ____**h**____

5. liberal ____**a**____

6. thrive ____**j**____

7. reactionary ____**g**____

8. ludicrous ____**b**____

9. supplant ____**c**____

10. defer ____**f**____

a. favoring gradual progress and reform

b. ridiculous

c. to replace

d. to arrest

e. favoring traditional beliefs

f. to delay

g. opposing progress in an extreme way

h. threatening evil

i. confusion

j. to grow vigorously

k. best example

l. favoring great change

■ *Words in Context*

Complete each sentence with the word that fits best. Use each choice only once.

a. apprehend   e. ludicrous   i. radical
b. chaos   f. ominous   j. liberal
c. defer   g. supplant   k. conservative
d. epitome   h. thrive   l. reactionary

1. The police wanted to __a, apprehend__ the thief.

2. His wife's death resulted in a(n) __i, radical__ change in the man's life, as he moved to another city and remarried.

3. It is __e, ludicrous__ to suggest that a dog could fly.

4. The __l, reactionary__ team owner wanted baseball to return to the way it was played in the early 1900s.

5. Plants __h, thrive__ in rich soil.

6. The __f, ominous__ sign read "Danger! Keep out!"

7. The brilliant physicist Albert Einstein is often considered the __d, epitome__ of genius.

8. If you want to please eight-year-olds, bring a(n) __j, liberal__ supply of chocolate bars.

9. In the future, cell phones may __g, supplant__ home phones.

10. Our guess that we would earn $100 was __k, conservative__, because we actually made $200.

■ *Using Related Words*

Complete each sentence by using a word from the group of related words above it. Use each choice only once.

1. chaotic, chaos

In the **chaotic** situation that followed the 2003 war in Iraq, there were many tragic losses. The lack of an effective

security force left the streets in **chaos** . Many people were killed.

2. defer, deference

Recently, an old tradition ended in England. For over 100 years, tennis players at England's Wimbledon court had to show

deference to the king or queen by bowing to the royal

seats. They were expected to **defer** starting their games until they had shown this sign of respect. In 2003, the Duke of Kent eliminated the custom, much to the relief of Martina Navratilova, Jennifer Capriati, and other players, who often forgot to do it.

3. apprehend, apprehended, apprehensive

In most cities it is illegal to dine in a restaurant with your dog, and

if you try, you may be **apprehended** by the police. But in New York, dogs can accompany owners to outdoor cafés. Although

an occasional diner may become **apprehensive** when a huge dog looks longingly at his hamburger, most dogs behave very well. In fact, at Fido's, the first dog spa, dogs are served biscuits while people eat. Fido's now hosts dog birthday parties for owners

who cannot **apprehend** how a dog's birthday can pass without a celebration.

4. conserve, conservative

In 1995, the U.S. Supreme Court decided to uphold a law to aid the spotted owl, an endangered species. The law forbids logging on several thousand acres of forest that provide the bird's habitat.

Although this helps to **conserve** the bird population, it harms business interests, including the jobs of loggers. The ban on logging has been opposed by

<u>**conservative**</u>_____ politicians. This case shows how difficult it can be to balance the existence of wildlife habitat with the needs of the economy.

■ *Reading the Headlines*

This exercise presents five headlines that might appear in newspapers. Read each headline and then answer the questions that follow. (Remember that small words, such as *is, are, the,* and *a,* are often left out of newspaper headlines.)

DESPITE OMINOUS SIGNS, ECONOMY CONTINUES TO THRIVE

1. Are the signs good? **no**_____

2. Is the economy doing well? **yes**_____

RADICAL PROPOSALS FOR CHANGE SEEM LUDICROUS

3. Are minor changes proposed? **no**_____

4. Do the changes seem sensible? **no**_____

CONSERVATIVES SUPPLANT LIBERALS IN PARLIAMENT

5. Are there more conservatives than before? **yes**_____

6. Are there more people favoring gradual progress and

    reform? **no**_____

CHAOS ERUPTS AS STUDENTS REFUSE TO DEFER TO REACTIONARY PRINCIPAL

7. Is the principal old-fashioned? **yes**_____

8. Is the school orderly? **no**_____

MAN APPREHENDED BY POLICE IS EPITOME OF SPORTS HERO

9. Was the person arrested? **yes**_____

10. Is the man a good example of a sports hero? **yes**_____

Chapter Exercises

■ *Practicing Strategies: Context Clues of Substitution*

In each of the following sentences, one difficult word is italicized. Using context clues of substitution, make an intelligent guess about the meaning of the word as it is used in this sentence. Your instructor may ask you to look up these words in your dictionary after you've finished the exercise.

1. The rotten food gave off a *noisome* odor.

   Noisome means **disgusting; terrible**_____.

2. *Corpulent* people often become healthier after they lose weight.

   Corpulent means **fat; overweight**_____.

3. The child was so *contrite* about losing the money that we found it easy to forgive him.

   Contrite means **sorry; regretful**_____.

4. The town hall was a large and beautiful *edifice*.

   Edifice means **building**_____.

5. The road was *truncated* when several miles were closed down.

   Truncated means **shortened**_____.

6. The *parsimonious* millionaire bought a cheap used car.

   Parsimonious means **cheap; frugal**_____.

7. On the exam, Antonio made a *grievous* error that lowered his grade from an A to a C.

   Grievous means **serious; bad**_____.

8. The fierce winds and below-zero temperatures made the weather *gelid*.

   Gelid means **very cold**_____.

9. The person of *paramount* importance was the ruler of the kingdom.

Paramount means **supreme, most** .

10. Injuries to their two best players had a *deleterious* effect on the football team.

Deleterious means **harmful; destructive; bad** .

■ *Practicing Strategies: New Uses of Familiar Words in Context*

Context clues can often help you determine the meaning of words used in unusual ways. Make an intelligent guess about the meaning of the italicized word or phrase in each of the following sentences.

1. The scientist *ran* an experiment to prove his theory.

Ran means **carried out; conducted; did** .

2. A young reporter *sat in* for the absent newscaster.

Sat in means **substituted** .

3. He couldn't vote because he was a few months *shy of* eighteen.

Shy of means **less than; younger than; short of** .

4. After spending the day at the library, they *repaired* to the restaurant.

Repaired means **went** .

5. The president was alone *save for* a few friends.

Save for means **except for** .

■ *Companion Words*

Complete each sentence with the word that fits best. Look back at the "Words to Learn" for help. Choose your answers from the words below. You may use each word more than once.

Choices: to, with, on, of, in, about

1. Queen Elizabeth I was the epitome **of**_____ a great ruler.

2. Monica thrived **on**_____ a healthy diet.

3. Children should defer **to**_____ the wishes of their parents.

4. During Halloween, children's consumption **of**_____ candy is very high.

5. Radioactivity had catastrophic effects **on**_____ plants and animals in the area.

6. Jules showed deference **to**_____ his boss by addressing him as "sir."

7. The child was apprehensive **about**_____ sleeping alone.

8. Nobody dared to intervene **in**_____ the fight between the two gang members.

9–10. Sophia's actions were **in**_____ accordance **with**_____ the rules of our club.

■ Writing with Your Words

This exercise will give you practice in writing effective sentences that use the vocabulary words. Each sentence is started for you. Complete it with an interesting phrase that also indicates the meaning of the italicized word.

1. I would never *intervene* in _____

_____.

2. I would like to *defer* _____

_____.

3. It is *ludicrous* to suggest that _____

_____.

4. I would like to *supplant* required courses with _____

_____.

5. *Conservatives* want _____

_____.

6. One *ominous* trend in society is _____

_____.

7. I cannot *apprehend* how _____

_____.

8. I would favor a *radical* change in _____

_____.

9. You could *pacify* me by _____

_____.

10. The *media* _____

_____.

■ *Making Connections*

These questions will help you relate the words you have learned in this chapter to your own life. Answer each question by writing a paragraph or more on a separate sheet of paper.

1. Is the amount of money a family has an important factor in whether children thrive?

2. Who is an epitome of a great star? Why do you think so?

3. Do you feel that the media is fair to celebrities? Why or why not?

Passage

Sneakers: A Multibillion-Dollar Industry

Once used only for sports, sneakers are now everywhere. Urban teenagers, sports figures, and rap stars have changed the lowly shoe to a world cultural symbol.

Sneakers have undergone dramatic transformations.

Back in 1964, Motown rocker **(1)** Tommy Tucker's hit song "Put on Your High-heeled Sneakers" seemed to suggest something **ludicrous.** But today, fashion designers around the world are producing and selling high-heeled sneakers for several hundred dollars a pair. In fact, nearly everybody wears sneakers and for just about every occasion. Economists estimate that **consumers** bought $16 billion worth in 2002.

It all started in 1899 when Humphrey O'Sullivan got a patent for a rubber heel. Rubber heels, which were more durable than leather, used the vulcanization process discovered by Charles Goodyear, the founder of Goodyear Tires. Keds, a company still in business, produced the first "sneakers." The name came from the fact that rubber heels allowed people to walk so quietly that they could "sneak up" on others.

After World War I, the German Dassler brothers started making shoes in their backyard. When Jesse Owens, the African-American runner, stunned the world by winning the 1936 Olympics, he was wearing Dasslers. The two Dassler brothers separated, **(2)** but each was to become a successful **entrepreneur.** Adolf started the Puma Company. Rudolf changed his name to Adidas.

Sneakers continued to be used as sports shoes. But beneath the surface, things were beginning to change. In **conservative** decades like the 1950s, renegade James Dean, dressed in sneakers for everyday wear, thrilled people in the movie *Rebel Without a Cause.* And in the 1970s, people started wearing sneakers on the street.

But it was Nike that brought sneakers to the public's attention. In 1980, Philip H. Knight imported a shoe from Japan and named his company Nike after the Greek goddess of victory. He paid an Oregon designer

$35 for the now-famous "swoosh" design, **(3)** hired Michael Jordan, the **epitome** of a great basketball player, to promote the shoe, and coined the phrase "Just do it." The **media** were flooded with Nike ads, and overnight, Air Jordan™ shoes became a sensation.

Basketball grew into an important sport in urban neighborhoods. And from these very neighborhoods, the new music of rap and hip-hop emerged. Words and music were clever, **radical,** and at times violent. Neighborhood kids often imitated great basketball players by buying the shoes they wore. No longer just an athletic shoe, sneakers became a status symbol. **(4)** As rap and hip-hop **thrived** in urban neighborhoods, they spread to the rest of America. The "Ghetto Fabulous" style of rappers came to define both song and fashion. When a famous Paris fashion house started designing "Ghetto Fabulous" clothes, they became a sensation. Soon everyone listened to rap and hip-hop, and wore sneakers.

Popular musicians celebrated sneakers in such songs as Nelly's "Air Force Ones." Run DMC's "My Adidas" thanked the company that introduced new sneakers named after their favorite Cadillacs: the Eldorado, Brougham, and Fleetwood. **(5)** Little by little, sneakers **supplanted** regular shoes as the most popular footwear in the United States.

White sneakers in one style only have become a thing of the past. Companies now produce sneakers in every imaginable color, shape, and finish. Rappers have become designers, as figures like Jay-Z and 50 Cent sell their ideas to such companies as Reebok. Prices have skyrocketed. Companies even issue "limited edition" sneakers. The Jackie Chan sold for $300. The Reebok shoe commemorating the reunification of Hong Kong and China cost $2,500. There is a legend that one pair of original Air Jordans sold for $10,000, **(6)** although this has not been **corroborated**.

Teenage "sneaker freaks" collect pairs by the hundreds, spending countless hours in specialty stores. **(7)** They beg their parents for ever more **liberal** allowances so they can buy the most desirable pairs. Some **defer** wearing their new shoes, storing them in closets until they become rare and valuable.

But is all of this a good thing? When "fly" sneakers became desirable, teens started stealing them from each other. There have even been incidents of people killed for their clothes. **(8)** School administrations have **intervened** with dress codes, seeking to prevent **catastrophe** by forcing teens to limit their styles. **(9)** In a truly **ominous** sign, the hit song "My Adidas" was sung by pallbearers, wearing matching white Adidas sneakers, for the funeral of Run DMC's murdered Jam Master Jay.

It has also been reported that several big sneaker companies employ workers in poor nations at low wages and under harsh working conditions. **(10)** The Christian Aid society has worked to reach **accords** between producers and factories and ensure that workers are treated more fairly.

Despite these problems, new sneakers continue to set fashion trends and record prices. A style started by urban teenagers has become a multibillion-dollar business. Thanks to them, **conservative** middle-aged business people throughout the United States wear sneakers to business lunches, to the opera, and to formal dinners. Some of us even "put on our high-heeled sneakers" when we're going out at night.

■ *Exercise*

Each numbered sentence below corresponds to a sentence in the Passage. Fill in the letter of the choice that makes the sentence mean the same thing as its corresponding sentence in the Passage.

1. The hit song suggested something ___d___.
   a. insane   b. changing   c. delayed   d. ridiculous

2. Each brother was to become a successful ___b___.
   a. firm   b. businessperson   c. buyer   d. agent for change

3. Jordan was the ___a___ of a great basketball player.
   a. example   b. salesman   c. advertiser   d. peace agent

4. Rap and hip-hop ___d___ in urban neighborhoods.
   a. were delayed   b. interfered   c. sold   d. grew

5. Sneakers ___a___ regular shoes as the most popular footwear.
   a. replaced   b. agreed with   c. grew with   d. helped

6. The report has not been ___d___.
   a. in the news   b. delayed   c. worn away   d. confirmed

7. They beg their parents for more ___c___ allowances.
   a. ridiculous   b. moderate   c. generous   d. delayed

8. School administrations have ___a___.
   a. interfered   b. agreed   c. been replaced   d. worn away

9. The sign was ___c___.
   a. replaced   b. delayed   c. frightening   d. growing

10. The society worked to reach ___d___.
    a. buyers   b. TV and radio   c. businessmen   d. agreements

■ *Discussion Questions*

1. Which cultures sparked the popularity of sneakers?

2. What are two ways this trend might be considered to have negative effects?

3. Do you think celebrities' involvement in promoting sneakers is good? Why or why not?

◄ ENGLISH IDIOMS

The Media and Communication

Although news sometimes comes to us *by word of mouth,* or through personal contact, we get most of our news from the media. On our way home from work or school, for example, we may *lend an ear to,* or listen to, the radio. If a reporter reading the news is not clear, we may not be able to *make heads or tails of,* or understand, what is being said. At other times, we may *see eye to eye with,* or agree with, a reporter's opinion.

On many television news broadcasts, newscasters talking about the weather *ham it up,* or joke and overact. This may *rub us the wrong way,* or annoy us. Increasingly, the subjects of talk shows are sex and violence. This practice has *raised eyebrows,* or shocked, some members of the public. Yet talk shows have also *brought to light,* or made public, many important issues.

Yellow journalism refers to newspaper reporting that concentrates on shocking and sensational news, such as brutal murders and scandals. The term comes from the "Yellow Kid," the first comic strip in the United States, which was printed in yellow ink to attract attention. Because the newspaper containing the strip, the *New York World,* was known for its shocking news, *yellow paper* or *yellow journalism* came to mean shocking and sensational reporting.

Words for Feeling, Expression, and Action

In this chapter you will learn new words for emotions, thoughts, and actions. Instead of saying you feel very happy, you can use the word *elated*. When you are bored by a speech, you can describe it as *bland*. When you see someone imitating a good model, you can say she is *emulating* it. The words in this chapter will help you use more exciting and precise language.

Chapter Strategy: Context Clues of Definition

Chapter Words:

Part 1

bland	confrontation	emulate
boisterous	dynamic	enigma
clarify	elated	skeptical
concise	emphatic	thwart

Part 2

appall	condemn	flaunt
articulate	contemplate	harass
belligerent	contend	prohibit
chagrin	elicit	undermine

Quiz Yourself

To check your knowledge of some of the chapter words before you begin to study, identify these statements as true or false. Answers are on page 409.

A **boisterous** person is noisy.	True	False
People enjoy being **harassed**.	True	False
When we **flaunt** something, we hide it.	True	False
A **chagrined** person is embarrassed.	True	False

You will learn the answers as you study this chapter.

Did You Know?

How Do Cars Get Their Names?

The process of naming cars involves feeling, expression, and action. A car's name is important to its image. By choosing names that *express* speed, power, glamour, or even economy, manufacturers hope to give you positive *feelings* about their cars that translate into *action* when you decide to buy one.

Long ago, Detroit auto pioneer Henry Leland named early cars after his own heroes.

Cadillac is taken from Antoine de La Mothe Cadillac, the French adventurer who founded Detroit in 1701.
The *Lincoln* honored President Abraham Lincoln, the man Leland voted for in the 1860 election.

The tradition of naming cars carefully continues to this day. Names for sport utility vehicles, pick-up trucks, and minivans often suggest the power and openness of the American west.

Sonoma—county in California famous for wine
Yukon—a mineral-rich territory in Canada; a lake in Canada and Alaska

The DaimlerChrysler Corporation seems to look upward for names. *Stratus* and *Cirrus* refer to types of clouds.

Sometimes carmakers simply create new names that suggest appealing images.

Cadillac *Escalade*—perhaps from *escalate,* meaning "go up," and *parade,* suggesting showy, upbeat travel

Nissan *Altima*—probably from *ultimate,* meaning "the last" and "best"

Oldsmobile *Bravada*—suggesting *bravado,* or showy courage (You will learn the word *bravado* later in this book.)

Car names chosen from the animal kingdom often suggest speed and power, like *Jaguar* and *Cougar.* Bird names have also been popular. Five car models have been named *Eagle.* But the 1912 *Dodo* was a disaster. It was named for an extinct bird that could not fly. Like the real dodo, the car "never got off the ground."

Learning Strategy

Context Clues of Definition

The learning strategy in this chapter will focus on *context clues of definition.* Often, words that you don't know will actually be defined for you as they are used in sentences. Context clues of definition appear often in textbooks. How do these clues work? Usually, a sentence provides a *synonym* (a word that means the same thing or nearly the same thing) for the unknown word. For example, look at the word *effervescent* as it is used in a sentence.

Coca-Cola® is an *effervescent,* or bubbly, beverage.

The word *effervescent* means? . . . bubbly. Thus, *bubbly* is a synonym for *effervescent.*

Such clues of definition are quite easy to use if you can recognize them. Here are some common methods:

1. Words or phrases set off by commas, dashes, or parentheses:

    The man's altruistic, *unselfish,* motives led him to donate money to charity. (This use of commas indicates an *appositive.*)

    The man's altruistic—*unselfish*—motives led him to donate money to charity.

    The man's altruistic *(unselfish)* motives led him to donate money to charity.

2. Direct definition:

> She thought his motives were altruistic, *which means unselfish.*
>
> She thought his motives were altruistic, *that is to say, unselfish.*

3. Indirect definition:

> He was an altruistic person *who often acted out of unselfish motives.*

4. The use of *or, and,* or *also:*

> The man's altruistic, *or unselfish,* motives pleased his family.
>
> (The use of commas with *or* is an extra hint signaling that a context clue of definition is being used.)
>
> The man's altruistic *and unselfish* motives pleased his family.
>
> (Sometimes, however, words joined by *and* and *or* do not mean the same thing. Examples are "The man was lazy and dishonest" and "People shouldn't be lazy or dishonest.")

5. Words signaling agreement, such as *therefore, likewise, in the same way, as well as,* and *similarly:*

> The man was altruistic; *therefore, he donated money to charity and did volunteer work with children.*

As you can see, the word *altruistic,* which you learned in Chapter 1, has been defined in each sentence. Many sentences use the synonym *unselfish.* Others provide a longer definition through examples, such as *donated money to charity* and *did volunteer work with children.*

Three more examples of context clues of definition are given below. Can you make an intelligent guess about the meaning of each italicized word?

1. The margin of the leaf was *sinuated,* and indented curves ran along the edge. (An *and* clue is used.)

2. The king took *draconian* measures against the rebels, and their supporters were also punished severely. (*And* and *also* clues are used.)

3. We used *tricot,* a heavy knitted cloth, to make a jacket. (A comma *appositive* structure is used.)

Answers are on page 409.

Now try using context clues to figure out the meanings of some words you will be learning in this chapter.

1. We were appalled, really shocked, by the violent movie. (An appositive is used.)

   Appalled means **(really) shocked**_____.

2. Manfred's *dynamic*, or energetic, personality amazed us. (An *or* clue and an appositive are used.)

   dynamic means **energetic**_____.

3. The French philosopher Pascal was a *skeptical* thinker who doubted many accepted beliefs. (Indirect definition is used.)

   Skeptical means **doubting**_____.

Answers are on page 409.

Words to Learn

Part 1

1. **bland** (adjective)   blănd

   calming; not spicy

   > The mayor's **bland** responses calmed the angry crowd.

   > After surgery, patients are often fed a **bland** diet of clear soup and gelatin.

   dull

   > Patsy changed her hair color from **bland** brown to fiery red.

   > A **bland** shopping mall, where all stores looked the same, replaced the colorful and varied shop fronts on the city street.

2. **boisterous** (adjective)   boi'stər-əs

   noisy; rowdy; rough

   > It was hard to hear the speaker over the **boisterous** crowd.

   Both New Orleans and Rio de Janeiro are home to *boisterous* Mardi Gras celebrations. People let go of their cares as they sing, dance, shout, parade, and joke. They often wear colorful costumes and masks. After a great time on Mardi Gras, or "Fat Tuesday," the cities settle into the quiet time of Ash Wednesday and Lent.

Mardi Gras celebrations are *boisterous*.

3. **clarify** (verb)   klăr′ə-fī′

to make clear or sensible

> This job description **clarifies** your responsibilities.

▶ *Related Word*
>   **clarification** (noun)   We asked our accountant for **clarification** of the instructions on our tax form.

4. **concise** (adjective)   kən-sīs′

short; clear but using few words

> Most students prefer a **concise** definition of a word to a more lengthy one.
>
> The three-minute speech was **concise,** but powerful.

5. **confrontation** (noun)   kŏn′frŭn-tā′shən

hostile meeting; direct fight

> To avoid a **confrontation** with her parents, Jane took the ring out of her lower lip when she went home.
>
> The coach and the referee had a **confrontation** after the umpire called a foul on the player.

▶ *Related Word*
>   **confront** (verb)   (kən-frŭnt′)   I would not want to **confront** a bear in the forest. (*Confront* means "to meet in a way that leads to a fight.")

6. **dynamic** (adjective)   dī-năm′ĭk

energetic; forceful

> The **dynamic** pastor doubled church membership and raised funds for a new building.

fast moving; fast changing

> Investors have made and lost fortunes within hours on **dynamic** stock futures markets.

▶ *Related Word*
dynamics (noun)   Sports psychologists often study team *dynamics*. Experts studied the *dynamics* of the hurricane. (*Dynamics* means "social or physical forces.")

7. **elated** (adjective)   ĭ-lā′tĭd

thrilled; very happy

> Fans were **elated** when their team won the Super Bowl.

8. **emphatic** (adjective)   ĕm-făt′ĭk

strong; definite

> The **emphatic** speaker waved his arms, pounded the table, and shouted into the microphone.

> The Los Angeles Lakers scored an **emphatic** victory over the Chicago Bulls.

▶ *Related Words*
emphasis (noun)   The professor's *emphasis* in lectures indicates what will be on the test.

emphasize (verb)   Mom *emphasized* her instructions to make them perfectly clear.

9. **emulate** (verb)   ĕm′yə-lāt′

to try to equal or excel through imitating; to imitate

> Competitors try to **emulate** the success of Starbucks at selling coffee.

▶ *Related Word*
emulation (noun)   Its excellent political and economic policies make the African country of Botswana worthy of *emulation*.

10. **enigma** (noun)   ĭ-nĭg′mə

something unexplainable or puzzling

"Idiot savants," who may be mathematical geniuses but cannot manage everyday life, remain **enigmas** to scientists.

▶ *Related Word*

enigmatic (adjective) The humming sounds made by Mississippi's Pascagoula River remain *enigmatic.*

Leonardo da Vinci's famous portrait *Mona Lisa* hangs in the Louvre in Paris. The look on her face is an *enigma.* Is she happy, sad, content, cruel, or displaying another emotion?

11. **skeptical** (adjective)   skĕp′tĭ-kəl

doubting; tending to disbelieve

> The doctor was **skeptical** about the herbal medicine until it cured his patient's flu.

▶ *Common Phrases*
skeptical of; skeptical about

▶ *Related Words*
skeptic (noun)   The *skeptic* did not believe the reports that aliens have visited Earth.

skepticism (noun)   Scientists should show *skepticism* and demand proof of every claim.

12. **thwart** (verb)   thwôrt

to prevent from happening

> A Spokane hotel clerk **thwarted** a theft by offering the thief food and a coat, rather than cash.

> The kidnapping was **thwarted** by a bodyguard.

> Poverty can **thwart** a student's wish to finish college.

Exercises

Part 1

■ Definitions

The following sentences deal with feelings, expressions, and actions. Complete each statement by matching each word with the letter of its definition. Use each choice only once.

1. A concise statement is ___**e**___.

2. Something bland is ___**g**___.

3. To thwart is to ___**d**___.

4. To be elated is to be ___**c**___.

5. An enigma is a(n) ___**j**___.

a. energetic

b. imitate

c. thrilled; very happy

d. prevent from happening

e. short

f. definite; strong

g. dull

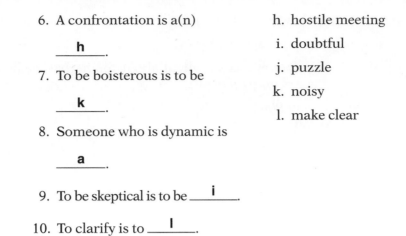

6. A confrontation is a(n) ___h___.

7. To be boisterous is to be ___k___.

8. Someone who is dynamic is ___a___.

9. To be skeptical is to be ___i___.

10. To clarify is to ___l___.

h. hostile meeting

i. doubtful

j. puzzle

k. noisy

l. make clear

■ *Words in Context*

Complete each sentence with the word that fits best. Use each choice only once.

a. bland	e. confrontation	i. emulate
b. boisterous	f. dynamic	j. enigma
c. clarify	g. elated	k. skeptical
d. concise	h. emphatic	l. thwart

1. Something strong and definite is **h, emphatic** _____.

2. When six-year-olds have a(n) **e, confrontation** _____, they fight and scream.

3. Telling my brother about the party will **l, thwart** _____ our plans to surprise him.

4. Ishmael hated spice and would only eat **a, bland** _____ food.

5. After he made his essay more **d, concise** _____, less paper was needed to print it.

6. I am **k, skeptical** _____ that anyone could walk twenty miles in a half hour.

7. Many teenagers try to __i, emulate_____ famous athletes.

8. The __f, dynamic_____ woman ran a company while raising three children.

9. The girl was __g, elated_____ when she was elected prom queen.

10. The mysterious 1937 disappearance of pilot Amelia Earhart remains a(n) __j, enigma_____ to this day.

■ *Using Related Words*

Complete each sentence by using a word from the group of related words above it. You may need to capitalize a word when you write it in a sentence. Use each choice only once.

1. clarify, clarification

In 2000, the U.S. presidential election was decided in the state of Florida, where votes were cast by punching holes in cards. Many cards were not punched through, however, resulting in "chads," or punched-out pieces that clung to the ballots. These could not be read accurately, so volunteers studied each card to try determine what each voter had wanted. Finally, the courts were asked to

__clarify_____ whether or not a "hanging chad" should

count as a vote. The __clarification_____ of this issue, which involved many court cases, resulted in the election of George W. Bush—and in better voting machines.

2. skeptics, skeptical, skepticism

Many computer advertisements, or spam, make ridiculous claims.

It seems only natural to be __skeptical_____ of a diet that results in a twenty-pound loss in one week. Claims of doubling stock investments in one month should also be greeted with

__skepticism_____. In fact, these ads are enough to turn even

the most gullible person into a __skeptic_____.

3. emulate, emulation

Eating disorders may arise when girls seek to **emulate** _____ extremely thin models. Since body types differ, a weight that is healthy for one girl may be too low for another.

Emulation _____ of a favorite star or model can actually result in death from starvation! A U.S. survey found that many eight-year-old girls felt they were overweight. In Argentina, it has been reported that one in ten teenage girls suffers from an eating disorder.

4. boisterous, boisterousness

Are you tired of the **boisterous** _____ children who play on your street daily? Does the **boisterousness** _____ of your neighbor's parties offend you? Do you wish the elderly lady next door would stop bothering you about the noise *you* make? Cities in Colorado, California, New York, and Illinois have joined the Neighborhood Mediation Task Forces. In this program, volunteers are trained to help neighbors address their complaints by working together to solve them.

5. enigma, enigmatic

In 1591, English explorers returning to the new colony of Roanoke, Virginia, found that everyone had vanished. The colonists' disappearance was an **enigma** _____. The word "Croatoan" carved into a tree was the only clue to this **enigmatic** _____ event. Were the people killed? Were they captured? Did they wander away? To this day, no one knows.

■ *True or False?*

Each of the following statements uses at least one word from this section. Read each statement and then indicate whether you think it is probably true or probably false. Your instructor may ask you to reword false statements to make them true.

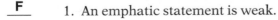

_**F**_   1. An emphatic statement is weak.

_**F**_   2. An enigma is something that has been fully clarified.

T	3. Dynamic forces are fast moving.
F	4. If a crime is thwarted, it takes place.
T	5. We would be skeptical if told that a dish made with twenty-five chili peppers was bland.
T	6. A concise report is short.
F	7. It is good to teach your children to emulate criminals.
T	8. Boisterous laughter is loud.
F	9. An elated person cries with sadness.
T	10. Confrontations are usually difficult.

Words to Learn

Part 2

13. **appall** (verb)   ə-pôl′

    horrify; fill with horror, dismay, or shock

    > The public was **appalled** when police found fourteen children living in a filthy, roach-infested apartment.
    >
    > Parents were **appalled** by the teacher's spelling mistakes.

    ▶ *Related Word*
    appalling (adjective)   Gabrielle found her date's table manners *appalling*.

14. **articulate** (adjective)   är-tĭk′yə-lĭt;   (verb)   är-tĭk′-yə-lāt′

    skilled in using language; well expressed (adjective)

    > An **articulate** person often has a well-developed vocabulary.
    >
    > Hillary Rodham Clinton is an **articulate** spokesperson for children's rights.

    to express clearly and distinctly (verb)

    > Children can't always **articulate** their thoughts and feelings.

▶ *Related Word*

articulation (noun)   Frank Sinatra's *articulation* was so clear that people understood every word he sang.

15. **belligerent** (adjective)   bə-lĭj′ər-ənt

hostile; engaged in warfare

Belligerent Afghans fired on U.S. troops.

The minor disagreement between drivers turned into a **belligerent** shouting match.

▶ *Related Word*

belligerence (noun)   Owners closed their shops for one day to protest the *belligerence* of local gangs.

Belligerent comes from the Latin words *bellum,* "war," and *gerere,* "to carry on." *Bellum* is also the root of the word *rebellion,* a war waged against a ruling power, and of the word *rebel,* a person who defies authority. Two other words that come from *bellum* are *bellicose* (warlike) and *antebellum,* the period in the United States before the Civil War (*ante-* means before).

---

16. **chagrin** (noun)   shə-grĭn′

embarrassment or unhappiness caused by failure

To my **chagrin,** I spilled spaghetti sauce all over my boyfriend's mother.

The kicker was filled with **chagrin** when his missed punt lost the game for his team.

▶ *Common Phrases*

to my (your/his/her/our/their) chagrin; filled with chagrin

17. **condemn** (verb)   kən-dĕm′

to express strong disapproval of

Animal rights activists **condemn** the use of dogs and cats in experiments.

to give a punishment; to find guilty

The judge **condemned** the criminal to life in prison.

His lack of education **condemned** him to a low-level job.

The city inspectors **condemned** the decayed old building. (In this case, *condemn* means "decide to destroy.")

► *Common Phrase*
condemn to

► *Related Word*
condemnation (noun) (kŏn'dĕm-nā'shən) The United Nations issued a *condemnation* of modern-day slavery.

18. **contemplate** (verb) kŏn'təm-plāt' to think about carefully

Some Britons **contemplate** what their country would be like without the royal family.

When Mario **contemplated** taking a vacation with his four children, he realized he would have to rent a minivan.

► *Related Word*
contemplation (noun) Long walks alone provide time for *contemplation*.

19. **contend** (verb) kən-tĕnd'

to compete; to struggle against something.

Greeks from Sparta, Athens, and many other cities **contended** in the ancient Olympic games.

Eighty high school students **contended** in the debate tournament.

Jolene had to **contend** with a class of thirty boisterous children.

NOTE: The phrase *contend with* often means "to cope with."

Can you match these **contenders** with their sports?

1. Oscar de la Hoya	a. tennis
2. Goldberg	b. ice skating
3. Annika Sorensen	c. boxing
4. Venus Williams	d. golf
5. Dick Weber	e. wrestling
6. Sasha Cohen	f. bowling

Answers are on page 409.

---

to put forth a point of view; argue

Some scientists **contend** that Mars once had enough water to support life.

► *Related Words*

contender (noun, person) Three *contenders* entered the Senate race.

contention (noun) It was the museum curator's *contention* that the famous painting was a fake. (*Contention* means "point of view.")

contentious (adjective) The fight for civil rights in the United States was often *contentious*. (*Contentious* means "argumentative.")

20. **elicit** (verb) ĭ-lĭs'ĭt

to draw forth (a response)

The tender love story **elicited** sighs from the audience.

The lawyer was famous for his ability to **elicit** information from closed-mouth witnesses.

21. **flaunt** (verb) flônt

to display obviously or showily; show off

The star **flaunted** her huge diamond.

The military government **flaunted** its strength with parades of well-armed soldiers.

NOTE: Be careful not to confuse *flaunt* (to display) with *flout* (to disregard or ignore).

22. **harass** (verb) hăr'əs or hə-răs'

to annoy or attack repeatedly

The class bully **harassed** boys who wouldn't fight back.

► *Related Words*

harassed (adjective) With a full-time job and three children, Milagros constantly felt *harassed*. (Here *harassed* means "bothered and under stress.")

harassment (noun) The police stopped the gang's *harassment* of elderly citizens.

Harass comes from the Old French *Hare!*—a command telling a dog to "Get it!" This cry was used in hunting, a traditional sport of nobles and rich landowners. Hunters set out on horseback with dogs that followed the scent (smell) of foxes. When the nobles finally saw the fox, they ordered "Hare!" and the dogs chased the fox.

23. **prohibit** (verb)   prō-hĭb′ĭt

to forbid

> People are **prohibited** from entering the dangerous area.
>
> Laws **prohibit** the sale of alcohol to people under the age of twenty-one.

▶ *Common Phrase*
  prohibit (someone) from

▶ *Related Word*
  prohibition (noun)   The city council issued a *prohibition* on new construction in the historic district.

NOTE: Prohibition is also the name of the period from 1919 to 1933, when no sales of liquor were allowed in the United States.

24. **undermine** (verb)   un′dər-mīn′

to weaken or injure slowly

> Our confidence in the press was **undermined** by false reporting.
>
> Constant criticism can **undermine** a person's confidence.

Recent evidence has revealed many problems in the trials of those accused of murder. Weak defense lawyers, faulty eyewitness evidence, and forced confessions have *undermined* justice. Innocent people have been convicted of murder and condemned to death. Fortunately, some have been later found innocent based on DNA or other physical evidence. Because of these problems, in 2000, Illinois governor George Ryan put a hold on all executions in that state.

Exercises

Part 2

■ Definitions

The following sentences deal with feelings, expressions, and actions. Complete each statement by matching each word with the letter of its definition. Use each choice only once.

1. To flaunt is to ___**b**___.

2. To contend is to ___**c**___.

a. annoy repeatedly

b. display obviously

c. compete

3. To condemn is to __h__.

4. To feel chagrin is to feel

   __e__.

5. A belligerent person is

   __k__.

6. To appall is to __f__.

7. To contemplate is to __d__.

8. When we elicit a response,

   we __g__.

9. To undermine is to __j__.

10. Articulate people are __l__.

d. think about carefully

e. unhappy and disappointed

f. fill with shock

g. draw it out

h. express disapproval

i. forbid

j. weaken

k. hostile

l. skilled in using language

■ *Words in Context*

Complete each sentence with the word that fits best. Use each choice only once.

a. appall   e. condemn   i. flaunt
b. articulate   f. contemplate   j. harass
c. belligerent   g. contend   k. prohibit
d. chagrin   h. elicit   l. undermine

1. People can __l, undermine__ their health by eating poorly.

2. A boring lecture might __h, elicit__ yawns from students.

3. The Senate majority leader is expected to __e, condemn__ the racist remarks made by a new senator.

4. Laws __k, prohibit__ drunk people from driving.

5. Dogs __j, harass__ cats by chasing and barking at them.

6. Others became jealous when the girl began to __i, flaunt__ her good grades.

7. Because he was **b, articulate**_____, Alphonse was often asked to give speeches.

8. To my **d, chagrin**_____, I fell on the stage during graduation.

9. The horrors of this brutal war will **a, appall**_____ the public.

10. Police had to put handcuffs on the **c, belligerent**_____ woman they arrested.

■ *Using Related Words*

Complete each sentence by using a word from the group of related words above it. Use each choice only once.

1. harass, harassment, harassed

Ducks and geese can annoy homeowners and damage their yards.

Some homeowners complain they feel **harassed**_____ when dozens of birds choose their property as roosting grounds.

Homeowners have tried several methods of **harassment**_____ to make the birds leave. Laws permit a homeowner to make loud noises and use chemicals that have short-term effects. However, people may not touch the birds or their eggs. If people

harass_____ the birds illegally, they may be charged with a crime.

2. appalled, appalling

In a famous play entitled *Pygmalion*, George Bernard Shaw

presents a language expert who is **appalled**_____ by the speech of a working-class woman. The professor and she work

hard to improve her **appalling**_____ articulation. After several months of work, she convinces others that she is a great lady! This play, remade as *My Fair Lady*, shows how important speech is to social standing.

3. contemplating, contemplation

Born into poverty, Auguste Rodin became one of France's best-known artists. His 1880 sculpture, "The Thinker," shows a man who is **contemplating**_____. The look on the man's face almost defines the nature of **contemplation**_____.

4. prohibition, prohibit

The durian, an unusual fruit, is popular in Thailand. Although it tastes wonderful, its terrible smell reminds people of garbage. Because of the odor, some hotels and airlines **prohibit**_____ the fruit. However, this **prohibition**_____ has not affected the popularity of this delicious but strange-smelling food.

5. contended, contender, contention, contentious

The great African-American athlete Jesse Owens **contended**_____ in the Olympic Games of 1936. These games, held in Germany, were presided over by Nazi leader Adolf Hitler. It was Hitler's racist

contention_____ that the white "Aryan" race was superior to

all others and that no black **contender**_____ could win. However, Owens earned four gold medals in running events. The

contentious_____ Nazi leader refused to attend the award ceremonies. Owens, who died in 1978, remains a symbol of black athletes' struggle for equality.

■ True or False?

Each of the following sentences uses at least one word from this section. Read each statement and then indicate whether you think it is probably true or probably false. Your instructor may ask you to reword false statements to make them true.

T   1. Athletes contend in the Olympics.

F   2. We take immediate action when we contemplate.

F   3. If you flaunt something, you hide it.

T   4. You would be chagrined if your five-year-old brother told all your secrets to the neighbors.

T   5. People should condemn a boss who forced employees to work under appalling conditions.

F   6. Belligerent people are peace-loving.

T   7. People who tell lots of lies undermine their own reputation for truthfulness.

T   8. Bosses should be prohibited from harassing employees.

F   9. When we articulate something, we keep it to ourselves.

T   10. A disabled child often elicits sympathy from adults.

Chapter Exercises

■ *Practicing Strategies: Context Clues of Definition*

In each of the following sentences, a difficult word is italicized. Using context clues of definition, make an intelligent guess about the meaning of the word as it is used in the sentence. Your instructor may ask you to look up these words in your dictionary after you have finished the exercise.

1. Carlos was *cognizant* of the responsibilities he was accepting, for he had been made aware of them beforehand.

    Cognizant means __aware; knowledgeable__.

2. That *charlatan*—the awful faker—gave my aunt something for her illness that almost killed her.

    Charlatan means __fraud; faker; imitator__.

3. The two close friends held a *tête-à-tête*, that is to say, a private conversation.

    Tête-à-tête means __private conversation__.

4. He *bilked* us, which, put more plainly, means he cheated us.

    Bilked means __cheated__.

5. President Calvin Coolidge was a *taciturn* person who seldom talked to others.

    Taciturn means __quiet; not talkative__.

6. Looking into the *limpid* water, we could clearly see the bright colors of the fish.

    Limpid means __clear__.

7. The child's *dyslexia*, a serious reading disorder, was being investigated by a specialist.

    Dyslexia means __serious reading disorder__.

8. For years great chefs have been using the *chanterelle,* that is, a trumpet-shaped mushroom.

   Chanterelle means **a trumpet-shaped mushroom**.

9. The teenager *embellished* the story to the police, as well as exaggerating it to his friends.

   Embellished means **exaggerated; elaborated falsely**.

10. The *vestige,* or small remaining part, of the fossil revealed the impression of a bird's wing.

   Vestige means **small remaining part; remnant**.

■ *Practicing Strategies: Using the Dictionary*

Read the following definition and then answer the questions below it.

> **hawk**[1] (hôk) *n.* **1.** Any of various birds of prey of the order Falconiformes, esp. of the genera *Accipiter* and *Buteo,* having a short hooked bill and strong claws for seizing. **2.** Any of various similar birds of prey. **3.** A person who preys on others; a shark. **4a.** One who demonstrates an aggressive or combative attitude. **b.** A person who favors military action to carry out foreign policy. ❖ *intr.v.* **hawked, hawk•ing, hawks 1.** To hunt with trained hawks. **2.** To swoop and strike in the manner of a hawk. [ME *hauk* < OE *hafoc.* See **kap-** in App.] —**hawk′ish** *adj.*

1. What two parts of speech can *hawk* be? **noun, intransitive verb**.

2. In which language is *hawk* first recorded? **Old English**.

3. What adjective is related to *hawk?* **hawkish**.

4. Give the definition number and part of speech of the definition that best fits this sentence: "In the middle ages, noblemen would *hawk* in the forests with birds on their wrists." **1, intransitive verb**.

5. Give the definition number and part of speech that best fits this sentence: "The representative was a *hawk* who repeatedly voted for war."

   4b, noun.

■ *Companion Words*

Complete each sentence with the word that fits best. Look back at the "Words to Learn" for help. Choose your answers from the words below. You may use words more than once.

Choices: to, of, by, from, for, about

1–2. The spies asked the head of intelligence **for**_____ clarification

of_____ their mission.

3. Many great artists were condemned **to**_____ lives of poverty.

4. Our outdoor picnic was thwarted **by**_____ rain.

5. The public was appalled **by**_____ the negative campaign ads.

6. The cause of cancer remains an enigma **to**_____ scientists.

7. **To**_____ my chagrin, my girlfriend kissed me in front of my boss.

8. Passengers are prohibited **from**_____ leaving their seats when an airplane is taking off.

9. I was skeptical **of, about**_____ my friend's driving abilities.

10. He undermined his happiness **by**_____ not marrying the woman he loved.

■ *Writing with Your Words*

This exercise will give you practice in writing effective sentences that use the vocabulary words. Each sentence is started for you. Complete it with an interesting phrase that also indicates the meaning of the italicized word.

1. My plans to have fun would be *thwarted* if _____

_____.

2. The *bland* meal consisted of _____

_____.

3. I would like to *articulate* my grievances about _____

_____.

4. I have always *contended* that _____

_____.

5. I had a *confrontation* with my brother about _____

_____.

6. The government should *prohibit* _____

_____.

7. I am *skeptical* that _____

_____.

8. Much to my *chagrin,* _____

_____.

9. It is an *enigma* to me how _____

_____.

10. It is *appalling* that _____

_____.

■ *Making Connections*

These questions will help you relate the words you have learned in this chapter to your own life. Answer each question by writing a paragraph or more on a separate sheet of paper.

1. Do you consider yourself articulate? Why?

2. Do you think people convicted of murder should ever be condemned to death? Why?

3. Whom would you like to emulate? Why?

Passage

Jackie Robinson, Baseball Hero

As incredible as it may seem today, at one time African Americans were prohibited from playing baseball in the major leagues. The ban was first broken by Jackie Robinson, a star athlete from the "Negro Leagues," who went on to enrich major league baseball with his exciting and competitive style. This is Robinson's story, but as you read it, you should also think of "Smokey" Joe Williams, Rube and Willie Foster, Josh Gibson, Cool Papa Bell, "Bullet" Joe Rogan, and all the other earlier African-American greats who were denied the chance to play major league baseball.

Almost sixty years ago, a quiet man made baseball history. In 1947, Jackie Robinson became the first African American to play major league baseball in the twentieth century. **(1)** He bravely faced **appalling** persecution and helped **undermine** racial prejudice in the United States. Jackie Robinson "broke the color line."

Before Robinson signed with the Brooklyn Dodgers, **(2)** blacks had been **prohibited** from playing in major league baseball. Although many black players were as good as, or better than, white major league players, blacks were **condemned** to receive almost no national attention.

(3) When the Dodgers' management decided to sign Robinson, they issued a purposely **bland** announcement: "The Brooklyn Dodgers today purchased the contract of Jackie Roosevelt Robinson from the Montreal Royals." The baseball world reacted strongly. Some applauded the move to end discrimination. Others predicted disaster. How could an African American succeed in white baseball? **(4)** Some critics **contended** that Robinson would never be able to live peacefully with white teammates or tolerate the insults of fans. Still others doubted Robinson's ability as a baseball player.

All the doubters were wrong.

The Dodgers' general manager, **(5)** Branch Rickey, had **contemplated** the problem before making his choice. Rickey ensured Robinson's success in the major leagues by working with him on how to respond to **harassment.** "Hey," he would say, impersonating a hotel clerk. "You can't eat here." He imitated a prejudiced white ballplayer and charged into Robinson, saying, "Next time get out of my way, you bastard." Robinson was puzzled: "Are you looking for a Negro who is afraid to fight back?" Replied Rickey, "I'm looking for a ballplayer with guts enough not to fight back. **(6)** Those **boisterous** crowds will insult you, **harass** you, do anything to make you start a fight. And if you fight back, they'll say, 'Blacks don't belong in baseball.'"

Of all the struggles Robinson was to have, the hardest one would be to keep calm in the face of insults. Nobody would be able to **elicit** an outburst from Jackie Robinson. This fiercely proud man, who had refused to sit in the back of an army bus, found the ultimate courage—the courage to be quiet.

In the 1947 season, Robinson was to face trouble that would have defeated a lesser man. Roars of "Go home!" and "Kill him!" were heard from **belligerent** crowd members. Robinson was hit in the head by more "beanballing" pitchers than any other player in the major leagues. Sometimes it became too much for his friends. Robinson's teammate Pee Wee Reese once challenged some **harassers** by shouting at them to take on somebody who could fight back. **(7)** But Robinson himself avoided **confrontations** and never **articulated** his grievances publicly.

Robinson gained revenge in another way. To the amazement of his critics, he succeeded brilliantly in the major leagues. **(8)** Although he never **flaunted** his skill, it was apparent that he was a marvelous ballplayer. For his first year in the majors, he had a batting average of .297, the team high, and was named Rookie of the Year. In his ten years in baseball, his superior playing helped his team win the pennant six times. He must have been **elated** when he was elected the first black member of the Baseball Hall of Fame.

Robinson is perhaps best remembered for his daring base stealing. Sleepy pitchers had to beware, for Robinson could steal a base at a moment's notice. As he ran from base to base, he confused infielders into making mistakes and losing control of the ball. A fellow player gave a **concise** description of Robinson as "a hard out." He stole home base eleven times! **(9)** Although many have tried to **emulate** him, this feat has never been equaled.

In his later years Robinson became ill with diabetes. Although he left baseball, he never stopped fighting for a just society. He championed civil rights and made investments to help build good housing in slum areas.

Jackie Robinson's name lives on in history. We all owe a debt to a brave man who bore the troubles of a prejudiced society. **(10)** No one could **thwart** the ambitions of this great baseball player and pioneer.

■ *Exercise*

Each numbered sentence below corresponds to a sentence in the Passage. Fill in the letter of the choice that makes the sentence mean the same thing as its corresponding sentence in the Passage.

1. He bravely faced ____**b**____ persecution.
   a. frightening b. shocking c. violent d. illegal

2. Blacks had been ____**c**____ from playing major league baseball.
   a. discouraged b. threatened c. forbidden d. discontinued

3. The Dodgers' management issued a purposely ____**d**____ announcement.
   a. short b. exciting c. long d. calm

4. Some critics ___d___ that Robinson would never live peacefully with white teammates.
   a. thought   b. wrote   c. hoped   d. argued

5. Branch Rickey had ___b___ the problem before making his choice.
   a. argued about   b. thought about   c. met with   d. planned for

6. Those ___a___ crowds will insult you.
   a. noisy   b. evil   c. shocking   d. excited

7. But Robinson himself avoided ___d___
   a. hotels   b. fans   c. baseball   d. fights

8. He never ___d___ his skill.
   a. talked about   b. thought about   c. tired of   d. showed off

9. Many have tried to ___d___ him
   a. defeat   b. upset   c. bother   d. imitate

10. No one could ___c___ the ambitions of this great man.
    a. accomplish   b. aid   c. block   d. know

■ Discussion Questions

1. What was Robinson's greatest skill as a baseball player?

2. Why was Robinson's refusal to lose his temper important?

3. In 1955, Rosa Parks refused to obey a law that required blacks to sit in the back of buses. How is Robinson's struggle similar to her act, and how is it different?

THE GREAT SATCHEL PAIGE, 1906–1982

Playing for the Negro League Crawfords and Monarchs, and even in the Dominican Republic, Satchel Paige was so famous that his pitches were given names such as "bee-ball," "jump-ball," and "trouble-ball." With his great skill, sense of fun, and willingness to take risks, Paige was a legendary figure. After Jackie Robinson "broke the color line" in major league baseball, Paige became the oldest rookie ever to play in the majors. St. Louis Browns fans remember that he relaxed in his personal rocking chair when not on the field. Paige, the oldest man to pitch in a major league game, ended his career at age fifty-nine.

◀ ENGLISH IDIOMS

Feelings and Actions

Many English idioms express feelings and actions. Some expressions deal with being bothered or confused. *To drive wild* and *to drive up the wall* mean to cause someone to become frantic or crazy. People who are *at loose ends* are unsettled and lack a clear direction for their lives. Such people may also have many *loose ends*, or undone things to finish. Other idioms deal with preciseness. When we *hit the nail on the head*, we get something exactly right.

When teachers tell students, *"don't sweat"* an exam, they mean don't worry about it. However, most students will improve their grades if they *hit the books*, or study. Computers, which are always improving, help us to study. If your old computer *can't hold a candle* to your new computer, your new computer is much better than your old one.

To *bury the hatchet* means to make peace. The early English settlers of the American colonies often fought and then made peace with Native American tribes. To symbolize that fighting had stopped, both sides buried a hatchet in the ground. In 1680, Samuel Sewall wrote that since the hatchet was a very important weapon for the Native Americans, this ceremony was more meaningful to them than a written agreement.

4

Other Useful English Words

If you read, "New technology is making pay phones *obsolete*," do you know what the author means? When a newscaster says, "The economy can't *withstand* more bad news," do you understand? This chapter presents a variety of words that college students have identified as useful. The author's classes collected them from textbooks, newspapers, magazines, and the media. Because students encountered these words often, they wanted to learn them. You, too, should find them valuable additions to your vocabulary.

Chapter Strategy: Context Clues of Opposition

Chapter Words:

Part 1

accolade	cryptic	meticulous
augment	indulge	obsolete
chivalrous	jeopardize	perpetual
complacent	mandatory	zealous

Part 2

accelerate	cultivate	pinnacle
adulation	euphemism	procrastinate
chronological	mammoth	successive
copious	mitigating	withstand

Quiz Yourself

To check your knowledge of some chapter words before you begin to study, identify these statements as true or false. Answers are on page 410.

The **pinnacle** is the top.	True	False
An **accolade** is an honor.	True	False
Adulation means hatred.	True	False
Something **mammoth** is small.	True	False

You will learn the answers as you study this chapter.

Did You Know?

How Does English Get New Words?

What language has the most words? What language is most used for international communication? The answer to both questions is English!

Mandarin Chinese is the most widely spoken language in the world, but English is number two, and the number of English speakers is constantly growing. Perhaps more important, English is the international language of technology and business. Most international scientific journals are published in English. Japanese and German companies, for instance, train many employees in English. English now influences other languages so powerfully that the French passed a law forbidding terms like *Walkman, leader, label, jeans,* and *disque jockey* in government communications and advertising.

New inventions, discoveries, and customs are constantly adding new words to English. In 1928, the first *Oxford English Dictionary* had ten volumes; it now has twenty. Editors are adding terms like *reality television, 24/7* (all the time), and *geekfest* (unfashionable people having a technical discussion). In fact, there are so many new words that *Barnhart's Dictionary of New English Words* has been created to catalog them.

Computers and the Internet have given us words like *software* and *text messaging.* Sometimes these words are made from older ones. *Retail* refers to buying at a store; *e-tail* means buying on the Internet. Similarly, an *e-zine* is a magazine on the Internet.

One new word can be formed from two old ones, as many Internet words show. *Netiquette* combines *Internet* and *etiquette*; it refers to how one behaves when using the Internet. *E-mail* merges the abbreviation for *electronic* and the word *mail*; *blog* combines *web* and *log*. Political protest also gives us new combined words. Those who object to genetically modified food call it *Frankenfood*, a combination of *Frankenstein* (from the famous horror story) and *food*.

The business world is a rich source of words. Hours in the office are called *face time*. The new European currency is called the *euro*. The Canadian government put a picture of a loon, a water bird found in Canadian lakes, on its dollar coin. People promptly nicknamed the coin *loonie*. Then, when the government issued a two-dollar coin, it was promptly called the *toonie*!

Parts of ancient Greek and Latin words are also used to create words. A person who is interested in the quality of sound reproduction is an *audiophile*. The word is formed from the Latin verb *audire* (to hear) and the ancient Greek noun *philos* (love). People may suffer from *cholesterophobia*, formed from *cholesterol* and *phobia* (the ancient Greek noun for fear). In this book, you will study many words from Greek and Latin.

Using old words in new ways has a time-honored tradition. The meanings of many words have changed over centuries of use. *Husband* once meant "master of the house." *Lady* meant "kneader of bread."

Can you match these new words and phrases with their definitions?

1. bloviate
2. hold the hail
3. aggie
4. bottom feeder
5. fly

a. no ice
b. fashionable, good
c. to write or speak in an unnecessarily long and complex manner
d. angry
e. a person who thrives on the bad luck of others

Answers are on page 410.

Learning Strategy

Context Clues of Opposition

Some sentences give the opposite definition or sense of a word you are trying to understand. A simple opposition clue is the word *not*. Take the following example:

The food was *not* hot, but cold.

Hot is, of course, the opposite of *cold*. Context clues of opposition can be used for more difficult words.

Since it was something not normal in nature, it was considered an *anomaly*. (An anomaly is something not normal or usual.)

Often a clue of opposition will provide an *antonym*, or a word opposite in meaning. In the first example, *hot* is an antonym of cold. Clues of opposition are easy to use if you become familiar with opposing structures in sentences. Some of the common structures are as follows.

1. The use of *not* and *no*.

   Peggy was *not happy*, but despondent.

2. Words signaling opposition. These include *but, nevertheless, despite, rather than, regardless of the fact, unless, if not,* and *although*.

   Peggy was despondent *despite* the fact that her sister was *happy*.

3. Words with negative senses. Certain words have a negative meaning, such as *merely, mere, barely, only, rarely, never, hardly, nowhere,* and *nothing*.

   Peggy was despondent and *rarely* felt happy.

4. Words containing negative prefixes, such as *anti-, un-, dis-, non-,* and *in-*. For example, when the prefix *un-* is added to *happy*, it forms *unhappy*, which means the opposite of *happy*.

   Peggy was despondent and felt *unhappy*.

From these examples, it is clear that *despondent* means "sad" or "depressed." In the examples, the antonym of *despondent (happy)* is given as a context clue.

Three examples of context clues of opposition are given below. Can you guess at the meaning of the italicized words? Remember that context clues of opposition, like all context clues, may give only the general sense of a word.

1. He was not shy and was, in fact, an *extrovert*. (A *not* clue is used.)

2. There was so much *enmity* between the two brothers that they almost never spoke to each other. (A word with a negative sense is used.)

3. Although Kristin thought the candidate was *despicable*, her friend thought he was wonderful. (A word signaling opposition is used.)

Answers are on page 410.

Now try context clues to determine the meaning of some words in this chapter.

1. The *meticulous* person rarely made a careless error. (A word with a negative sense is used.)

   Meticulous means **careful**_____.

2. Unable to *withstand* the force of the waves, the boat broke apart. (A negative prefix is used.)

   Withstand means **resist, tolerate, bear**_____.

3. Because the course was not *mandatory,* we did not have to take it. (A *not* clue is used.)

   Mandatory means **required**_____.

Answers are on page 410.

Words to Learn

Part 1

1. **accolade** (noun)   ăk′ə-lād′

   praise, honor, award

   > South African Nelson Mandela was awarded the **accolade** of the Nobel Peace Prize for his fight against apartheid.
   >
   > The high-performing school district received many **accolades**.

   NOTE: Accolade used in the singular means an award or honor; in contrast, *accolades,* the plural, usually signifies general praise or applause.

   The word *accolade* comes from a ceremony during the Middle Ages in which a warrior was made a knight. The ruler gave the knight an accolade (an embrace) and dubbed him (tapped him on the shoulder with a sword). Thus, the word *accolade* is related to the word *chivalrous,* the third word in this section.

In the code of *chivalry*, a warrior was made a knight by being given
an *accolade* and being dubbed, as shown here.

2. **augment** (verb)   ôg-měnt′

to increase

> I **augmented** my income by taking a second job.
>
> People can **augment** their height by wearing high-heeled shoes.

▶ *Related Word*
> **augmentation** (noun)   Websites often result in considerable
> *augmentation* of a company's sales.

3. **chivalrous** (adjective)   shĭv′-əl-rəs

having qualities of honor, including courtesy, bravery, and loyalty

> The **chivalrous** man held the door open for his date.

The **chivalrous** knight used his own body to shield his master from attack.

▶ *Related Word*
chivalry (noun)   In a famous act of *chivalry*, Sir Walter Raleigh laid his cloak across a puddle so that Queen Elizabeth I would not get her feet wet.

NOTE: Chivalry usually refers to the actions of men.

Chivalry was the code of conduct for European knights in the Middle Ages. A true knight was brave, loyal, and fair; he showed mercy to the defeated and loyalty to his overlord, or master. In the tradition of courtly love, a knight dedicated poems to his lady and fought tournaments in her name. However, this idealized passion involved only worship from afar. *Chivalrous* gestures are considered somewhat old-fashioned in today's society, but in the Middle Ages they represented an improvement in the treatment of women.

---

4. **complacent** (adjective)   kəm-plā′sənt

overly self-satisfied

People in the United States were **complacent** about airline security before the September 11 terrorist attacks.

After years of good health, Michael became **complacent** and stopped going for yearly checkups.

NOTE: Complacent is a somewhat negative word.

▶ *Related Word*
complacency (noun)   The *complacency* of the company allowed its competitors to succeed.

5. **cryptic** (adjective)   krĭp′tĭk

puzzling; mysterious in meaning

I was puzzled by the **cryptic** messages on my computer screen.

Egyptian hieroglyphics remained **cryptic** until the discovery of the Rosetta Stone enabled them to be translated.

6. **indulge** (verb)   ĭn-dŭlj′

to pamper; to yield to desires

Grandparents often **indulge** their grandchildren.

I wanted to **indulge** myself by buying an expensive new pair of shoes.

▶ *Common Phrases*
indulge in; indulge oneself (Indulge often uses a reflexive pronoun, such as myself, yourself, or herself.)

▶ *Related Word*
indulgence (noun)   After a hard year, the cruise to the Bahamas was a great *indulgence*.

7. **jeopardize** (verb)   jĕp′ər-dīz′

to risk loss or danger

Marcus **jeopardized** his savings by putting them in a risky investment.

A single computer virus can **jeopardize** an entire hard drive.

▶ *Related Word*
jeopardy (noun)   The soldier's loud whispering put the secret attack in *jeopardy*.

8. **mandatory** (adjective)   măn′də-tôr′ē

required; commanded

English 101 was **mandatory** for college graduation.

Military service is **mandatory** in some countries.

▶ *Related Words*
mandate (noun)   (măn′dāt′)   The court issued a *mandate* that stopped the factory from polluting the river. (Here *mandate* means "command.")

The governor interpreted the wide margin of his election victory as a *mandate* to reduce taxes. (Here *mandate* refers to the unspoken wishes of the people who have elected an official.)

mandate (verb)   The company *mandated* computer training for all employees.

9. **meticulous** (adjective)   mĭ-tĭk′yə-ləs

extremely careful; concerned with details

Performing open-heart surgery is **meticulous** work.

My English professor is **meticulous** about correcting grammatical errors.

10. **obsolete** (adjective)   ŏb′sə-lēt′

no longer in use; outmoded; old-fashioned

> Electricity has made gas lamps **obsolete.**
>
> **Obsolete** words, like *welkin* and *grece,* make Shakespeare's plays difficult to understand.

▶ *Related Word*
obsolescent (adjective) (ŏb′sə-lĕs′ənt) No one wants to buy an *obsolescent* computer. (*Obsolescent* means "becoming obsolete.")

11. **perpetual** (adjective)   pər-pĕch′o͞o-əl

lasting forever; eternal

> Many religions teach that the human soul is **perpetual.**

continuous and long lasting

> The inefficient college registration system is a source of **perpetual** student complaints.

▶ *Related Words*
perpetually (adverb) Ann Marie is *perpetually* late.
perpetuate (verb) (pər-pĕch′o͞o-āt′) The country name of Bolivia *perpetuates* the memory of South American freedom fighter Simón Bolívar.

12. **zealous** (adjective)   zĕl′əs

extremely dedicated or enthusiastic

> Champion athletes are **zealous** in their pursuit of victory.
>
> The **zealous** teacher stayed after school every day to help struggling readers.

▶ *Related Word*
zeal (noun) (zēl) We admired the *zeal* of the priest who dedicated his life to his faith.

The first *zealots* were religious Jews who fought against Roman rule. After Romans destroyed the second Jewish temple in 70 CE, the Zealots retreated to the ancient mountaintop fortress of Masada. There, 1,000 people held off a Roman force of 15,000 for more than two years. Preferring death to defeat, the Zealots committed suicide when they realized they could not win.

NOTE: Zealous can refer to enthusiasm that is excessive, and thus, often negative.

Exercises

Part 1

■ Matching Words and Definitions

Check your understanding of useful words by matching each word with the letter of its definition. Use each choice only once.

1. cryptic ___f___
2. jeopardize ___e___
3. complacent ___a___
4. obsolete ___i___
5. zealous ___g___
6. augment ___j___
7. perpetual ___k___
8. accolade ___c___
9. meticulous ___h___
10. mandatory ___l___

a. overly self-satisfied
b. having qualities of honor
c. award
d. yield to desires
e. to risk loss or danger
f. mysterious in meaning
g. dedicated or enthusiastic
h. very careful
i. no longer used
j. to increase
k. lasting forever
l. required

■ Words in Context

Complete each sentence with the word that fits best. Use each choice only once.

a. accolade   e. cryptic   i. meticulous
b. augment   f. indulge   j. obsolete
c. chivalrous   g. jeopardize   k. perpetual
d. complacent   h. mandatory   l. zealous

1. In some states a breath test is **h, mandatory** ___ if you are stopped on suspicion of drunk driving.

2. In a(n) **c, chivalrous** ___ gesture, the man bowed and kissed the woman's hand.

3. Patrick Henry was so __l, zealous__ in pursuing liberty that he said, "Give me liberty or give me death."

4. I would like to __f, indulge__ myself by taking a vacation.

5. The horse and chariot are now __j, obsolete__ in warfare.

6. The __a, accolade__ of the Purple Heart has been awarded to many soldiers serving in Iraq and Afghanistan.

7. After earning straight A's, Rick became __d, complacent__ and stopped studying.

8. We could not understand the __e, cryptic__ code.

9. Failure to wear a seat belt in a car can __g, jeopardize__ your safety.

10. The farm workers tried to be __i, meticulous__ about separating the good strawberries from the spoiled ones.

■ *Using Related Words*

Complete each sentence by using a word from the group of related words above it. Use each choice only once.

THE GREAT ELEANOR OF AQUITAINE

1. chivalry, chivalrous

   The tradition of __chivalry__ owes much to Eleanor of Aquitaine, 1122–1204. As perhaps the most powerful woman of her century, she ran the court of Aquitaine (now part of France), which

   invited poets and performers to celebrate the __chivalrous__ deeds of legendary knights.

2. augment, augmentation

   The province of Aquitaine, which Eleanor inherited, was actually larger than France at the time. Thus, by marrying Eleanor, any king could considerably **augment**_____ the land under his control. In those days, when there was little commerce and hardly any currency, land was the only real source of power. Thus, an

augmentation_____ of territory meant an increase in power. Eleanor was a sought-after bride, and her first marriage was to the French king Louis VII.

3. indulged, indulgences

   But in her youth, Eleanor **indulged**_____ in some wild behavior. In fact, King Louis VII divorced her for unfaithfulness. As the heir to enormous lands, she soon remarried. Unfortunately, her second marriage, to King Henry II of England, was also

   unhappy. This time, it was Henry's **indulgences**_____ with other women that caused problems.

4. perpetual, perpetually, perpetuate

   Life was stressful for Eleanor. Nobles of this time traveled extensively, moving among their many properties. Even when pregnant,

   Eleanor was **perpetually**_____ moving by horseback or small, often unsafe, boats. Unfortunately, her arguments with

   Henry proved to be **perpetual**_____. She spent much of her time apart from him, ruling her court in Aquitane. She even supported a revolt against Henry. In revenge he imprisoned her for sixteen years. She was freed only when their son Richard the Lion-Hearted assumed the throne. In her last years, she remained strong. When almost eighty, she crossed the English Channel from England to present-day France twice—a dangerous journey in those days—to fetch her granddaughter. One recorder described Eleanor as "beautiful and just, imposing and

   modest, humble and elegant." We **perpetuate**_____ her memory every time we tell stories of knights in shining armor and courtly love.

■ *True or False?*

Each of the following statements contains at least one word from this section. Read each statement and then indicate whether you think it is probably true or probably false. Your instructor may ask you to reword false statements to make them true.

__F__   1. People want to use obsolete technology.

__F__   2. When people indulge themselves, they work hard.

__F__   3. Complacent people are not satisfied.

__T__   4. Most people want to augment their income.

__F__   5. Cryptic behavior is easily understood.

__T__   6. Perpetual care is long lasting.

__F__   7. A chivalrous person is often rude.

__F__   8. A person may choose to do something mandatory.

__T__   9. A computer programmer who is not meticulous may jeopardize her work.

__T__   10. A zealous worker would be likely to receive the accolade of "Employee of the Month."

Words to Learn

Part 2

13. **accelerate** (verb)   ăk-sĕl′ə-rāt′

    to speed up; to go faster

    > Our heartbeats **accelerate** when we run.

    > Discoveries of large oil deposits are **accelerating** Azerbaijan's economic development.

    ▶ *Related Words*
    acceleration (noun)   *Acceleration* helps airplanes to lift off the ground.

    accelerator (noun)   The race car driver pressed the *accelerator* to the floor.

    accelerated (adjective) An *accelerated* degree program enabled Frasier to earn an MBA in less than a year.

14. **adulation** (noun) ăj′ə-lā′shən

extreme admiration or flattery

> The bride looked at the groom with **adulation** as she said, "I do."
>
> Adoring fans greeted the Latin rock band Mana with **adulation.**

▶ *Related Word*
  adulate (verb)   Boys often *adulate* famous athletes.

15. **chronological** (adjective) krŏn′ə-lŏj′ĭ-kəl

arranged in order of time

> Jamal's job application listed his work experience in **chronological** order.

▶ *Related Word*
  chronology (noun)   (krə-nŏl′ə-jē)   A *chronology* of Egyptian pharaohs is listed in the front of the textbook.

16. **copious** (adjective) kō′pē-əs

plentiful; abundant

> The student's **copious** lecture notes filled ten pages.

NOTE: Copious cannot be used to refer to a single large thing. We cannot say "a copious piece of cake." We can, however, refer to "copious notes," "a copious amount of sand," and "copious supplies." These are all composed of many things.

▶ *Common Phrase*
  copious amount

17. **cultivate** (verb) kŭl′tə-vāt′

to grow deliberately; to develop

> Parents try to **cultivate** their children's athletic abilities.
>
> California's Kearny Agricultural Center **cultivates** papayas, a fruit from the tropics, in the United States.
>
> The lobbyist **cultivated** contacts with important senators.
>
> The college student **cultivated** a relationship with his rich aunt, who he hoped might pay his tuition.

▶ *Related Words*
  cultivated (adjective)   Going to college helps a person to become more *cultivated*. (*Cultivated* often describes people who are cultured and have interests in history, art, classical music, literature, etc.)

cultivation (noun)   Stefano's musical *cultivation* impressed us.

NOTE: Cultivated is used in many common phrases, including *to cultivate a taste for* (something), and *to cultivate an image. Cultivated pearls* are created from grains of sand placed inside oysters, rather than gathered from the oysters found in the ocean.

Corn, or maize, is the most important product *cultivated* in the Americas. When Christopher Columbus first saw corn in Cuba, he remarked on the meticulous efficiency of its cultivation. Early Americans developed modern corn over thousands of years, and efforts to improve corn continue. Researchers in Mexico, Nigeria, and the United States are currently cooperating to develop corn that contains more vitamin A.

---

18. **euphemism** (noun)   yo͞o′fə-mĭz′əm

a more positive word or phrase substituted for a negative one

> "Cul-de-sac" is a **euphemism,** taken from French, for "dead end."

▶ *Related Word*
euphemistic (adjective)   "Peacekeeping forces" can be a *euphemistic* expression for soldiers.

Euphemisms are used frequently. A bank recently announced that it was "downsizing" by "lowering payroll costs through reducing head count." In other words, it was firing people.

Do you know what these common euphemisms stand for?

1. These people are *economically disadvantaged.*

2. He has gone to *meet his maker.*

3. He is *mentally challenged.*

4. This will be a slightly *uncomfortable* procedure.

5. She *stretched the truth a bit.*

Answers are on page 410.

---

19. **mammoth** (adjective)   măm′əth

huge; very large

> Millions of years ago, the **mammoth** arthropleura, an insect over six feet long, lived on forest floors.

NOTE: The word *mammoth* originates in the Russian name for a huge woolly elephant that is now extinct. Other animal names have now become common words in English. A *chicken* is a coward. To *parrot* means to repeat. For more animal idioms, see the "English Idioms" box on page 343 in Chapter 10.

20. **mitigating** (adjective)   mĭt′ĭ-gāt′ĭng

making less severe or intense; moderating

> An ocean breeze has a **mitigating** effect on tropical heat.
>
> Good music **mitigated** the boredom of our wait.
>
> Declaring the thief's young age a **mitigating** circumstance, the judge reduced his jail term.

▶ *Common Phrase*
  mitigating circumstance(s)

▶ *Related Word*
  mitigate (verb)   Grandmother *mitigated* her harsh words with a wink.

21. **pinnacle** (noun)   pĭn′ə-kəl

top; highest point

> The **pinnacle** of Mount Everest is the highest point on Earth.
>
> The British Empire reached the **pinnacle** of its power in the late 1800s.

22. **procrastinate** (verb)   prō-krăs′tə-nāt′

to delay; to put off

> Because Leshan **procrastinated** about seeing a dentist, he ended up losing a tooth.

▶ *Related Words*

procrastinator (noun, person)   The National *Procrastinators'* Club celebrates New Year's Day in October.

procrastination (noun)   *Procrastination* is the strategy I use when my wife asks me to wash the dishes.

23. **successive** (adjective)   sək-sĕs′ĭv

following one after another without interruption

> For three **successive** years, our town has raised taxes.

> My family lived on this farm for four **successive** generations.

▶ *Related Words*

successor (noun, person)   John Adams, second president of the United States, was the *successor* to George Washington, the first president.

succession (noun)   After a *succession* of rude students, the teacher finally met a polite one.

> The prince's *succession* to the throne was greeted with joy. (*Succession* can mean the inheritance of a crown or title.)

24. **withstand** (verb)   wĭth-stănd′ (past tense: **withstood**)

not to surrender; to bear (the force of)

> Russia has **withstood** many attacks, but has never been conquered.

> Shakespeare's plays have **withstood** the test of time.

> Unable to **withstand** the force of the hurricane, the tree broke in half.

When you meet smiling, friendly Mike, it is difficult to understand the hardships he *withstood* as a soldier in the Vietnam War. Drafted at eighteen, he lived in the midst of mud and roaches for months. He had to kill, or be killed. He was captured by the enemy and tortured. Finally, he was able to escape only by killing his guard. For comfort from the terrible conditions he endured and to rid himself of the ghosts that haunted him, he turned to opium. When he returned from the war, it took him thirteen years to overcome his addiction. Mike must also *withstand* the burden of his guilt. He has apologized to the Vietnamese people for his role in what he considers a tragedy for Vietnam—and for U.S. soldiers.

Exercises

Part 2

■ Matching Words and Definitions

Check your understanding of useful words by matching each word with the letter of its definition. Use each choice only once.

1. procrastinate __c__

2. accelerate __d__

3. chronological __k__

4. euphemism __b__

5. successive __e__

6. adulation __i__

7. pinnacle __a__

8. mitigating __j__

9. withstand __g__

10. copious __h__

a. top

b. use of a more positive word or phrase in place of a negative one

c. to delay

d. to speed up

e. following without interruption

f. very large

g. not to surrender

h. plentiful

i. extreme admiration

j. making less severe

k. in order of time

l. to grow deliberately

■ Words in Context

Complete each sentence with the word that fits best. Use each choice only once.

a. accelerate   e. cultivate   i. pinnacle
b. adulation   f. euphemism   j. procrastinate
c. chronological   g. mammoth   k. successive
d. copious   h. mitigating   l. withstand

1. Thanksgiving dinners usually include a(n) **d, copious** amount of food.

2. Today's newest roller coasters **a, accelerate** very rapidly.

3. The **g, mammoth** blue whale is 100 feet long and weighs 400,000 pounds.

4. The English teacher used the **f, euphemism** "not quite acceptable" to describe the failing paper.

5. Students who **j, procrastinate** starting papers may find themselves staying up all night the night before the papers are due.

6. Most parents want their children to **e, cultivate** a taste for healthy food.

7. Events listed by date are given in **c, chronological** order.

8. So far, the dancers in the marathon have been on the dance floor for eighteen **k, successive** hours.

9. At the **i, pinnacle** of her career, the newscaster earned $1 million per year.

10. The boy's apology had a(n) **h, mitigating** effect on his mother's anger.

■ *Using Related Words*

Complete each sentence by using a word from the group of related words above it. Use each choice only once.

THE LIFE OF ELVIS PRESLEY

Elvis receiving the *adulation* of fans.

1. adulated, adulation

   Elvis Presley, perhaps rock 'n' roll's most legendary performer,

   was **adulated**＿＿＿＿＿＿ by millions. So great was their

   adulation＿＿＿＿＿＿ that, thirty years after his death, his former home, Graceland, in Memphis, Tennessee, remains a popular tourist attraction.

2. chronology, chronological

   The **chronology**＿＿＿＿＿＿ of Elvis's life is simple. He was born in 1935 in Tupelo, Mississippi. He served in the army, married, had a daughter, and divorced. At the time of his sudden death at Graceland in 1977, his records had sold over 500 million copies, and he had made thirty-five movies. This

   chronological＿＿＿＿＿＿ retelling of his life, however, cannot capture his enormous influence.

3. cultivate, cultivating, cultivation, cultivated

Growing up, Elvis was surrounded by the music of the American south. He listened to the Grand Ole Opry on the radio; he **cultivated**_____ a taste for gospel and sang in a church choir; and he studied African-American blues artists. Although these artists were largely unrecognized by white audiences of the time, many people of musical **cultivation**_____ borrowed from the great heritage of the blues. Elvis's knowledge of blues later inspired him to **cultivate**_____ an intensely personal style.

His performances also became known for **cultivating**_____ sex appeal, which gave him the nickname "Elvis the Pelvis."

4. withstand, withstood

Elvis's performances **withstood**_____ attacks from many sources. In his early days, he was criticized by racists, who did not like the popularity of blues music. Later, his reputation had to **withstand**_____ the attacks of those who felt he built his fame on the work of such magnificent blues artists as Muddy Waters and B. B. King. Yet Elvis also gathered accolades. Twice he was awarded the Grammy for gospel music.

5. mitigated, mitigating

Tremendous success was **mitigated**_____ by personal problems. His marriage failed, and, by the end, he was probably addicted to mood-controlling pills. Yet Elvis's abiding love for his mother, even after her death, was a **mitigating**_____ factor that counterbalanced his flaws. Today he is remembered for such classics as "Love Me Tender," "Hound Dog," "All Shook Up," and "Don't Be Cruel." Can you hum any of these tunes?

■ *Reading the Headlines*

This exercise presents five headlines that might appear in newspapers. Read each headline and then answer the questions that follow. (Remember that small words, such as *is, are, a,* and *the,* are often left out of newspaper headlines.)

COPIOUS SPRING RAIN MITIGATES EFFECTS OF DRY WINTER

1. Did it rain much in the spring? **yes**

2. Did the rain make the effects of the winter stronger? **no**

**MAMMOTH HURRICANES POUND EAST COAST
FOR THIRD SUCCESSIVE YEAR**

3. Are the hurricanes small? **no**

4. Did the hurricanes hit for three years in a row? **yes**

CULTIVATION OF LAND ACCELERATES IN DESERT

5. Are crops being grown? **yes**

6. Is the cultivation speeding up? **yes**

**CEO, UNABLE TO WITHSTAND CRITICISM, RESIGNS
AFTER PROCRASTINATING ABOUT MAKING CHANGES
TO IMPROVE COMPANY**

7. Did the CEO improve the company right away? **no**

8. Could the CEO bear the criticism? **no**

**AT PINNACLE OF CAREER, OPERA STAR RECEIVES
ADULATION OF CROWD**

9. Is the opera star at the height of her career? **yes**

10. Does the crowd act positively toward the opera star? **yes**

Chapter Exercises

■ *Practicing Strategies: Context Clues of Opposition*

In each of the following sentences, a difficult word is italicized. Using context clues of opposition, make an intelligent guess about the meaning of the word as it is used in the sentence. Your instructor may ask you to look up each word in your dictionary after you have finished the exercise.

1. Although the editor's efforts were usually *disparaged*, she was occasionally praised.

   Disparaged means **criticized; spoken badly about**.

2. The *dauntless* speaker was not at all frightened by the hostile crowd.

   Dauntless means **without fear; fearless; brave**.

3. He *dissipated* his money on parties and cars, and soon he was broke.

   Dissipated means **spent wastefully; wasted everything**.

4. The politician decided to ignore his prepared speech and give an *extemporaneous* address.

   Extemporaneous means **unrehearsed; unprepared; spur of the moment**.

5. Alpa displayed *fortitude* in climbing the mountain, for nothing could make her quit.

   Fortitude means **strength to finish; endurance**.

6. The *pusillanimous* soldier lacked courage.

   Pusillanimous means **cowardly**.

7. Barbara is *reticent* about revealing her background, despite the fact that she talks freely about other things.

   Reticent means **hesitant; shy; not willing**.

8. She thought she would be *recompensed*, but she was never paid.

   Recompensed means **paid**.

9. This *diminutive* type of hummingbird almost never grows to be more than three inches long.

   Diminutive means **tiny; small**.

10. Although she was usually *garrulous*, Anna became quiet at the party.

    Garrulous means **talkative**.

■ *Companion Words*

Complete each sentence with the word that fits best. Choose your answers from the words below. You may use each word more than once.

myself, about, to, by, in, of, with, amount, circumstances

1–2. I would like **to**_____ indulge **myself**_____ by taking a bubble bath.

3. There were mitigating **circumstances**_____ that explained her lateness.

4. After a succession **of**_____ career failures, Harry Truman achieved success as U.S. president.

5. The calendar lists holidays **in**_____ chronological order.

6. The pope was greeted **with**_____ adulation.

7. The complacency **of**_____ the defending champion cost him the title.

8. Halle Berry was awarded the accolade **of**_____ the Oscar.

9. The augmentation **of**_____ the company's workforce meant less overtime pay for workers.

10. There is a copious **amount**_____ of water in the sea.

■ *Writing with Your Words*

This exercise will give you practice in writing effective sentences that use the vocabulary words. Each sentence is started for you. Complete it with an interesting phrase that also indicates the meaning of the italicized word.

1. When I saw the *mammoth* lion _____

_____.

2. I use the *euphemism* _____

_____.

3. I find it hard to *withstand* _____

   _____ .

4. I would never want to *jeopardize* _____

   _____ .

5. When you begin to *procrastinate*, you need to _____

   _____ .

6. With each *successive* step, _____

   _____ .

7. It's important to be *meticulous* when _____

   _____ .

8. It is *mandatory* to _____

   _____ .

9. When I saw the *cryptic* message _____

   _____ .

10. The crowd showed its *adulation* by _____

   _____ .

■ *Making Connections*

These questions will help you relate the words you have learned in this chapter to your own life. Answer each question by writing a paragraph or more on a separate sheet of paper.

1. How could you jeopardize your school career?

2. If you could choose one course to make mandatory in college, what would it be? Defend your answer.

3. Identify two things that have become obsolete, and describe what has replaced them.

Passage

Crazy Laws

People are often surprised to learn that many silly laws are still in effect. It seems that no one has taken the time or trouble to get rid of them.

As good citizens, people should obey the law. But, if they were to obey all of the laws on the books, they might find themselves very confused. Many were passed long ago and **(1)** are simply **obsolete.** It is, for example, illegal to cross Boston Common (in Boston, Massachusetts) without carrying a shotgun to protect against bears!

Other laws regulate behavior between men and women. In New York, men are prohibited from turning around and **indulging** in an admiring look at a woman. After two convictions, a man must wear horse blinders on the street. Similarly, in Ottumwa, Iowa, a man may not wink at a lady he does not know. In another state, men must speak like gentlemen. They may not say "Oh, boy," but instead **(2)** must find a **euphemism** for this dangerous phrase.

Of course, women also have responsibilities under the law. In Virginia, **(3)** it is **mandatory** for women to wear corsets, tight girdle-like garments worn in the early 1900s. In contrast, in Missouri corsets are forbidden. In Illinois, women must address unmarried men by calling them "master," not "mister." In California, a 1925 law states that women may not wiggle their bottoms while dancing.

(4) A man in Idaho, feeling **chivalrous, (5)** may want to **indulge** his sweetheart by buying her a box of candy. However, it is against the law to buy candy for his love unless it weighs at least fifty pounds. It takes a special kind of **adulation** to buy—and carry—such a **mammoth** box, and, on the part of the lady, it takes a special love of candy to eat it.

However, once a man has won his lady love, there are laws that ensure that he not become **complacent.** In Alexandria, Minnesota, a husband may not enjoy marital relations with his wife if his breath smells like garlic, onions, or sardines. Other laws **cultivate** marital happiness by protecting it from outsiders. In Michigan, women must have their husbands' permission to cut their own hair. On the Paiute Indian reservation in California, a mother-in-law may spend no more than thirty days visiting her children. It is felt that a longer time might **jeopardize** the marriage.

Laws also govern eating and drinking. In New York, people may not walk on Sundays with ice cream cones in their pockets. **(6)** This law seems **cryptic** in two ways. First, what situation might have led to passing it? Second, why is it acceptable to have an ice cream cone in one's pocket on days other than Sunday?

Other laws, although just as silly, at least have some purpose. Apparently, lawmakers in St. Louis, Missouri, **(7)** wanted to prevent the consumption of **copious** amounts of alcohol when they passed a law prohibiting people from sitting on street curbs and drinking beer from a bucket.

Yet some laws actually seem to be dangerous. One community will have a hard time putting out fires, since their fire trucks are prohibited from traveling faster than twenty-five miles per hour. **(8)** That's not much **acceleration** when you're on your way to a burning building!

Bathing is a subject that governments love to regulate. People living in Massachusetts must be **zealous** about their cleanliness, for the law requires a full bath each night before going to bed. If residents **procrastinate** about taking a bath, they will never get to bed! In contrast, **(9)** Virginians may be less **meticulous** about personal care, as bathtubs may not be kept in the house. They are allowed only in yards.

Laws also govern our treatment of animals. In Honolulu, Hawaii, it is illegal to annoy birds in parks. A Texan cannot shoot a buffalo from the second story of a hotel. California permits people to keep potbellied pigs as pets, but snails, elephants, and big-horned sheep are illegal. It also is legal to drive as many as 2,000 sheep up Hollywood Boulevard. But **augment** your flock by just one, and it will be illegal. In Michigan, one may not tie an alligator to a fire hydrant. In 1924, a monkey in Indiana was convicted and fined for smoking a cigarette.

At times, lawmakers try to regulate things they cannot control. Kirkland, Illinois, forbids bees to fly in its village. Another Illinois city, Urbana, prohibits monsters. The Arkansas legislature passed a law that, **(10)** despite any **mitigating** circumstances, the Arkansas River can rise no higher than to the Main Street bridge in Little Rock. The legislature did not state what it would do to punish the river if it broke the law.

Are you feeling that you might not be able to **withstand** the strain of living with these laws? If so, go to South Dakota on the Fourth of July, for no one can be arrested there on that date.

■ *Exercise*

Each numbered sentence below corresponds to a sentence in the Passage. Fill in the letter of the choice that makes the sentence mean the same thing as its corresponding sentence in the Passage.

1. Many laws are simply ____**d**____
   a. very stupid   b. very wise   c. not within the power of lawmakers
   d. out of date

2. They must find a ____**c**____ to replace "Oh, boy."
   a. worse phrase   b. less descriptive phrase   c. nicer phrase
   d. funnier phrase

3. It is ____**a**____ for women to wear corsets in Virginia.
   a. necessary   b. useless   c. fun   d. not allowed

4. A man in Idaho might feel ____**a**____.
   a. courteous   b. self-satisfied   c. careful   d. mysterious

5. He may want to ____**a**____ his sweetheart.
   a. pamper   b. hurt   c. disturb   d. convince

6. This law seems ____**c**____ in two ways.
   a. exciting   b. cruel   c. puzzling   d. radical

7. Missouri wanted to forbid people from drinking ____**c**____ amounts of alcohol.
   a. strong   b. small   c. large   d. appropriate

8. That's not too much ____**d**____.
   a. slowing down   b. fast turning   c. government efficiency
   d. speeding up

9. Virginians are less ____**b**____ about their bathing.
   a. confused   b. careful   c. insane   d. cultured

10. Despite ____**b**____ circumstances, the river cannot rise above the Main Street bridge.
    a. personal   b. moderating   c. weather   d. harsh

■ *Discussion Questions*

1. Give two examples of laws that limit romance.

2. Imagine and describe an incident that might have inspired one of these crazy laws. Be sure to identify the law.

3. Which law do you think is the silliest? Why?

◀ ENGLISH IDIOMS

Rhyme and Repetition

Speakers of English create many idioms by combining two words that sound almost alike. Most of these idioms are informal and more appropriate to everyday speech than to formal conversation and writing.

To *dilly-dally* means to delay, or to take too much time. People who change their minds easily are called *wishy-washy.*

To *hobnob* means to associate closely with, as in "He *hobnobs* with the rich people in town." If you *hobnob* with the rich, you may be considered *hoity-toity,* which means snobby. (A snob is also referred to as *stuck up*.)

Something that contains many things that don't fit together is said to be a *hodgepodge.* For example, an essay might be a *hodgepodge* of unrelated ideas. However, if the essay contained many false or silly ideas, it could be called *claptrap.*

Cartoonist Billy DeBeck created the comic strip "Barney Google," about the adventures of a man and his racehorse. On October 26, 1923, DeBeck coined the phrase *heebie-jeebies* to describe nervousness. Since then, "to have the *heebie-jeebies*" is to be nervous or upset. So popular was the term that trumpeter Louis Armstrong even made a record called *"Heebie Jeebies."*

REVIEW

Chapters 1–4

■ Reviewing Words in Context

Read the passage below. Then complete each sentence with a word from the group of words below.

THE "TROUBLE TWINS"

a. adroit	e. chronological	i. epitome	m. intrepid
b. articulate	f. conservative	j. exuberant	n. ludicrous
c. belligerent	g. contemplate	k. fraternal	o. meticulous
d. chagrined	h. enigma	l. frugal	p. thwarted

Background: Sophia and Rocio, students in the author's class, are identical twins who have been together since they shared a cradle. They sometimes find that they are independently humming the same song or thinking the same thoughts. Here is more about them.

1. Rocio and Sophia are identical twins, not **k, fraternal** _____ twins.

2. Both have **j, exuberant** _____ personalities; they are bubbly and get excited over things.

3. In addition, they both are **b, articulate** _____ people who express themselves forcefully and well.

4. In **e, chronological** _____ order, Sophia, who was born five minutes before Rocio, came first.

5. Their wonderful relationship is the **i, epitome** _____ of how sisters should get along.

6. Being twins made them feel secure, so they grew up to be **m, intrepid** _____ and afraid of nothing.

7. In fact, it is difficult for them to **g, contemplate** _____ what life would be like if they didn't have each other.

8. However, there are some differences between them; Rocio is **l, frugal** _____ and shops carefully, but Sophia spends money freely.

9. Rocio, who is more **f, conservative** _____, values marriage and family more highly than Sophia, who values independence.

10. They are both **a, adroit** _____ musicians who move their fingers skillfully when playing the violin and piano.

11. When they were young, their mother **p, thwarted** _____ their desire to look like individuals by dressing them the same; people teased them by calling them "Trouble Twins."

12. To most people, it is a(n) **h, enigma** _____ which twin is Rocio and which is Sophia.

13. However, if you examine their faces with <u>**o, meticulous**</u> care, you can see that Rocio, who is called "la gorda" ("fat one"), has slightly rounder cheeks than Sophia, who is called "la flaca" ("thin one").

14. Once a <u>**c, belligerent**</u> playmate, who was angry with Rocio, started to fight with Sophia!

15. More recently, Sophia's boyfriend was <u>**d, chagrined**</u> when he realized he was trying to kiss Rocio!

■ *Passage for Word Review*

Complete each blank in the Passage with the word that makes the best sense. The choices include words from the vocabulary lists along with related words. Use each choice only once. You will need fifteen of the words below.

a. accord	g. deference	m. prohibited
b. adulation	h. emulate	n. successive
c. bland	i. intrepid	o. venerable
d. bureaucratic	j. ludicrous	p. zeal
e. capricious	k. meticulous	
f. confrontation	l. procrastinate	

Background: This passage continues the discussion of names that appears in Chapter 1. It presents naming practices from several different traditions.

NAMES, NAMES, AND MORE NAMES

Have you ever met a couple who couldn't agree on a name for their newborn? One parent might want a common name like *John* or *Kimberly*; the other, feeling that these are **(1)** <u>**c, bland**</u> choices, might prefer something more unusual like *Drusilla* or *Menus*. To avoid a(n) **(2)** <u>**f, confrontation**</u>, some parents **(3)** <u>**l, procrastinate**</u>, perhaps registering "boy" or "girl" on the birth certificate, and waiting until they reach a(n) **(4)** <u>**a, accord**</u>. In other families, a grandfather or other **(5)** <u>**o, venerable**</u> relative is given the honor of naming the baby.

The choice of a name may show **(6) b, adulation** _____ of a personal hero. Perhaps the family hopes that the baby will

(7) h, emulate _____ this idol. In the 1700s, the Scots fought to put "Bonnie Prince Charlie" (Charles Stuart) on the throne. Although they failed, many people remained loyal to him. One man showed his

(8) p, zeal _____ for this cause by naming all fourteen of his sons *Charles*.

In some cultures religious leaders, rather than parents, name babies.

Traditional Buddhist parents often show their **(9) g, deference** _____ to monks by asking them to choose names. After a name is given, the

parents are **(10) m, prohibited** _____ from eating meat for a year.

Many Korean families give all the boys of one generation the same middle name. Five names meaning *wood, fire, earth, metal,* and *water* are passed from father to son. The name is changed in each

(11) n, successive _____ generation. If two brothers are named *wood*, their sons are named *fire* and their grandsons are named *earth*.

Today, many English-speaking parents give children hyphenated last names. This practice is similar to naming customs in Spanish-speaking countries. For instance, a Costa Rican woman named Beatrice has a father whose last name is *Sandino* and a mother named *Rodriguez*. Beatrice's full name is *Beatrice Sandino-Rodriguez*.

In Russia, a "patronymic" middle name shows family ties. The middle name contains the father's first name plus *-ovich* for a son or *-ovna* for a daughter. Alexander Fekson's son Gennady is *Gennady Alexandrovich Fekson*. Alexander's daughter Sophia is *Sophia Alexandrovna Fekson*. The most respectful way to address a Russian is by his or her first name and patronymic, as in *Gennady Alexandrovich*. As difficult as these names are

to pronounce, Russians take care to be **(12) k, meticulous** _____ about getting them correct.

People who don't like the names they have been given have the right to change them when they are adults. In fact, New Yorkers are doing this at a record rate. Applications for name changes rose by 40 percent in three years, partially because new laws simplified a difficult

(13) d, bureaucratic _____ process. Although the process is now less difficult, some restrictions remain. People may not give themselves titles. Thus, *Sultan of Swing* and *Queen of Brooklyn* are not allowed. The new law also states that a person may not change his or her name,

without any apparent reason, in a totally **(14) e, capricious** _____

way. Nevertheless, some of the names people choose are
(15) <u>j, ludicrous</u>. One man who worked with children in a
local hospital changed his name to *A. Fluffy Bunny*. Another is now
known as *Human Being*.

■ *Reviewing Learning Strategies*

Dictionary Skills   Complete each sentence with the answer that fits
best.

1. An etymology gives the <u>**c, history**</u> of a word.
   a. pronunciation   b. meaning   c. history

2. The most complete dictionary is called a(n) <u>**a, unabridged**</u>.
   dictionary.
   a. unabridged   b. college   c. pocket

Context Clues   Using context clues, make an intelligent guess about the
meaning of the italicized word in each sentence.

3. He had a *propensity* to be lazy; in other words, he tended to avoid
   work.

   Propensity means <u>**tendency**</u>.

4. The *refractory* mule refused to move from the spot, despite our
   urging.

   Refractory means <u>**stubborn**</u>.

5. As a child, Beverly Sills *evinced* so much musical talent that she gave
   her first performance at the age of three.

   Evinced means <u>**showed**</u>.

6. There was *bedlam*, or total confusion, after the riot.

   Bedlam means <u>**total confusion**</u>.

7. Since the dodo bird died out centuries ago, it is no longer *extant*.

   Extant means <u>**living**</u>.

8. The *fervor* of his plea was emphasized by his wild gestures.

   Fervor means <u>**passion; wildness; urgency**</u>.

9. The *noxious* gas caused sickness and death.

   Noxious means **harmful**_____.

10. You are *niggling* again, and I'd be grateful if you would not argue about small points and discuss the issues instead.

    Niggling means **arguing about small points**_____.

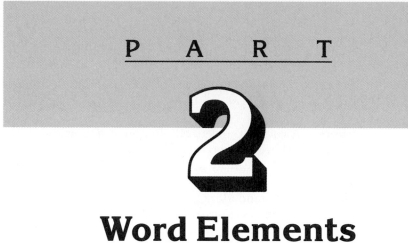

PART

2

Word Elements

In Part 1 of this book, you learned about context clues. Part 2 focuses on word elements, the parts of words that have their own meanings. Unlike context clues, which provide hints from the sentence, word elements give hints within the word itself. For example, the parts *re-* (meaning "back") and *tract* (meaning "pull") are the two elements in the word *retract* (meaning "to pull back"). If you break up an unknown word into separate elements, you can often figure out its meaning. If you combine context clues with the word element clues you will learn in Part 2, you will have a powerful approach to understanding new words.

Prefixes, Roots, and Suffixes

There are three kinds of word elements: prefixes, roots, and suffixes. A **prefix** is a group of letters that is attached to the beginning of a word root. A **root** is the central, or main, portion of a word. A **suffix** is a group of letters that is attached to the end of a root. An example of a word that contains all three elements is *impolitely: im-* is the prefix, *polite* is the root, and *-ly* is the suffix. Now let us look at each element separately.

Prefixes. A prefix such as *im-* attaches to the beginning of a root. The hyphen at the end of *im-* shows where the root attaches. When a prefix joins a root, the result is a new word with a different meaning. In the word *impolite,* for example, the prefix *im-* means "not." When *im-* is joined to the root *polite,* the new word formed by the prefix and root means "not polite." Next, we can see what happens when the prefix *co-,* which means "together," is joined to two familiar word roots.

137

co- (together) + *exist* = *coexist* (to exist together)
co- (together) + *operate* = *cooperate* (to work or operate together)

In both of these examples, the prefix *co-* changes the meaning of the root word.

Roots. A root is the central portion of a word, and it carries the basic meaning. There are two types of roots: base words and combining roots. A **base word** is simply an English word that can stand alone, such as *polite* or *operate*, and may be joined to a prefix or a suffix. **Combining roots** cannot stand alone as English words; they are derived from words in other languages. For example, the combining root *ject* is derived from the Latin word *jacēre*, which means "to throw." Although the root *ject* is not an English word by itself, it can combine with many prefixes to form words. Two examples are *reject* and *eject*.

e- (a prefix meaning "out") + *ject* (a root meaning "throw") = *eject*
re- (a prefix meaning "back") + *ject* (a root meaning "throw") = *reject*

How do a prefix and a root create a word with a new meaning? Sometimes the new word's meaning is simply the combination of its root and prefix. Thus, *eject* means "to throw out." At other times the meaning of a word may be somewhat different from the combined prefix and root. *Reject* does not mean "to throw back"; rather, "it means not to accept." These two meanings are related, since we could imagine that someone who did not accept something might throw it back. In fact, "to throw back" gives an imaginative mental picture of *reject*. Prefixes and roots often give an image of a word rather than a precise definition. This image can help you remember the meaning of a word. The formation of several words from *ject* is illustrated below.

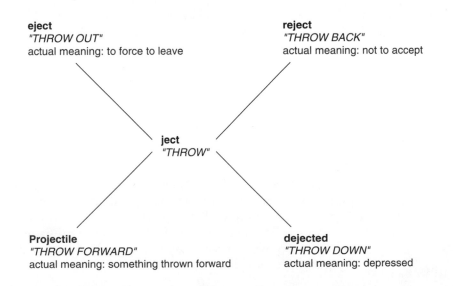

eject
"THROW OUT"
actual meaning: to force to leave

reject
"THROW BACK"
actual meaning: not to accept

ject
"THROW"

Projectile
"THROW FORWARD"
actual meaning: something thrown forward

dejected
"THROW DOWN"
actual meaning: depressed

Suffixes.   A suffix, such as -*ly* is added to the end of a root. The hyphen at the beginning shows where the root attaches. Most suffixes change a base word from one part of speech to another (see the table on pages 5 and 6). For example, -*able* changes a verb *(reach)* to an adjective *(reachable).* Suffixes may also indicate a plural or a past tense, as in boy*s* and reach*ed.* A few suffixes extend the basic meaning of a word root. The root *psych* (mind), and the suffix -*logy* (study of) are joined to form *psychology* (the study of the mind).

Many common words contain word elements. Each of the following words consists of a prefix, a root, and a suffix: *reaction, unlikely, exchanges, reviewing,* and *invisibly.* Can you identify each element?

Answers are on page 410.

Using Word Elements

Word elements provide valuable clues to the meanings of unknown words, but they must be used carefully.

Some word elements have more than one spelling. For example, the root *ject* can be spelled *jet* (as in *jet* and *jettison*). The prefix *anti-* is also spelled *ant-* (as in *antacid* and *antagonist*). Some spelling differences make words easier to pronounce. Others reflect the history of a word element. Fortunately, spellings usually vary by only one or two letters. Once you learn to look for the common letters, you should easily be able to identify word elements.

Some word elements have more than one meaning. For example, the combining root *gen* can mean both "birth" and "type." This book gives all the common meanings of many combining roots, prefixes, and suffixes, and some hints about when to use them. When you encounter word elements that have more than one meaning, remember to use the context clues you learned in Part 1 of this book. If you combine your knowledge of word elements with context clues, you can usually determine the most appropriate meaning.

Finally, when you see a certain combination of letters in a word, those letters may not always form a word element. For instance, the appearance of the letters *a-n-t-i* in a word does not mean that they always form the prefix *anti-*. To find out whether or not they do, you must combine context clues with your knowledge of word elements. To illustrate this, *a-n-t-i* is used in two sentences below. Which sentence contains the prefix *anti-* (meaning "opposite" or "against")?

1. The *antihero* was a villain.

2. We *anticipate* you will come.

The answer is the first sentence; *antihero* ("villain") is the opposite of *hero*. (The *anti-* in *anticipate* is actually a varied spelling of the prefix *ante-*, meaning "before.")

Despite these cautions, the use of word elements is an excellent way to increase your vocabulary. Prefixes, roots, and suffixes can help you unlock the meanings of thousands of difficult words. The chapters in Part 2 of this book present many different word elements. Each one is illustrated by several new words that will be valuable to you in college. If you relate these words to the word elements they contain, you will remember both more effectively.

As you work through the word elements in Part 2, keep in mind the context clues that you learned in Part 1. Together, word elements and context clues will give you very powerful strategies for learning new words on your own.

5

Word Elements: Prefixes

The rich cultural heritage that the ancient Greeks and Romans left to us includes many word elements that are still used in English. This chapter introduces some prefixes from ancient Greek and from Latin, the language of the ancient Romans. Learning these prefixes will help you figure out the meanings of many unfamiliar words.

Chapter Strategy: Word Elements: Prefixes

Chapter Words:

Part 1

anti-	antidote	re-	reconcile
	antipathy		revelation
	antithesis		revert
equi-	equilibrium	sub-	subconscious
	equitable		subdue
	equivocal		subordinate

Part 2

auto-	autobiography	im-, in-	impartial
	autocratic		incongruous
	autonomous		ingenious
ex-	eccentric		interminable
	exorbitant		invariably
	exploit		
	extricate		

Quiz Yourself

To check your knowledge of some chapter words before you begin to study, identify these statements as true or false. Answers are on page 410.

Something **interminable** is short.	True	False
An **impartial** person is fair.	True	False
An **exploit** is an adventure.	True	False
Equilibrium is balance.	True	False

You will learn the answers as you study this chapter.

Did You Know?

Where Does English Come From?

The origins of language are lost in the mists of time. Archaeologists have found examples of ancient jewelry, weapons, and art, but no one knows how or why people first spoke. We do know that most of the languages of Europe, the Middle East, and India are descended from a common source. Linguists trace these languages back to a possible parent language called *Indo-European,* which would have been spoken at least 5,000 years ago. The Indo-European root *mater* (mother), for example, shows up in many different languages.

Languages No Longer Spoken

Ancient Greek	mētēr
Latin	mater
Old English	modor

Modern Languages

English	mother
German	mutter
Italian	madre
Spanish	madre
French	mère
Polish	matka

English vocabulary descends from Indo-European through several other languages that are no longer spoken. Much of the higher-level vocabulary of modern English comes from ancient Greek and Latin.

(These are often called the *classical languages*.) A knowledge of the Greek and Latin word elements used in English will help you master thousands of modern English words.

Who were these Greeks and Romans from whom so much language flows? The civilization of the ancient Greeks flourished between 750 and 250 BCE. Greece was a land of small, separate city-states that created the first democracies and the first concept of citizenship. Sparta and Athens were two important city-states. The citizens of Sparta excelled in warfare, whereas Athens became a center of art and learning. Athenians produced the first lifelike sculpture, wrote the first tragedies and comedies, and learned philosophy from Socrates and Plato. Unfortunately, ancient Greek civilization also had its dark side. The economic system was based on slavery, and only a small percentage of the population—free men—were full citizens. Women had few political rights. Tragic wars between city-states also marred Greek history.

In contrast to the divided Greek city-states, the city of Rome steadily took over first the whole of Italy, and then more territory, until it finally ruled over a vast empire. From about 200 BCE to 450 CE Rome brought its way of life to much of the Mediterranean world and beyond. Roman officials introduced a highway system, a postal service, water supplies, public baths, and border patrols to many less advanced areas. They also spread their language, Latin. But, like ancient Greece, Rome had its problems. After the first emperor, Augustus, died, plots and murders became common in the Roman court. Several Roman emperors were poisoned, stabbed, or smothered. Meanwhile, officials and the army continued to rule the empire efficiently.

If you have studied the ancient Greeks and Romans, you may be able to answer these questions.

1. An epic poem, the *Iliad*, tells of a Greek war that started when Helen, the daughter of Zeus, was stolen from her husband. Helen is often

   called "Helen of __**d**__."
   a. Athens   b. Sparta   c. Crete   d. Troy

2. __**a**__ was a famous Roman leader who said, "I came, I saw, I conquered."
   a. Julius Caesar   b. Brutus   c. Cato   d. Augustus

3. Cleopatra, queen of Egypt, did *not* have a romance with __**c**__.
   a. Mark Antony   b. Julius Caesar   c. Augustus

Answers are on page 410.

Learning Strategy

Word Elements: Prefixes

Our heritage from the Greeks and Romans includes many word elements that are still used in English. The Learning Strategy in this chapter concentrates on *prefixes,* word elements "added to" the beginning of word roots. The seven prefixes presented in this chapter are very common, and learning them will help you build a large vocabulary. One dictionary lists over 400 words that use *ex-* and more than 600 formed from *in-* or *im-.*

Prefix	*Meaning*	*Origin*	*Chapter Words*
Part 1			
anti-, ant-	against; opposite	Greek	antidote, antipathy, antithesis
equi-, equa-	equal	Latin	equilibrium, equitable, equivocal
re-	back; again	Latin	reconcile, revelation, revert
sub-	below; under; part of	Latin	subconscious, subdue, subordinate
Part 2			
auto-	self	Greek	autobiography, autocratic, autonomous
ex-, e-, ec-	out of; former	Latin	eccentric, exorbitant, exploit, extricate
im-, in-	not; in	Latin	impartial, incongruous, ingenious, interminable, invariably

When prefixes join with word roots, the prefixes give clues to word meaning. Let us look first at how prefixes can combine with roots that are base words.

anti- (against) + war makes *antiwar,* meaning "against war"
  The *antiwar* protesters demonstrated in Washington, DC.
sub- (below) + *normal* makes *subnormal,* meaning "below normal."
  Subnormal temperatures are colder than usual.
auto- (self) + *suggestion* makes *autosuggestion,* meaning "a suggestion made to yourself."
  Some people use *autosuggestion* when they try to stop smoking.

See if you can use prefixes to determine the meaning of the following words. Write in the word and its meaning.

re- (again) + *marry* makes **remarry**_____, meaning

marry again_____.

in- (not) + *secure* makes **insecure**_____, meaning

not secure_____.

equi- (equal) + *distant* makes **equidistant**_____, meaning

equal in distance_____.

Answers are on page 410.

Now let's look at how prefixes join with combining roots (roots that cannot stand alone as English words). The Latin root *scrib* or *script* (meaning "write") combines with some prefixes in our list to make English words whose meanings are the combined meanings of the prefix and root

in- (in) + *scrib* makes *inscribe,* "to write in."
   People often *inscribe* their names in books.
sub- (under) + *script* makes *subscript,* "written under."
   A *subscript* is a tiny number or letter written beneath a line, such as the 2 in H_2O, the chemical symbol for water.

At other times, the meaning of a word is not precisely the combined meanings of a prefix and a combining root. Still, these word elements will give you valuable clues to the meaning of the word. The Latin root *vert* (to turn) combines with three prefixes that you will study in this chapter to make different English words. The idea of "turn" appears in each one.

re- (back) + *vert* (turn) makes *revert,* or "turn back."
   When people *revert* to an old habit, they start to do it again. Perhaps you know a child who *reverted* to sucking his thumb after having outgrown the behavior.
in- (in) + *vert* (turn) makes *invert,* or "turn in."
   Invert means to turn inside out or upside down, or to change in order. If you *invert* a glass, you turn it upside down.
sub- (under) + *vert* (turn) makes *subvert,* or "turn under."
   Subvert means to make something worse by corrupting it or trying to overthrow it. Traitors seek to *subvert* their countries' governments.

As you can see, using prefixes sometimes requires a little imagination. Prefixes and roots may not give the *entire* meaning of an unknown word, but they do provide excellent hints. If you combine the use of context clues with the use of word elements, you can often figure out the precise meaning of an unfamiliar word.

Two words formed from a prefix and a root are presented below. The meanings of the roots and prefixes are given, followed by a sentence using the word. Write in the meaning of each word.

revive, from *re-* (again) and *vivere* (to live).
   The plant *revived* after we gave it water.

   Revive means **to live again**_____.

incredulous, from *in-* (not) and *cred* (to believe)
She grew *incredulous* as she listened to the weird story.

Incredulous means **not believing**_____.

Answers are on page 410.

Prefixes

Part 1

The four prefixes presented in Part 1 of this chapter are described below.

anti-, ant- (against; opposite)
> The two meanings of *anti-* are related and therefore easy to remember. *Antiaircraft* missiles are fired **against** aircraft, and *antigambling* laws outlaw gambling. New English words continue to be formed with *anti-,* since people always seem to find things to protest **against.**

equi- equa- (equal)
> *Equi-* is used in many English words. Two homes that are *equidistant* from a school are the same, or **equal,** distance from the school. *Equivalent* sums of money have the same, or **equal,** value. For example, one dollar is *equivalent* to four quarters. Two **equally** powerful forces may be called *equipotent.*

re- (back; again)
> *Re-* has two distinct meanings. It usually means "again" when it is attached to other English words (or base words). For example, when *re-* is added to the base words *start* and *do,* it forms *restart* (start **again**) and *redo* (do **again**). However, when *re-* is added to combining roots, which cannot stand alone, it often means "back." *Recede,* for instance, means "to go **back**" and comes from *re-* (back) and *cēdere* (to go).

sub- (below; under; part of)
> In the word *substandard, sub-* means "below": "**below** the standard." *Sub-* can also refer to a classification that is "part of" something else, as a *subdivision,* which is **part of** a division. In biology, animals from one species may be further classified into several *subspecies.*

Words to Learn

Part 1

anti-, ant-

1. **antidote** (noun)   ăn′tĭ-dōt′

   From Greek *anti-* (against) + *didonai* (to give) (to give a remedy against something harmful)

   a substance that acts against a poison or a medical problem

   > Dimercaprol is used as an **antidote** to arsenic poisoning.

   > Some people claim that breathing into a paper bag is an **antidote** to hiccups.

   something that acts against a harmful effect

   > Long walks, soft music, and relaxing baths are **antidotes** to stress.

   > Conservatives often promote tax cuts as an **antidote** to economic problems.

   The prefix *anti-* is widely used in medicine. Health care professionals prescribe *antibiotics* such as penicillin and neomycin to kill organisms that can cause disease. The word *antibiotic* comes from *anti-* and *bio,* meaning "life." We take an *antihistamine* to stop the sneezing and runny nose of a cold or an allergy. *Antihistamine* comes from *anti-* plus *histi,* the ancient Greek word element meaning "tissue," or body substance. Immunizations against smallpox, measles, polio, and tuberculosis allow us to form *antibodies* that prevent these diseases. Currently, medical researchers are trying to locate substances that will form *antibodies* against the deadly AIDS virus, SARS, BSE, and avian flu.

   ---

2. **antipathy** (noun)   ăn-tĭp′ə-thē

   From Greek: *anti-* (against) + *patho* (feeling)

   great hatred, opposition, or disgust

   > Carlos began to feel **antipathy** toward the neighbors who blasted their stereo all night long.

   > Mara's **antipathy** toward her abusive father made her move to another city.

3. **antithesis** (noun)   ăn-tĭth′ĭ-sĭs   (plural: **antitheses**)

From Greek: *anti-* (against) + *tithenai* (to put)

contrast; opposite

> Female superheroes in movies are the **antithesis** of the stereo-type of the weak woman.
>
> Censorship is the **antithesis** of freedom of expression.

▶ *Common Phrases*
  antithesis of; antithetical to

▶ *Related Word*
  antithetical   (adjective)   (ăn′tĭ-thĕt′ĭ-kəl)   Rigid thinking is *antithetical* to creativity.

equi-, equa-

4. **equilibrium** (noun)   ē′kwə-lĭb′rē-əm

From Latin: *equi-* (equal) + *libra* (balance)

balance between forces; stability

> Traditional Chinese philosophy values keeping the forces of yin (passivity) and yang (activity) in **equilibrium.**
>
> The tightrope walker almost lost his **equilibrium.**
>
> She lost her **equilibrium** and began to cry.

▶ *Common Phrase*
  in equilibrium

NOTE: The concept of balance can be used to describe both nonphysical conditions, such as evenness of temperament or fairness, and physical conditions, such as the ability to walk along a narrow curb without falling.

5. **equitable** (adjective)   ĕk′wĭ-tə-bəl

From Latin: *equi* (equal)

fair; just

> The judge divided the divorcing couple's money in an **equitable** fashion.
>
> Laws should provide for **equitable** payment to victims of crimes.

NOTE: In *equitable,* the word element *equi* is used as a root.

In 1972, the U.S. Congress enacted Title IX, which required *equitable* treatment for women who wanted to participate in athletics in all institutions receiving federal funds. This bill made a tremendous difference in women's sports. In 1972, for example, only 300,000 American girls played high school sports; in 2003, 2,700,000 participated.

6. **equivocal** (adjective)   ĭ-kwĭv′ə-kəl

From Latin: *equi-* (equal) + *vox* (voice) (When something is equivocal, it seems as if two equally strong voices are sending different messages.)

open to different interpretations, often misleading or avoiding the truth

> Studies of the effects of welfare payments on family stability have shown **equivocal** results. (There is no intention to mislead in this sentence.)

> The president's **equivocal** reply, "I will serve our national interest," did not answer the question of whether he would support a war. (In this sentence, there is an intention to mislead or avoid the truth.)

doubtful

> Although people pay high prices for her paintings, her position as a great artist is **equivocal.**

NOTE: Equivocal statements can be meant to mislead and even deceive people.

▶ *Related Words*
> **equivocate** (verb)   (ĭ-kwĭv′ə-kāt′)   Don't *equivocate;* answer directly.

> **equivocation** (noun)   The defendant's *equivocation* about where he was on the night of the robbery made him look guilty.

re-

7. **reconcile** (verb)   rĕk′ən-sīl′

From Latin: *re-* (back) and *concilare* to bring together (to bring back together)

To bring to peace, agreement, or understanding

> Married couples seek to **reconcile** their differences.

> Computer programs help me **reconcile** my bank statement with my checking account records.

After he lost his job, LeShan had to **reconcile** himself to living on a lower budget.

▶ *Related Word*
reconciliation (noun)   The *reconciliation* of ex-presidents Thomas Jefferson and John Adams ended a long rivalry.

According to Lakota Sioux tribal legend, the birth of a white buffalo will bring *reconciliation* among nations. A story is told that a beautiful woman once appeared to rescue the people from starvation. As she left, promising to return, she turned into a white buffalo. In the 1990s, a rare white buffalo was born in Wisconsin. Named "Miracle," it has captured the imagination of many who hope for world peace.

---

8. **revelation** (noun)   rĕv′ə-lā′shən

From Latin: *re-* (back) + *vēlāre* (to veil) This makes *revēlāre*, "to draw back the veil." (When a veil is drawn back, something surprising or even shocking may be discovered.)

dramatic disclosure; surprising news

The Islamic holiday of Ramadan marks God's **revelation** of the Koran to the prophet Mohammed. (Here, *revelation* has a positive, religious meaning.)

The nation was shocked by the **revelation** that the top official was a spy. (Here *revelation* has a negative meaning.)

▶ *Related Word*
reveal (verb)   (rĭ-vēl′)   Mystery novels usually *reveal* the identity of a murderer in the last few pages.

9. **revert** (verb)   rĭ-vûrt′

From Latin: *re-* (back) + *vert* (turn)

to return to a former practice or condition

The abandoned farmland **reverted** to its natural prairie state.

Whenever his brother was around, my boyfriend **reverted** to childish behavior.

After her divorce, Lakesha **reverted** to using her maiden name.

▶ *Common Phrases*
revert to; revert back to

sub-

10. **subconscious** (adjective, noun)   sŭb-kŏn′shəs

    From Latin: *sub-* (under) + *conscius* (aware of)

    not aware (or conscious) in the mind (adjective)

    > Advertisers try to appeal to our **subconscious** desires.

    the part of the mind that is beneath awareness (noun)

    > Some say memories from earliest childhood are buried deep in the **subconscious**.

    NOTE: The *unconscious* (not conscious) part of the mind can *never* become conscious. The word *unconscious* also describes a sleeping person or someone in a coma. The *subconscious* can become conscious, but only with great effort or through a traumatic event.

11. **subdue** (verb)   səb-do͞o′

    From Latin: *sub-* (under) + *dūcere* (to lead) (Someone who is subdued is led by, or placed under, the control of another.)

    to conquer or bring under control

    > Over 2,500 years ago, Cyrus the Great of Persia **subdued** lands from Greece to India.

    > It is difficult to **subdue** a desire to overeat when faced with a tempting buffet.

    to make less intense or noticeable

    > The soft lighting **subdued** the bright colors in the room.

    ▶ *Related Word*
    > **subdued** (adjective)   The *subdued* voices of golf tournament sportscasters contrast with the loud announcers at football games.

12. **subordinate** (adjective, noun)   sə-bôr′də-nĭt; (verb)   sə-bôr′də-nāt

    From Latin: *sub-* (under) + *ōrdināre* (to arrange in order)

    less important; of lower rank (adjective)

    > District courts and courts of appeals hold **subordinate** positions to the Supreme Court.

    a person of lower rank or importance (noun)

    > The vice president is the **subordinate** of the president.

to place in a lower or less important position (verb)

> Mothers **subordinate** their own needs to the needs of their children.

▶ *Common Phrases*
subordinate to (adjective); a subordinate of (noun)

NOTE: The pronunciation of the verb *subordinate* differs from the adjective and noun forms.

▶ *Related Word*
subordination (noun)   The southern portion of the Sudan has not freed itself from economic *subordination* to the north.

Exercises

Part 1

■ Definitions

Match each word in the left-hand column with a definition from the right-hand column. Use each choice only once.

1. subdue ___a___

2. equitable ___h___

3. revelation ___k___

4. antithesis ___d___

5. equilibrium ___b___

6. subconscious ___l___

7. antipathy ___f___

8. equivocal ___i___

9. revert ___g___

10. antidote ___e___

a. conquer

b. balance

c. bring to agreement

d. opposite

e. something that acts against a poison

f. hatred

g. return to a former practice

h. fair

i. doubtful

j. less important in rank

k. surprising news

l. beneath awareness

■ Meanings

Match each prefix to its meaning. Use each choice only once.

1. re- __b__

2. equi-, equa- __c__

3. anti-, ant- __d__

4. sub- __a__

   a. under, below, part of

   b. again, back

   c. equal

   d. against

■ Words in Context

Complete each sentence with the word that fits best. Use each choice only once.

a. antidote	e. equitable	i. revert
b. antipathy	f. equivocal	j. subconscious
c. antithesis	g. reconcile	k. subdue
d. equilibrium	h. revelation	l. subordinate

1. We are barely aware of our __j, subconscious__ thoughts.

2. After he married, Maurice had to __g, reconcile__ himself to living with two spoiled stepsons.

3. When we feel dizzy, we lose our __d, equilibrium__.

4. After the __e, equitable__ decision everyone felt that justice had been done.

5. The CEO was so busy that her __l, subordinate__ had to handle many details for her.

6. We feel __b, antipathy__ for our bitter enemy.

7. Although the man was the __c, antithesis__ of everything Cherise had been looking for, she fell in love with him.

8. After a dangerous snakebite, a(n) __a, antidote__ to the poison must be administered quickly.

9. Using a stun gun, the forest rangers were able to __k, subdue__ the bear that invaded our campsite.

10. Many recovering alcoholics are tempted to **i, revert**_____ to drinking alcohol in tense situations.

■ *Using Related Words*

Complete each sentence by using a word from the group of related words above it. Use each choice only once.

A BRIEF HISTORY OF ANCIENT ROME

Ancient Rome was ruled by the Senate until about 40 BCE.

1. reconcile, reconciliation

For almost 500 years, until about 40 BCE, a Senate governed the Roman republic. However, continual fighting among

Senators, with few attempts at **reconciliation**_____, led to greater concentration of power. Eventually, the Romans had to **reconcile**_____ themselves to living under an emperor. The story starts with the great Julius Caesar, born poor, but noble.

2. subordinate, subordination

After achieving much political success, Julius Caesar set out to

subordinate_____ Gaul (now France and Belgium) to the

Romans. He achieved this **subordination**_____ and returned home a hero.

3. equivocated, equivocation

After some **equivocation**_____, Julius Caesar, Crassus, and Pompey formed a triumvirate, or group of three, to rule Rome. Pompey was Caesar's son-in-law, yet their position as allies was short-lived. Pompey envied Caesar's popularity; Caesar hungered for power. Eventually they fought, and Caesar won. As Caesar

equivocated_____ about whether he wanted to be emperor, Senate members murdered him.

4. revelation, revealed

While Augustus, Caesar's nephew, was in Illyria, a letter from his

mother brought the shocking **revelation**_____ that Caesar had been murdered. His mother warned Augustus to flee. Instead,

his decision **revealed**_____ his character: he immediately went to Rome. This courage later helped him become Rome's first emperor. For the next 500 years, Rome remained an empire.

5. antithesis, antithetical

Centuries after Augustus took power, a series of barbarian invasions weakened the city of Rome. Their lack of technology and art made the

invaders' culture **antithetical**_____ to the highly civilized Roman culture. The destructive violence of the attacks was the

antithesis_____ of the principles on which the Roman Empire stood. After many invasions, the last Roman emperor was forced to resign in 467 CE.

■ *Reading the Headlines*

This exercise presents five headlines that might appear in newspapers. Read each headline and then answer the questions that follow. (Remember that small words, such as *is, are, a,* and *the,* are often left out of newspaper headlines.)

REVELATION THAT SUBORDINATE BETRAYED CEO SHOCKS BUSINESS WORLD

1. Has something been made public? __yes__

2. Was the betrayer the boss? __no__

THERAPY IS THE ANTIDOTE THAT ENDS ANTIPATHY, SO MARRIED COUPLE RECONCILES

3. It therapy the cure for antipathy? __yes__

4. Has the couple made peace? __yes__

AFTER UNSUCCESSFUL EFFORTS TO SUBDUE SUBCONSCIOUS URGES, ROCK STAR REVERTS TO DRUG ADDICTION

5. Did the rock star try to conquer the urges? __yes__

6. Has the rock star ever stopped being a drug addict? __yes__

EQUIVOCAL STATEMENT IS ANTITHESIS OF CLARITY

7. Was the statement clear? __no__

8. Is the statement the opposite of clarity? __yes__

AFTER EQUITABLE SETTLEMENT OF RICH MAN'S ESTATE, FAMILY SETTLES BACK INTO EQUILIBRIUM

9. Was the settlement fair? __yes__

10. Is the family now balanced and calmer? __yes__

Prefixes

Part 2

The following three prefixes are introduced in Part 2 of this chapter.

auto- (self)

This prefix comes from the Greek word for *self*. The word *automobile* comes from *auto-* and *mobile,* meaning "moving." When the automobile was invented, it was named for the amazing sight of something moving all by **itself.**

ex-, e-, ec- (out of; former)

When *ex-* is combined with a base word, it usually means "former." The words *ex-wife* (*former* wife) and *ex-president* (**former** president) show *ex-* used in this sense. The hyphens in these words give a hint that the **former** meaning is being used. When *ex-* is used with a combining root, it usually means "out of," as in *exhale* (to breathe **out**). The words introduced in this lesson join *ex-* to combining roots, so *ex-* means "out of" in all these words. However, you should remember that *ex-* can also mean "former."

im-, in- (not; in)

This prefix is commonly spelled in two different ways, and either spelling may have two different meanings. The most common meaning of *im-* and *in-* is "not," as in the words *impure* (**not** pure) and *indecent* (**not** decent). *Im-* and *in-* can also mean "in," as in *inhale* (to breathe **in**) and *import* (to carry **into** a country). This prefix is spelled *ir-* or *il-* before roots that begin with *r* or *l,* such as in *irregular* and *illogical.* The *il-* and *ir-* spellings always mean "not."

Words to Learn

Part 2

auto-

13. **autobiography** (noun)   ô′tō-bī-ŏg′rə-fē

    From Greek: *auto-* (self) + *bio* (life) + *graph* (to write)

    account of a person's life written by that person

    > Although blind and deaf, Helen Keller composed a moving **autobiography** titled *The Story of My Life.*

Can you match these famous people with the names of their auto-biographies?

1. Hillary Rodham Clinton
2. Howard Stern
3. Christopher Reeve
4. Michael Jordan
5. David Beckham
6. Billy Joel

a. *Piano Man*
b. *Living History*
c. *Private Parts*
d. *Still Me*
e. *My Side*
f. *For the Love of the Game*

Answers are on page 410.

▶ *Related Word*
  autobiographical (adjective)   Many of rapper Eminem's songs are *autobiographical*.

14. **autocratic** (adjective)   ô′tə-krăt′ək

From Greek: *auto-* (self) + *krates* (ruling)

having absolute power; domineering

> Fidel Castro has been the **autocratic** ruler of Cuba since 1959.
>
> Teachers accused the principal of being so **autocratic** that he never consulted anyone else when making a decision.

▶ *Related Words*
  autocrat (noun; person)   (ô′tə-krăt′)   The *autocrat* Peter the Great ruled Russia from 1682 to 1725.

  autocracy (noun)   (ô-tŏk′rə-sē)   Chileans rejected the *autocracy* of General Augusto Pinochet Ugarte when they voted for a multiparty leadership in 1989.

15. **autonomous** (adjective)   ô-tŏn′ə-məs

From Greek: *auto-* (self) + *nomos* (law)

self-governing; independent

> Chechnya has fought to leave Russia and become an **autonomous** nation.
>
> To become more **autonomous,** people open their own businesses.

▶ *Related Word*
  autonomy (noun)   Slaves have no *autonomy*.

ex-, e-, ec-

16. **eccentric** (adjective)   ĕk-sĕn′trĭk

    From Greek: *ek-* (out) + *kentron* (center)

    odd; different from normal or usual

    > The **eccentric** man ate exactly 200 Cheerios each morning for breakfast.

    ▶ *Related Word*
    eccentricity (noun) (ĕk′sĕn-trĭs′ə-tē) One of Thomas Jefferson's *eccentricities* was soaking his feet in cold water every morning.

17. **exorbitant** (adjective)   ĭg-zôr′bĭ-tənt

    From Latin: *ex-* (out) + *orbita* (path)

    expensive; unreasonable; exceeding proper limits

    > The kidnapper's **exorbitant** demands included a helicopter and $20 million.

    > We paid an **exorbitant** price for a special coffee drink.

18. **exploit** (verb) ĭk-sploit′; (noun) ĕks′ploit′

    From Latin: *ex-* (out) + *plicāre* (to fold), making *explicāre* (to unfold) (When we *exploit* something, we "fold it out" and make it work for us.)

    to take advantage of; to use (verb)

    > In the early 1900s, U.S. industries **exploited** laborers in low-paying jobs at dangerous factories. (Here *exploit* has a negative meaning.)

    > Alaska **exploited** its rich oil and natural gas reserves while trying not to harm the environment.

    great adventure; great deed (noun)

    > English legends tell of the **exploits** of King Arthur and his Knights of the Round Table.

    ▶ *Related Word*
    exploitation (noun) (ĕk′sploi-tā′shən) Consumers have protested the *exploitation* of child labor in clothing factories.

NOTES: (1) *Exploit* and *exploitation* often suggest taking unfair advantage (as in the exploitation of minorities). However, the words can mean simply "to take advantage of" or "to use wisely." (2) Notice the difference in pronunciation stress between *ex-ploit′* (verb) and *ex′ploit* (noun).

Child beauty pageants feature girls as young as four or five wearing adult clothes and makeup. They are judged on their charm and appearance and compete for big cash prizes. Is this harmless fun, or is it child *exploitation* that can leave girls psychologically damaged?

Are child beauty pageants *exploitation*?

19. **extricate** (verb)   ĕk′strĭ-kāt′

From Latin: *ex-* (out) + *tricae* (difficulties), making *extricāre* (to disentangle, to free)

to free from difficulty; to disentangle

Rescue personnel worked for two hours to **extricate** the woman from her crushed car.

To **extricate** herself from the bad date, Jolene claimed to be sick and left.

▶ *Common Phrase*
to extricate (oneself) from

Harry Houdini (1874–1926) was a world-famous escape artist. Houdini *extricated* himself from many seemingly escape-proof devices, including ten pairs of handcuffs, jail cells, nailed crates, and an airtight tank filled with water. Once, tied into a straitjacket and hung upside down from the top of a tall building, he *extricated* himself within minutes.

---

im-, in-

20. **impartial** (adjective)   ĭm-pär′shəl

From Latin: *im-* (not) + *pars* (part)

fair; just; not biased

To ensure that the scholarship board remained **impartial,** names of students were removed from applications.

The relief agency remained **impartial** toward both sides of the war, giving aid to all who came.

▶ *Common Phrase*
impartial toward

▶ *Related Word*
impartiality (noun)   (ĭm′pär-shē-al′ə-tē)   It is difficult to judge a good friend with *impartiality.*

21. **incongruous** (adjective)   ĭn-kŏng′groo-əs

From Latin: *in-* (not) + *congruere* (to agree)

out of place; not consistent or in harmony

The eighty-year-old grandfather and the twenty-five-year-old model made an **incongruous** couple.

The modern furniture looked **incongruous** in the ancient castle.

The patron's stingy tip seemed **incongruous** with his expensive limousine.

▶ *Related Word*
incongruity (noun)   News reporters noted the *incongruity* of the woman's mild manner and the terrible crime police charged her with.

22. **ingenious** (adjective)   ĭn-jēn′yəs

    From Latin: *in-* (in) + *gen* (born), making *ingenium* (inborn talent)

    clever; inventive

    > An **ingenious** engineer invented air conditioning to prevent temperature changes from affecting the paper in a printing plant.

    > Critics believe the pop star's fame depended more on **ingenious** advertising than on talent.

    ▶ *Related Word*
    > **ingenuity** (noun)   (ĭn′jə-no͞o′ĭ-tē)   Technological *ingenuity* has led to cell phones that access the Internet.

    Velcro®, an *ingenious* invention appreciated by kindergarten teachers who have to fasten many pairs of shoes each day, is actually two strips of nylon. One has tiny hooks and the other has tiny loops. When the strips are pressed together, the hooks catch the loops, and the two strips stick together. George de Mestral invented Velcro after walking in the woods and looking at how burrs stuck to his socks.

    ---

23. **interminable** (adjective)   ĭn-tûr′mə-nə-bəl

    From Latin: *in-* (not) + *terminus* (end, boundary)

    endless; too long

    > The five-hour wait inside a plane seemed **interminable.**

    NOTE: 1. *Interminable* has a negative connotation. 2. This word often describes something that seems endless rather than something that actually is endless.

24. **invariably** (adverb)   ĭn-vâr′ē-ə-blē

    From Latin: *in-* (not) + *variabilis* (changeable)

    consistently; always

    > My brother **invariably** loses his temper when we ask him to do the dishes.

Exercises

Part 2

■ **Definitions**

Match each word in the left-hand column with a definition from the right-hand column. Use each choice only once.

1. autocratic ___a___   a. holding all power

2. exorbitant ___j___   b. endless; too long

3. eccentric ___d___   c. the story of one's own life

4. autobiography ___c___   d. odd

5. ingenious ___e___   e. clever

6. exploit ___f___   f. to take advantage of

7. impartial ___h___   g. to free from difficulty

8. interminable ___b___   h. not biased

9. extricate ___g___   i. self-ruling

10. incongruous ___l___   j. very expensive

                             k. always; consistently

                             l. out of place; not in harmony

■ **Meanings**

Match each prefix to its meaning. Use each choice only once.

1. im-, in- ___b___   a. out; former

2. ex-, e-, ec- ___a___   b. in; not

3. auto- ___c___   c. self

■ *Words in Context*

Complete each sentence with the word that fits best. Use each choice only once.

a. autobiography
b. autocratic
c. autonomous
d. eccentric

e. exorbitant
f. exploit
g. extricate
h. impartial

i. incongruous
j. ingenious
k. interminable
l. invariably

1. African-American athlete, singer, and actor Paul Robeson wrote a(n) __a, autobiography__ detailing his life as a performer and political activist.

2. The __d, eccentric__ man attached strings to large bugs and walked them like dogs.

3. Mom objected to the __e, exorbitant__ prices her teenage daughter paid for clothes.

4. The Vatican is a(n) __c, autonomous__ country that rules itself but sits within the country of Italy.

5. In a(n) __j, ingenious__ plan to prevent water shortages, Alaska's plentiful water may be shipped in huge bags to dry areas.

6. The sophisticated computer system seemed __i, incongruous__ with the dirt floor and straw roof of the hut.

7. The time I spent waiting to find out whether I got the job seemed __k, interminable__.

8. People __l, invariably__ close their eyes when they sneeze, since it is not possible to keep them open.

9. When my dog got its paw caught in a mousetrap, we tried to __g, extricate__ it carefully.

10. The __b, autocratic__ ruler suddenly announced that everyone had to pay a new tax.

■ *Using Related Words*

Complete each sentence by using a word from the group of related words above it. Use each choice only once.

FACT AND FICTION FROM ANCIENT GREECE

1. incongruously, incongruity

    It might sound like an **incongruity**_____ for a scientist to make a famous discovery while sitting in a bathtub. But that's where Archimedes discovered an important principle of physics.

    Even more **incongruously**_____ this distinguished scientist supposedly yelled "Eureka!" (I have found it!)

2. autonomy, autonomous

    In 490 BCE, Darius, king of the vast Persian empire, decided to

    conquer the city-state of Athens and end its **autonomy**_____.
    Against all odds, Athens defeated the Persian army on the

    Plain of Marathon and remained **autonomous**_____.
    Pheidippides ran twenty-six miles to deliver news of the victory to Athens. Since then, a race of twenty-six miles, or any long, difficult contest, has been called a "marathon."

3. impartial, impartiality

    The philosopher Socrates was a famous teacher in ancient Athens. Unfortunately, when he criticized city leaders, they brought him to trial for corrupting youth. The trial was so emotional that it was

    impossible to be **impartial**_____ in the debate. In 399 BCE, the authorities condemned Socrates to die by drinking poison hemlock. Although the city elders stated that they had acted with

    impartiality_____, others disagreed.

4. exploitation, exploited

    Is there anyone who has never heard of Aesop's fables? Aesop lived in ancient Greece in about 500 BCE. In one fable, a couple had a goose that laid one golden egg each day. When the couple

exploited_____ their good fortune wisely, they grew wealthier. However, one day they decided to get all the gold immediately. They killed the goose, only to find that there was no gold

inside it. Thus, their attempt at greedy **exploitation**_____ cost them dearly. From this fable comes the phrase "to kill the goose that lays the golden egg."

5. eccentric, eccentricity

Modern voting machines have led to many errors, but imagine how

eccentric_____ a modern voter would consider the ancient Greek method of voting on pieces of pottery. Using pieces of clay jars, the Greeks voted to expel dangerous citizens. This

eccentricity_____ has given us a modern English word. The clay pieces were called *oster,* and to snub or exclude someone is now "to ostracize."

■ *Reading the Headlines*

This exercise presents five headlines that might appear in newspapers. Read each headline and then answer the questions that follow. (Remember that small words, such as *is, are, a,* and *the,* are often left out of newspaper headlines.)

AUTOCRATIC RULER LIMITS CITIZENS' AUTONOMY

1. Does the ruler have absolute power? __**yes**__

2. Is the people's freedom growing? __**no**__

ECCENTRIC MAN PAYS EXORBITANT PRICE FOR SECURITY SYSTEM GUARDING AGAINST ALIENS

3. Is the man odd? __**yes**__

4. Is the man paying a low price? __**no**__

IN AUTOBIOGRAPHY, FORMER FARM WORKER TELLS HOW HE EXTRICATED HIMSELF FROM EXPLOITATION

5. Did the former farm worker write the story of someone else's life?

__**no**__

6. Did he escape from exploitation? __**yes**__

INGENIOUS TEXT MESSAGING PROVIDES AMUSEMENT DURING INTERMINABLE WAITS

7. Is the text messaging clever? __**yes**__

8. Is the wait short? __**no**__

IMPARTIAL REFEREE INVARIABLY RECEIVES ACCOLADES FROM PROFESSIONAL ORGANIZATIONS

9. Is the referee fair? __**yes**__

10. Does the referee receive many accolades? __**yes**__

Chapter Exercises

■ *Practicing Strategies: New Words from Word Elements*

See how your knowledge of prefixes can help you understand new words. Complete each sentence with the word that seems to fit best. Use each choice only once.

a. antifreeze
b. antislavery
c. autoinoculation
d. equator
e. equipotential
f. impression
g. income
h. irresponsible
i. reattach
j. refill
k. subcontractor
l. subliminal

1. After I finished my coffee, the waiter offered to __**j, refill**__ my cup.

2. Money that comes in to you is called __**g, income**__.

3. The __**b, antislavery**__ movement fought for the right of African Americans to be free.

4. In a process called __**c, autoinoculation**__, chemicals from your own body are injected back into you to fight disease.

5. The general contractor hired a(n) __**k, subcontractor**__ to do the plumbing.

6. The __d, equator__ divides the earth equally into the Northern and Southern hemispheres.

7. That __h, irresponsible__ person never does what he is supposed to do.

8. I poured __a, antifreeze__ into my radiator to prevent the water from turning to ice.

9. Something __l, subliminal__ is beneath the limits of your hearing or vision.

10. He made a(n) __f, impression__ when his shoe pressed into the soft cement.

■ Practicing Strategies: Combining Context Clues and Word Elements

You can use context clues with word elements to help figure out the meaning of unknown words. In the following sentences, each italicized word contains a word element that you have studied in this chapter. Using the meaning of the prefix and the context of the sentence, make an intelligent guess about the meaning of the italicized word. Your instructor may ask you to check the meaning in your dictionary after you have finished the exercise.

1. Despite the fact that he had never attended school, the *autodidact* had a wealth of knowledge.

   Autodidact means __self-educated person__.

2. During the war, there was an exodus of people from the country.

   Exodus means __exit; leaving__.

3. At the time of an *equinox*, there are twelve hours of daylight and twelve hours of darkness.

   Equinox means __the time of year when day and night are of equal length__.

4. Since our computer is *infallible*, the mistake must be due to human error.

   Infallible means __perfect; never wrong__.

5. You need to redo this substandard paper.

Substandard means <u>**lower than standard, failing**</u>.

■ *Practicing Strategies: Using the Dictionary*

Read the following definition and then answer the questions that follow.

> **bloom**[1] (bloom) *n.* **1.** The flower of a plant.   **2a.** The condition of being in flower.   **b.** A condition or time of vigor and beauty; prime: *"the radiant bloom of Greek genius"* (Edith Hamilton).   **3.** A fresh, rosy complexion: *"She was short, plump, and fair, with a fine bloom"* (Jane Austen).   **4a.** A waxy or powdery bluish coating on the surface of certain plant parts, as on plums or cabbage leaves, that forms naturally to prevent the loss of fluids.   **b.** A similar coating, as on newly minted coins.   **c.** Grayish marks on the surface of chocolate produced by the formation of cocoa butter crystals.   **d.** *Chemistry* See **efflorescence** 3a.   **5.** Glare that is caused by a shiny object reflecting too much light into a television camera.   **6.** A colored area on the surface of water caused by planktonic growth. ❖ *v.* **bloomed, bloom•ing, blooms** —*intr.*   **1a.** To bear a flower or flowers.   **b.** To support plant life in abundance.   **2.** To shine; glow.   **3.** To grow or flourish with youth and vigor.   **4.** To appear or expand suddenly. —*tr.*   **1.** To cause to flourish.   **2.** *Obsolete* To cause to flower. [ME *blom* < ON *blōm.* See **bhel-** in App.] —**bloom'y** *adj.*

1. Which common word in the dictionary key contains a vowel pronounced like the *oo* in *bloom?* <u>**boot**</u>

2. What is the definition number and part of speech of the definition in which a quote is used from author Edith Hamilton to define *bloom?*

    <u>**2b, noun**</u>

3. What is the definition of *bloom* that is no longer in use?

    <u>**2, transitive verb**</u> : "to cause to flower"

4. What is the definition number and part of speech of the definition that best fits this sentence? "To avoid the *bloom,* the assistant on the TV show took the metal pans off the wall." <u>**5, noun**</u>

5. In which language did *bloom* appear just before it entered modern English? <u>**Middle English**</u>

■ *Companion Words*

Complete each sentence with the word that fits best. Choose your answers from the words below. You may use each word more than once.

Choices: to, toward, of, from

1. The sun lamp supplied an antidote **to**_____ her depression.

2. We felt antipathy **toward**_____ our enemy.

3. The corporal is a subordinate **of**_____ the lieutenant.

4. The corporal is subordinate **to**_____ the lieutenant.

5. We enjoyed hearing about the exploits **of**_____ people who have climbed Mt. Everest.

6. It is difficult to maintain an impartial attitude **toward**_____ our own children.

7. We extricated ourselves **from**_____ the stuck elevator by climbing up to the next floor.

8. The revelations **of**_____ child abuse shocked the neighborhood.

9. When I smell fresh baked bread, my thoughts revert back **to**_____ my childhood.

10. After his divorce, Ken had to reconcile himself **to**_____ living alone.

■ *Writing with Your Words*

This exercise will give you practice in writing effective sentences that use the vocabulary words. Each sentence is started for you. Complete it with an interesting phrase that also indicates the meaning of the italicized word.

1. If I had to *subdue* a lion, _____

_____.

2. In her *autobiography,* the famous star _____

_____.

3. First she lost her *equilibrium,* and then _____

_____.

4. A person would be considered *autocratic* if _____

_____.

5. I *invariably* have difficulty _____

_____.

6. If I felt *exploited* _____

_____.

7. It seems *incongruous* that _____

_____.

8. The world needs an *ingenious* solution to the problem of _____

_____.

9. Her *subconscious* was bothered by hidden memories of _____

_____.

10. I would pay an *exorbitant* price for _____

_____.

■ *Making Connections*

These questions will help you relate the words you have learned in this chapter to your own life. Answer each question by writing a paragraph or more on a separate sheet of paper.

1. What factors do you feel most affect the equilibrium of a marriage? How?

2. Describe a situation in which a person was autocratic.

3. If you were to write your autobiography, what event would you give most attention to?

Passage

Food of the People

It has fed our nation for more than sixty years, inspiring poetry and song. It has even been counted among the one hundred greatest inventions of the twentieth century. Yet it has come under attack for its nutritional value as well as its strange appearance. What is it? The SPAM® Family of Products, of course!

The SPAM® Family of Products was first produced in 1935. A few years later, **(1)** Hormel Foods Corporation f/k/a Geo. A Hormel & Company invented an **ingenious** process that allowed meat to be preserved in a can, without refrigeration. But sales didn't really take off until the company changed the name of the product. It ran a contest, choosing the suggestion of "Spam." The person who coined the name received $100. Although this would not be considered **equitable** by today's standards, it was quite a bit of money at the time.

(2) The seemingly **interminable** economic depression of the 1930s made the price of many fresh meats **exorbitant.** SPAM was a cheaper alternative. So with its new, appealing name, SPAM found its way into many U.S. homes. A can of SPAM was easy to get, store, and prepare.

World War II (1939–45) made SPAM luncheon meat a truly common food. With its new, square-cornered cans, designed to meet military needs, SPAM could easily be shipped to provide protein to soldiers. **(3)** Its high calorie count quickly **subdued** hunger. SPAM fed the armies of many nations. **(4)** In his **autobiography,** *Khrushchev Remembers,* the for-

SPAM is a registered trademark for pork and poultry products by Hormel Foods LLC and is used with permission by Hormel Foods Corporation.

mer head of the Soviet Union credited SPAM with saving the Russian army from starvation. And, back in the United States, when other meats were rationed, SPAM was not.

SPAM luncheon meat continued to feed troops in other wars. Jess Loya, a Vietnam veteran, remembers SPAM as an **antidote** to his homesickness. **(5)** Opening a can would **invariably** remind him of his childhood when, living with a single father, he ate it many times.

With its former gelatin-like coating and odd, boxlike shape, SPAM has long been a source of conversational fun. Its pink color, similar to ham but more intense, seems to spark strong reactions of **(6) antipathy** as well as devotion. Advertisements have also added to the popularity of SPAM. Radio featured "SPAMMY™ the Pig" and the musical "Hormel Girls," who toured the United States. In 1940, SPAM became quite possibly the subject of the world's first singing commercial. Sung to the tune of "My Bonny Lies Over the Ocean," it went "SPAM, SPAM, SPAM, SPAM, Hormel's new miracle meat in a can. Tastes fine, saves time. If you want something grand, ask for SPAM."

Although Hormel called it "the miracle meat in a can," others have referred to it as "the mystery meat." This is unfair, for, **(7) as impartial** observers have pointed out, the ingredients are listed on the can. (They are chopped pork shoulder with ham meat added, salt, water, sugar, and sodium nitrite.) In these more health-conscious times, the calorie count and high percentage of calories from fat have also become a concern. In fact, Hormel Foods now makes SPAM Lite and SPAM Oven Roasted Turkey.

SPAM is now manufactured in several countries. In fact, in Korea, SPAM is sold in stylish gift boxes. **(8)** It seems **incongruous** to see SPAM alongside expensive watches and perfume, but South Koreans consider it a great treat. Within the United States, Hawaiians eat the most SPAM per capita, averaging four cans per person each year. SPAM can be prepared in many ways, including grilled, baked, microwaved, or eaten cold right from the can. There are thousands of different recipes that include SPAM. SPAM cooking contests are popular throughout the United States.

(9) It may come as a **revelation** that some uses for SPAM Products have nothing to do with food. Joey Green has become famous for using it to polish furniture and bathroom fixtures. Reporter James Barron, however, noted that it left a greasy film. Others have found that SPAM can be used to spackle a wall, fill holes in a canoe, and soothe a black-and-blue eye. These seem like **eccentric,** but amusing, uses for a food. Would you want your furniture, wall, or canoe—not to mention your eye—to smell like meat?

SPAM has also been the subject of verse, including haiku, a form of poetry originally from Japan. One author writes:

> Pretty pink Spam ham
> Shining on the white platter.
> Where did my fork go?

Sonnets and limericks have also been written to SPAM.

With all the fun and nutrition that SPAM has given us over the years, it is good to know that the product is doing well. **(10)** Hormel Foods continues to be an **autonomous,** family-originated company. The continuing popularity of the SPAM Family of Products is illustrated by the fact that if all the cans ever sold were laid end to end, they would circle the earth at least twelve times!

■ *Exercise*

Each numbered sentence below corresponds to a sentence in the Passage. Fill in the letter of the choice that makes the sentence mean the same thing as its corresponding sentence in the Passage.

1. Hormel Foods Corporation invented a(n) __c____ process.
   a. independent   b. interesting   c. clever   d. speedy

2. The economic depression of the 1930s seemed __d____.
   a. unfair   b. hopeless   c. tragic   d. endless

3. Its high calorie count __c____ hunger.
   a. increased   b. caused   c. conquered   d. resulted in

4. In his __a____ Khrushchev credits SPAM with saving the Russian army.
   a. book about his life   b. book about the war   c. book about food
   d. book about Russia

5. Opening a can would __d____ remind him of his childhood.
   a. never   b. sometimes   c. often   d. always

6. SPAM has sparked **b**_____ as well as devotion.
   a. love   b. hatred   c. anger   d. unhappiness

7. **a**_____ observers have pointed out that the ingredients are listed on each can.
   a. Unbiased   b. Strange   c. Bossy   d. Alert

8. It may seem **b**_____ to see SPAM alongside expensive watches and perfume.
   a. not acceptable   b. out of place   c. inventive   d. natural

9. It may come as a **c**_____ that some uses for SPAM have nothing to do with food.
   a. joke   b. rumor   c. surprise   d. fact

10. Hormel continues to be a(n) **c**_____ company.
    a. profitable   b. well run   c. independent   d. large

■ Discussion Questions

1. List two nonfood uses for SPAM.

2. Describe two things that appeal to you about SPAM and two things you find unappealing.

3. Why do you think SPAM has drawn so much attention in our culture?

Spam has a new meaning related to computers. Sending out large numbers of unwanted advertisements by e-mail is called *spamming*. The name originated with *Monty Python's Flying Circus*, when comedians sang, "SPAM, SPAM, SPAM" to drown out conversation. In the same way, spam is said to overwhelm personal e-mail messages. Lawmakers are considering ways to limit it.

◀ ENGLISH IDIOMS

Beginnings, Endings, and Time

Beginnings, endings, and time form the basis of many idioms. To *start from scratch* means to start from the beginning. However, to *start up with someone* means to start an argument.

To *wind up* means to end something, as in "I'm winding up my assignment." People *at the end of their rope* or *at the end of their tether* are desperate and do not know what to do.

If a woman *takes her time,* she does things slowly, at her own rate. If she *has time on her hands,* she has time to spare, or extra time. If she has *the time of her life,* she really enjoys herself.

When something is done that is long overdue, we say, "It's *high time*" for it to be done. When something is no longer in fashion or up to date, we call it *behind the times.*

Until the invention of quartz controls, most clocks and watches were driven by small wheels with notches, or *nicks,* in them. You may actually have some clocks with these ticking gears. The nicks catch on a wheel and move as frequently as every second. Therefore, to be *in the nick of time* means to be on time to the second, or nearly late. A person who catches a train *in the nick of time* almost misses it.

6

Word Elements: People and Names

Words that come from names fill the English language. The *petrie* dish, the *ferris* wheel, and *nicotine* were named for their discoverers. In this chapter you will learn more words formed from names. In addition, this chapter presents combining roots that relate to people and two prefixes that come from names in Greek mythology.

Chapter Strategy: Word Elements About People

Chapter Words:

Part 1

anthrop	anthropological	*nom*	nominal
	misanthrope		pseudonym
	philanthropist		renowned
gen	congenital	*viv*	viable
	genesis		vital
	genocide		vivacious

Part 2

pan-	pandemonium	*Name Words*	boycott
	panorama		chauvinism
psych-	psyche		gargantuan
	psychosomatic		martial
			maverick
			odyssey
			quixotic
			spartan

Quiz Yourself

To check your present knowledge of some of the chapter words, identify these statements as true or false. Answers are on page 410.

Vivacious means lacking energy.	True	False
You are born with a **congenital** condition.	True	False
A **maverick** willingly follows rules.	True	False
A **psychosomatic** illness has a physical basis.	True	False

You will learn the answers as you study this chapter.

Did You Know?

Which Words Come from Names?

Many English words are taken from names in classical myths. The ancient Greeks and Romans had well-developed and colorful mythologies, whose legends reflected the violence and passion of life in a time when humans were at the mercy of disease and natural forces.

The mythological king of the gods, Jupiter, ruled thunder—a fearful force to ancient people. His many exploits included dethroning his father and turning himself into a swan in order to seduce a young girl. He loved nasty jokes. The word *jovial*, meaning "merry," comes from Jove, another name for Jupiter.

Mercury, often shown with wings on his feet, was the messenger of the gods. The metal *mercury*, used in thermometers, is a quick-moving liquid at room temperature. A quick-tempered person is often called *mercurial*. Venus, or Aphrodite, was the goddess of love. An *aphrodisiac* is a drug or food that is said to increase sexual desire.

Other words come from the names of real people. The Earl of Sandwich (1718–1792) loved to gamble so much that he refused to leave the game, even to eat. Instead he had meat brought to him between two pieces of bread. U.S. Union Civil War general Ambrose Burnside, a fashion leader, allowed his hair to grow down the side of his face, inventing a style we still call—reversing Burnside's name—*sideburns*.

Some words come from the names of organizations. The coffee drink *cappuccino* comes from the Italian Capuchin order, a group of Roman Catholic monks. The idea for the *frisbee* came from the easy-to-catch pie tins manufactured by the Frisbie company in Bridgeport, Connecticut.

Places also have contributed their names. The word *dollar* comes from *taler,* shortened from *Joachimstal,* the city in Bohemia where it was first used. *Peach* is taken from the Latin word for Persia (now Iran), where this fruit originated.

Even imaginary places have lent their names to English. In about 1500, a Spanish novelist described a beautiful, imaginary island inhabited by strong women. When exploring the Americas, a Spaniard used the novelist's word to name a real place of great natural beauty, at first thought to be an island. The name, *California,* is still used today.

In this chapter, you will learn several words derived from names. Perhaps one day a word will be coined from your name!

Can you match the word to the person or place of its origin?

1. Oscar
2. Melba toast
3. ritzy
4. Atlas
5. Pulitzer Prize

a. the founder of the *St. Louis Post-Dispatch*

b. uncle of the secretary of the Motion Picture Academy

c. mythical being who supported the world on his shoulder

d. a hotel founder who was the thirteenth child of a peasant couple

e. an Australian opera star on a diet

Answers are on page 410.

Learning Strategy

Word Elements About People

This first part of Chapter 6 discusses roots and how they function in words. Four roots related to people are used as examples. The second part of the chapter continues with prefixes, presenting two taken from names.

Element	Meaning	Origin	Function	Chapter Words
Part 1				
anthrop	human	Greek	root	anthropological, misanthrope, philanthropist
gen	birth; type	Latin; Greek	root	congenital, genesis, genocide

| *nom, nym* | name | Latin; Greek | root | nominal, pseudonym, renowned |
| *vit, viv* | life | Latin | root | viable, vital, vivacious |

Part 2

| *pan-* | all | Greek | prefix | panorama, pandemonium |
| *psych-* | mind; soul | Greek | prefix | psyche, psychosomatic |

A root is the word element that carries the central meaning of a word. Although prefixes and suffixes may alter the meaning of a root, they do not carry as much meaning as the root itself.

Remember that there are two kinds of roots—base words and combining roots. Base words can stand alone as English words. They may or may not have prefixes and suffixes attached to them. *Work* is an example of a base word.

Combining roots cannot stand alone as English words. They require a prefix, a suffix, or at least a change in spelling, in order to form a word. Most of the roots you will study in this book are combining roots that come from ancient Greek and Latin. Although they were words in these ancient languages, they appear in modern English only as word elements.

The root *anthrop* (human) is an example of a combining root. It forms a word when it is attached to a prefix (*misanthrope*) or a suffix (*anthropological*).

Nom or *nym,* meaning "name," is another example of a combining root. This root has more than one spelling because it comes from both Latin and Greek. It forms over thirty English words. Slight changes in spelling give us the words *name* and *noun;* adding a suffix gives us *nominate;* adding different prefixes gives us *antonym* and *synonym.*

Each of the words formed from the root *nom* or *nym* carries a meaning related to "name." Sometimes the meaning is directly related; at other times the root gives a hint about a word's meaning rather than supplying the meaning. The word *name* has the same meaning as the root *nom* or *nym;* thus, the word and the root are directly related. Other words have an indirect relationship to *nom* and *nym:*

A *noun* is a word that **names** a person, place, idea, or thing.
To *nominate* is to **name** somebody to a position, or to **name** somebody as
    a candidate in an election.
A *synonym* is a word that means the same thing as another word; two syn-
    onyms **name** the same thing. (*Syn* means "same.")
An *antonym* is a word opposite in meaning to another word; two
    antonyms **name** opposite things. (As you learned in Chapter 5, *ant-*
    means "opposite.")

Word Roots

Part 1

The four roots presented in Part 1 of this chapter are all related to people and their lives.

anthrop (human)

The root *anthrop* comes from the Greek word for "human," *anthropos*. Perhaps you have taken a course in *anthropology*, the study of **human** life.

gen (birth; type)

Because *gen* forms more than fifty English words, it is an extremely useful root. *Gen* has two meanings: "birth" and "type." The ancients felt that these meanings were related because when someone was **born**, he or she was a certain **type** of person. *Gen* means **birth** in the word *gene*, which refers to the hereditary information in each cell of a living plant or animal. We are all **born** with our genes. Recently, an enormous *genome* research project defined the function of all human genes. Another word, *generation*, refers to people who are **born** during the same time period.

Gen means "type" in the word *gender*, which tells what **type** of person you are, male or female. Perhaps you buy *generic* foods at the grocery. These have no brand names and are of a general **type.** The use of context clues will help you to determine whether *gen* means "birth" or "type" when you see it in a word.

nom, nym (name)

This root comes from both Latin and Greek. *Nomen* is Latin for "name," and the word originally appeared in Greek as *onoma*.

vit, viv (life)

In Latin, *vita* means "life." *Vit* forms such words as *vitamin*, chemicals necessary for human **life.** Manufacturers have used this root in brand names, such as *Vitalis*, which is supposed to add **life** to your hair. *Victuals* (pronounced and sometimes spelled informally as *vittles*) means "food." It comes from *vivere*, "to live," for food enables us to **live.**

Words to Learn

Part 1

anthrop-

1. **anthropological** (adjective)   ăn′thrə-pə-lŏj′ĭ-kəl

   From Greek: *anthrōpos* (human being)

   referring to the study of human beings and their cultures

   > In landmark **anthropological** research, Annette Weiner ex-
   > plored the complex society of the Trobriand Islanders in the
   > Pacific.

   ▶ *Related Words*
   anthropologist (noun, person)   Richard Lee, the noted *anthropologist*, described the changing lives and respect for nature of
   the southern African Dobe !Kung people.

   anthropology (noun)   In one application of *anthropology*,
   research into ancient Peruvian canals is improving modern-
   day farming methods.

2. **misanthrope** (noun, person)   mĭs′ən-thrōp′

   From Greek: *misein* (to hate) + *anthrop* (human)

   a person who hates or distrusts other people

   > A failure in business and personal life, the **misanthrope**
   > resented the happiness of others.

   ▶ *Related Word*
   misanthropic (adjective)   (mĭs′ən-thrŏp′ĭk) *Misanthropic* people can make cruel remarks to salespeople and waiters.

   Two famous literary characters exemplify the *misanthropic* spirit.
   Ebenezer Scrooge, created by Charles Dickens in the classic novella *A
   Christmas Carol*, mistreats his employee and wishes ill to everybody,
   especially at Christmas. Scrooge has become famous for his classic
   expression "Bah, Humbug!" A more modern *misanthrope*, the Grinch,
   actually steals Christmas. The Grinch was created by children's author
   Theodor Geisel, better known as Dr. Seuss.

   ---

3. **philanthropist** (noun)   fĭ-lăn′thrə-pĭst

   From Greek: *philos* (loving) + *anthrop* (human)

one who wishes to help humanity; a person who makes large gifts to charity

> **Philanthropists** Bill and Melinda Gates have donated millions of dollars for health care research.

▶ *Related Words*

philanthropic (adjective) (fĭl′ən-thrŏp′ĭk) The *philanthropic* efforts of the American Jewish community helped build the state of Israel.

philanthropy (noun) Mexicans working in the United States often demonstrate *philanthropy* by donating money to improve their home towns.

gen

4. **congenital** (adjective)   kən-jĕn′ĭ-təl

From Latin: *com-* (together; with) + *gen* (birth) (If something is *congenital,* you are born with it.)

existing at birth

> Tim Brandau, a victim of *congenital* deafness, received a cochlear implant that enables him to hear.

Duncan Kennedy, three-time contestant in the Olympics and the American who had won the most sledding awards in history, was diagnosed with a *congenital* condition affecting the formation of his brain. He also fought shoulder and back problems. However, Kennedy's response was not to give up, but to switch sports! He turned to competing in the sport of snowboarding.

NOTE: Congenital can also mean habitual, as in "He is a *congenital* liar."

5. **genesis** (noun)   jĕn′ĭ-sĭs

From Greek: *gen* (birth) (*Genesis* meant "birth" or "origin" in ancient Greek.)

origin; beginning

> The **genesis** of writing dates back 3,500 years to the Sumerians.

> Many scientists think that the **genesis** of the universe was an enormous explosion called the "big bang."

Genesis, the first book of the Bible, tells the story of a great flood survived only by Noah, his family, and two of each type of animal. Many other religions and cultures have tales of a large flood. In southern Mesopotamia (now largely Iraq), references to a flood are recorded on a stone tablet (dated 2100 BCE) and in the Babylonian Epic of Gilgamesh (about 700 BCE). Other references are found in India, Burma, Australia, and among Native American tribes. Was there ever a great flood? In 1929, after exploring lower Mesopotamia, Sir Leonard Woolley concluded that a widespread area had been badly flooded in about 3000 BCE.

6. **genocide** (noun)   jĕn′ə-sīd′

From Greek: *gen* (type) + Latin: *-cidium* (killing) (*Genos* meant "race" in ancient Greek, so *genocide* means "the killing of an entire race.")

the planned murder of an entire group

> The **genocide** of Armenians during World War I resulted in over a million deaths.

▶ *Related Word*
> **genocidal** (adjective)   The *genocidal* Khmer Rouge regime killed hundreds of thousands of fellow Cambodians.

The most horrible example of *genocide* occurred from 1939 to 1945, when the leader of Nazi Germany, Adolf Hitler, planned the destruction of all of Europe's Jews. This dreadful plan, often called the Holocaust, resulted in the deaths of over 6 million people. Another 5 million civilians were murdered by the Nazis because of their ethnic origins, beliefs, disabilities, or resistance to oppression.

nom; nym

7. **nominal** (adjective)   nŏm′ə-nəl

From Latin: *nom* (name)

in name only

> Although Queen Elizabeth II is the **nominal** ruler of England, the prime minister and Parliament hold most of the power.

a very small amount

> The nonprofit group paid the city a **nominal** sum of $25 for a year's rent.

8. **pseudonym** (noun)   sōōd'n-ĭm'

From Greek: *pseudes* (false) + *nym* (name)

assumed name; pen name

> Stephen King has published successful novels using the **pseudonym** Richard Bachman.

> Paul Westerberg sometimes performs under the **pseudonym** Grandpaboy.

NOTE: The word *pseudonym* often refers to authors or artists. In contrast, *alias,* which usually refers to names assumed by criminals, has a negative connotation.

▶ *Common Phrases*
    under the pseudonym of; using the pseudonym

Many celebrities have adopted *pseudonyms*. Can you match the following pseudonyms to the real names?

1. Ice Cube		a. O'Shea Johnson
2. Eminem		b. Marshall Mathers
3. Alice Cooper		c. Reginald Kenneth Dwight
4. Elton John		d. Sean Combs
5. Ice T		e. Vince Furnier
6. P. Diddy		f. Tracy Marrow

Answers are on page 410.

---

9. **renowned** (adjective)   rĭ-nound'

famous; well regarded

From Latin: *re-* (again) + *nom* (to name) (A person who is "named repeatedly" becomes famous.)

> Scientist Jane Goodall is **renowned** for her work with wild chimpanzees.

> Hawaii is **renowned** for its beautiful beaches.

▶ *Related Word*
    renown (noun)   The chef won *renown* for her excellent cheesecake.

vit; viv

10. **viable** (adjective)   vī-'ə-bəl

    From Latin: *vit* (life), becoming French *vie* (life)

    capable of living; capable of success; workable

    > Mosquito eggs remain **viable** for four years, awaiting enough rain to hatch.

    > For many people, a second career has become a **viable** alternative to retirement.

11. **vital** (adjective)   vīt'l

    From Latin: *vit* (life)

    referring to life

    > The doctor measured her pulse, blood pressure, and other **vital** signs.

    necessary; essential

    > Food is **vital** to life.

    > A day off is **vital** to my sanity.

    lively; full of life; busy

    > Seattle's **vital** downtown area attracts many tourists.

    ▶ *Common Phrase*
      vital to

    ▶ *Related Word*
      vitality (noun)   (vī-tăl'ĭ-tē)   The teacher's *vitality* enabled him to work long hours in after-school programs. (*Vitality* means "life energy.")

12. **vivacious** (adjective)   vĭ-vā'shəs

    From Latin: *viv* (to live) (*Vivax* meant "lively.")

    lively; full of spirit

    > No picture could capture the **vivacious** spirit of the high school cheerleader.

    ▶ *Related Word*
      vivacity (noun)   (vĭ-văs'ə-tē)   The teenager's **vivacity** captured the boy's attention.

    NOTE: *Vivacious* is usually used to describe women.

Exercises

Part 1

■ *Definitions*

Complete each sentence in the left-hand column with a definition from the right-hand column. Use each choice only once.

1. Genesis is __e__.

2. Anthropology is __l__.

3. A vivacious person is __h__.

4. Something congenital is

   __j__.

5. A pseudonym is __c__.

6. A philanthropist is __b__.

7. Renowned means __d__.

8. Genocide is __a__.

9. A viable idea is __g__.

10. A person in nominal control

    is __i__.

a. the planned murder of an entire group

b. a charitable person

c. an assumed name

d. famous

e. a beginning

f. a person who hates others

g. workable

h. lively

i. not really in power

j. present at birth

k. necessary

l. the study of human beings

■ *Meanings*

Match each word element to its meaning. Use each choice only once.

1. vit, viv __a__

2. nom, nym __b__

3. gen __c__

4. anthrop __d__

a. life

b. name

c. birth; type

d. human

■ *Words in Context*

Complete each sentence with the word that fits best. Use each choice only once.

a. anthropology   e. genesis   i. renowned
b. misanthrope   f. genocide   j. viable
c. philanthropist g. nominal   k. vital
d. congenital   h. pseudonym   l. vivacious

1. The company's founder is now only its __g, nominal__ head, since his daughter makes all the decisions.

2. Some people are born with hemophilia, a(n) __d, congenital__ condition that slows the ability of their blood to clot.

3. Many Mexican holiday customs have their __e, genesis__ in pre-Hispanic times.

4. The newborn hamster was not __j, viable__, and it soon died.

5. Jonas Salk became __i, renowned__ for developing a vaccine against polio.

6. Speed is __k, vital__ to a champion runner.

7. Jason Rekulak uses the __h, pseudonym__ Danny Cassidy for the books of romantic poetry he edits.

8. The __c, philanthropist__ gave money to build a new hospital.

9. Only a(n) __b, misanthrope__ would dislike this scene of human happiness.

10. In the horror movie *Plan 9 from Outer Space*, evil creatures from another planet plot the __f, genocide__ of the entire human race.

■ *Using Related Words*

Complete each sentence by using a word from the group of related words above it. Use each choice only once.

TALES AND TRADITIONS FROM THE ANCIENT GREEKS

1. vivacious, vivacity

   In one of Aesop's fables, as a **vivacious**_____ girl walked to town carrying a jug of milk on her head, she thought of how the milk would make cream that she could sell to buy eggs. The eggs would make chickens, and she could sell the chickens for a gown, which would attract a rich husband. As she fantasized, her

   vivacity_____ overcame her. She tossed her head and spilled the milk. From this story comes the proverb "Don't count your chickens before they're hatched."

2. misanthrope, misanthropic

   In the ancient Greek classic the *Odyssey,* Odysseus, the hero, has to

   choose between sailing near two **misanthropic**_____ monsters, Scylla, a six-headed horror that eats people for lunch, and Charybdis, a whirlpool that sucks in ships. Deciding that the less dangerous

   misanthrope_____ is Scylla, he loses only six men, rather than his entire crew. Today, to face two bad choices is referred to as being "between Scylla and Charybdis."

3. vital, vitality

   In Greek mythology, the hero Achilles was **vital**_____ to the success of the Greeks in conquering Troy. At his birth, Achilles' goddess mother wanted to make her son immortal, so she dipped him in the River Styx to preserve his

   vitality_____. However, the heel she held him by was not touched by the protective water. As battle raged in Troy, an arrow struck Achilles in that heel, killing him. A point of weakness is now called an "Achilles heel."

4. renown, renowned

   When Odysseus, a hero of great **renown**_____, went to fight in the Trojan War, he entrusted his son's education to the

renowned_____ tutor Mentor. Today a coach or adviser is often called a "mentor."

5. anthropological, anthropologist

Originally staged by the ancient Greeks, the Olympic Games took place from 776 to 394 BCE. In the 1800s, Frenchman Pierre de Coubertin spent his life reviving them. The modern Olympics, begun in 1896, are now a tradition. John MacAloon, an

anthropologist_____ at the University of Chicago, studies the meaning of the games. He concludes that, from an

anthropological_____ point of view, they give a sense of national identity and allow people throughout the world to share a common event.

■ *Reading the Headlines*

This exercise presents five headlines that might appear in newspapers. Read each headline and then answer the questions that follow. (Remember that small words, such as *is*, *are*, *a*, and *the*, are often left out of newspaper headlines.)

MANY BABIES WITH CONGENITAL HEART PROBLEMS ARE NOW VIABLE

1. Are the babies born with the heart problems? **yes**_____

2. Will the babies now live? **yes**_____

VIVACITY OF MUSEUM DIRECTOR VITAL TO CONVINCING PHILANTHROPIST TO HELP PROJECT

3. Is the museum director lively? **yes**_____

4. Will the philanthropist ask someone else for money? **no**_____

POLICE UNCOVER MISANTHROPE'S GENOCIDAL PLOT

5. Does the misanthrope like people? **no**_____

6. Is the misanthrope planning to kill people? **yes**_____

MAN WINS RENOWN UNDER PSEUDONYM

> 7. Is the man famous? <u>**yes**</u>

> 8. Is he using his own name? <u>**no**</u>

NOMINAL DONATION FUNDS GENESIS OF ANTHROPOLOGICAL RESEARCH

> 9. Was the donation large? <u>**no**</u>

> 10. Is the research ending? <u>**no**</u>

Prefixes and Name Words

Part 2

Part 2 of this chapter first presents two prefixes that come from names in Greek mythology. Then it introduces several words taken directly from names.

pan- (all)

The prefix *pan-* is the Greek word for "all." It appears in two names from Greek mythology. Pan was the god of woods, fields, and shepherds. He had the lower body of a goat and the upper body of a man. He got his name because, as Homer wrote, "he delighted **all.**" Pandora (*pan-,* **all,** + *dora,* gifts) was the first woman. The gods gave her a box that she was told not to open, and sent her to Earth. Curious, she disobeyed, and out flew **all** the world's troubles. Only Hope remained inside the box. (Like Eve in the Bible, Pandora was a woman blamed for causing **all** the world's problems.) The prefix *pan-* is used in such words as *pan-American,* which refers to **all** of the Americas: North, South, and Central.

psych-; psycho- (mind; soul)

The Greek word *psyche* originally meant "breath" and refers to the soul or the spirit of a person. This is personified in Greek mythology as Psyche, a beautiful mortal, who was loved by Eros (or Cupid), the god of love. Eros visited **Psyche** every night but told her never to look at him. One night, overcome by curiosity, Psyche held a lamp up to Eros as he slept. A drop of oil dripped on his shoulder, waking him, and he fled. Psyche searched frantically for Eros, performing many difficult tasks to win the favor of the gods. As a reward, they made her immortal and allowed her to marry Eros. Psyche, with her beauty and dedication, symbolizes the soul. Her immortality shows

Only Hope remained in Pandora's box.

how the human soul finally goes to heaven. In modern words, *psych-* usually means "mind" rather than "soul." *Psychobiology* is the study of the biology of the **mind.** In some words, *psych* functions as a root. Perhaps you have taken a class in *psychology,* the study of the **mind.**

Words to Learn

Part 2

pan-

13. **pandemonium** (noun)   păn′də-mōʹnē-əm

From Greek: *pan-* (all) + *daimōn* (demon)

chaos, wild disorder, and noise

> A fire in the restaurant caused **pandemonium** as patrons fled and trampled each other.

In John Milton's poem *Paradise Lost,* published in 1667, *Pandaemonium* is the principal city of Hell, where "all the demons" live.

14. **panorama** (noun)   păn′ə-răm′-ə

From Greek: *pan-* (all) + *horan* (to see)

an unbroken view over a large area

> From the top of the Eiffel Tower, visitors see a **panorama** of the Paris skyline.

a wide-ranging survey

> The college course offered a **panorama** of world history.

▶ *Related Word*
>   **panoramic** (adjective)   Looking down from the Colorado ski slope, we had a *panoramic* view of the beautiful mountains.

NOTE: Panorama can refer either to a physical view of something or a "view" in one's mind, as in a wide-ranging presentation of a subject.

psych-

15. **psyche** (noun)   sī′kē

From Greek: *psych-* (soul)

mental state; soul

> Mozart's superb music gives no clue to his troubled **psyche.**
> Psychologists believe that basic needs for food and love govern the human **psyche.**

NOTE: Psyche usually refers to the part of the mind that is not rational and is related to feelings such as self-esteem and happiness.

16. **psychosomatic** (adjective)   sī′kō-sō-măt′ĭk

From Greek: *psych-* (mind; soul) + *soma* (body)

referring to physical disorders that are caused by the mind

Parents can develop **psychosomatic** illnesses from the stress of raising teenagers.

Name Words

17. **boycott** (verb, noun)   boi'kŏt'

to refuse to use or buy something as an act of protest (verb)

> The Professional Golf Association decided to **boycott** country clubs that did not admit minorities.

the act of boycotting (noun)

> The International Labor Organization may urge a **boycott** of cocoa harvested by young children.

The Irish potato famine of the mid 1800s made farmers so poor that a law was passed in 1881 to reduce rents. Captain Charles C. Boycott, a cruel English land agent, angered people by insisting on the old payments, thus forcing many farmers out of business. In response, the Irish Land League *boycotted* him by refusing to associate with him in any way.

---

18. **chauvinism** (noun)   shō'və-nĭz'əm

prejudiced devotion to a group or country

> Jim's **chauvinism** was evident from the dozens of "Buy American" bumper stickers on his pickup truck.
>
> The men of the primitive Yanomamo tribe display **chauvinism** when they say that women are too clumsy to make pottery.

▶ *Related Words*

chauvinist (noun, person)   Slam poets frequently attack male *chauvinists*.

chauvinistic (adjective)   To avoid using a *chauvinistic* label, the city of Sacramento renamed a "manhole" as a "maintenance hole."

NOTE: The term *male chauvinism* refers to the view that men are superior to women, and a *male chauvinist* is a person who holds this view.

Nicholas Chauvin was a legendary lieutenant in the French army who was extremely devoted to his general, Napoleon Bonaparte. Even after Napoleon's defeat, Chauvin continued in his blind loyalty. Such excessive devotion is now called *chauvinism*.

---

19. **gargantuan** (adjective)   gär-găn′chōō-ən

huge; immense

> The **gargantuan** fossil skeleton of "Sue," a *Tyrannosaurus rex*, is forty feet long.
>
> I couldn't finish the **gargantuan** "super burrito."
>
> The man was shocked by the **gargantuan** legal fees from his divorce.

Gargantua and Pantagruel is a series of stories written by French author François Rabelais between 1532 and 1562. Gargantua is a giant with an appetite to match. At one point, he eats five people in a salad! He arranges his hair with a *gargantuan* comb 900 feet long. Right after his birth, he cries out, "Drink, drink!" The book may be a satire—a work that makes fun—of Francis I, the French king. Rabelais led an eventful life, which is reflected in the vitality of his book's hero.

This *gargantuan* window washer can reach the windows of a high-rise building while standing on the ground.

20. **martial** (adjective)   mär′shəl

referring to war or soldiers

> Dressed in armor and carrying a sword, the knight had a splendid **martial** appearance.

▶ *Common Phrases*

martial law In 1981, when Poland was placed under *martial law,* U.S. President Ronald Reagan halted trading with the country. (Martial law is rule by military authorities imposed on a civilian population.)

martial arts *Martial arts* were featured as Olympic sports for the first time in 2004. (Martial arts are sports such as karate and tae kwon do that teach one how to defend oneself.)

Mars, the Roman god of war, gives his name to the month of March. He is also the source of the name for Mars, the planet that appears to be faintly red, suggesting the color of blood. Except for Earth, each of the planets in our solar system is named for a Greek or Roman god. Closest to the sun is *Mercury,* the quickly rotating planet named for the messenger god. *Venus,* named for the god of love, is followed by *Earth* and *Mars. Jupiter* is named for the king of the gods. *Saturn* is Jupiter's father, and *Uranus* is his grandfather. *Neptune* is ruler of the sea. Finally, *Pluto,* the planet farthest from the sun, honors the gloomy god of the underworld, the region of the dead.

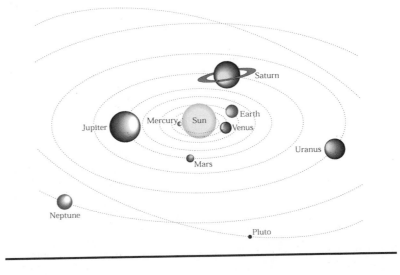

21. **maverick** (noun, person)   măv′ər-ĭk

an independent-minded person who does not conform or adhere to rules

> Tom was a **maverick** who refused to wear the school uniform.

NOTE: Maverick can also function as an adjective, as in "The *maverick* politician refused to follow party leaders."

In the 1800s, cattlemen began branding their calves to indicate ownership. Samuel Maverick, a Texan rancher of independent spirit, refused to follow this custom. This annoyed the other ranchers, who called all unbranded cattle *mavericks*. Maverick led a colorful life, fighting duels, spending time in prison, and serving in the Texas legislature.

22. **odyssey** (noun)   ŏd′ĭ-sē

a long and adventurous journey

> In an unusual **odyssey,** David Hempleman-Adams became the first person to cross the Atlantic Ocean by balloon.

> As the result of a spiritual **odyssey** that led him to join the Nation of Islam, Malcolm Little changed his name to Malcolm X.

The *Odyssey,* a classic ancient Greek poem by Homer, details the journey of Odysseus (also known as Ulysses) home from the Trojan War. His adventures include a shipwreck, a visit to the underworld, the irresistible songs of the dangerous Sirens, and a choice between meeting one of two monsters, Scylla and Charybdis (mentioned earlier in this chapter). Since this work appeared, an intense physical or spiritual journey has been called an *odyssey* in honor of Homer's epic poem.

23. **quixotic** (adjective)   kwĭk-sŏt′ĭk

noble, but not practical; having unreachable ideals; idealistic

> Scott spent three years in a **quixotic** effort to block the construction of a high-rise in a neighborhood others had lost interest in.

Miguel de Cervantes published his classic novel *Don Quixote* in 1605. In it, an old man, Don Quixote, decides to become a wandering knight and does noble but foolish deeds. He duels with a windmill that he thinks is a giant. He mistakes an inn for a castle and a peasant girl for a noble lady. His squire (helper), Sancho Panza, sees how ridiculous all of this is, but remains loyal to his master.

Although *Don Quixote* was originally written in Spanish, many of its famous phrases are used in modern-day English. These include "in a pickle," "too much of a good thing," "a wink of sleep," "a stone's throw," "smell a rat," "honesty is the best policy," "turn over a new leaf," and "faint heart never won fair lady."

Don Quixote traveled with his squire, Sancho Panza.

24. **spartan** (adjective)   spär′tn

lacking in comfort; requiring self-discipline

Richard's **spartan** diet included only brown rice and vegetables.

Professional football players were annoyed when they had to stay at a **spartan** college dorm rather than a luxurious hotel.

The ancient Greek city of Sparta was known for its devotion to athletics and the art of warfare. Spartans valued physical stamina, rough living, and bravery. So *spartan* was their training process that boys were taken away from their mothers and put in training camps when they were seven years old.

NOTE: The word *spartan* is sometimes capitalized.

Exercises

Part 2

■ Definitions

Complete each sentence in the left-hand column by choosing a word or phrase from the right-hand column. Use each choice only once.

1. Chauvinism is ___c___.

2. A quixotic person is ___h___.

3. A spartan life is ___e___.

4. Pandemonium is ___d___.

5. A panorama is ___i___.

6. A psychosomatic illness has ___b___.

7. An odyssey is ___j___.

8. To boycott is ___a___.

9. A martial man is ___g___.

10. A maverick is ___f___.

a. not to buy or use

b. a mental cause

c. prejudiced devotion

d. confusion

e. without comforts

f. an independent-minded person

g. warlike

h. idealistic

i. a wide view

j. a journey

k. huge

l. mental state or soul

■ *Meanings*

Match each word element to its meaning. Use each choice only once.

1. pan-___**b**___   a. mind; soul

                 b. all

2. psych-___**a**___

■ *Words in Context*

Complete each sentence with the word that fits best. Use each choice only once. You may have to capitalize some words.

a. panorama	e. boycott	i. maverick
b. pandemonium	f. chauvinistic	j. odyssey
c. psyche	g. gargantuan	k. quixotic
d. psychosomatic	h. martial	l. spartan

1. The political **i, maverick** refused to vote as his party wanted him to.

2. Madeline Albright met some **f, chauvinistic** men who didn't think a female should serve as secretary of state.

3. Lan's **d, psychosomatic** headaches disappeared when her nasty boss left.

4. **b, Pandemonium** broke out as the crowd realized that someone was firing a gun.

5. The **g, gargantuan** tree was over 300 feet tall.

6. We organized a(n) **e, boycott** of the store that treated its workers badly.

7. In Bev's **j, odyssey** across Russia, she traveled through eleven time zones.

8. Disturbing thoughts troubled Keisha's **c, psyche**.

9. For over a year, **k, quixotic** Julia Hill lived in a 600-year-old redwood tree to prevent it from being cut down.

10. Our **l, spartan** cabin lacked electricity and plumbing.

■ *Using Related Words*

Complete each sentence by using a word or phrase from the group of related words or phrases above it. Use each choice only once.

1. martial, martial arts

You have probably heard of **martial arts**_____ like judo and karate, but have you heard of Capoeira? Afro-Brazilians invented it at a time when most of them were slaves. Capoeira served the

martial_____ function of defense, but, perhaps to fool slave owners, appeared to be a dance. Still, it was outlawed in Brazil until 1937. Today Capoeira is considered a national treasure.

2. psyche, psychosomatic, psychosomatically

How much does the **psyche**_____ govern the body? A study done at Ohio State University found that healing may be

affected by **psychosomatic**_____ factors. Wounds inside the mouth healed more slowly during exam time, indicating that

the body is **psychosomatically**_____ affected by stress.

3. panorama, panoramic

Traveling up Highway 160, one reaches Colorado's Mesa Verde. From the top of the Mesa Verde, the traveler sees a vast

panorama_____ of valleys once farmed by the ancient Anasazi people. Over centuries, their homes changed from fire places with roofs to large stone apartment buildings. From the cliffs they inhabited, these people enjoyed the same

panoramic_____ view that tourists see today.

4. chauvinism, chauvinists, chauvinistic

During World War II, when British men went off to fight, women called "land girls" took their places working on farms. Some

chauvinists_____ doubted that the women would be able to tend to crops. But despite outdated equipment, they succeeded, proving that male <u>**chauvinism**</u> was unjustified. Season

after season, they proved their <u>**chauvinistic**</u> critics to be wrong.

■ *True or False?*

Each of the following statements uses at least one word from this section. Read each statement and then indicate whether you think it is probably true or probably false. Your instructor may ask you to reword false statements to make them true.

<u>F</u>   1. A gargantuan meal would consist of one egg.

<u>F</u>   2. A quixotic person is realistic.

<u>F</u>   3. Pandemonium has a calming effect on our psyches.

<u>F</u>   4. Citizens' rights are respected if there is martial law.

<u>F</u>   5. Spartan living conditions are comfortable.

<u>F</u>   6. An odyssey is a short trip.

<u>F</u>   7. A maverick obeys all the rules.

<u>F</u>   8. If we boycott a store, we buy things there.

<u>T</u>   9. The cause of a psychosomatic headache is in our minds.

<u>F</u>   10. A panorama is an in-depth study.

Chapter Exercises

■ *Practicing Strategies: New Words from Word Elements*

See how your knowledge of roots and prefixes can help you understand new words. Complete each sentence with the word that seems to fit best. Use each choice only once.

a. anonymous   e. genotype   i. psychopath
b. anthropoids   f. nomenclature   j. patronym
c. genealogy   g. pan-Asian   k. rematch
d. generation   h. psychobiography   l. vivisection

1. The root *path* can mean "sick," so a person with a sick mind is a(n)

   i, psychopath_____.

2. Scholars often use scientific **f, nomenclature**_____ when referring
   to plants and animals.

3. The word **g, pan-Asian**_____ refers to all of Asia.

4. Apes that resemble human beings are called **b, anthropoids**_____.

5. A(n) **j, patronym**_____ is a name that comes to you through
   your father, or paternal relative.

6. After Tom lost the first chess championship, he wanted to play a(n)

   k, rematch_____.

7. A(n) **h, psychobiography**_____ is a book about a person's life that
   explores his or her mind.

8. *A* means "without," so a(n) **a, anonymous**_____ song is one for
   which we don't know the name of the composer.

9. When scientists cut into, or section, live animals, they are performing

   l, vivisection_____.

10. Since *-logy* means "study of," **c, genealogy**_____ is the study of
    your heredity, or your family history.

■ *Practicing Strategies: Combining Context Clues and Word Elements*

Combining the strategies of context clues and word elements is a good
way to figure out the meaning of unknown words. In the following sentences, each italicized word contains a word element that you have studied in this chapter. Using the meaning of the word element and the
context of the sentence, make an intelligent guess about the meaning of
the italicized word. Your instructor may ask you to check the meaning in
your dictionary after you have finished the exercise.

1. The camera operator *panned* the room to make sure everyone present was in the video.

   Panned means **went all around; covered all** .

2. James Butler Hickok was known by the *cognomen* "Wild Bill Hickok."

   Cognomen means **a name by which a person is known; a nickname** .

3. It is a *misnomer* to call only citizens of the United States "Americans," for America includes North, Central, and South America.

   Misnomer means **wrong term; mistaken name** .

4. It is impossible to find a *panacea* for all the problems of humanity.

   Panacea means **cure; complete cure** .

5. A person suffering from psychosis has a very sick mind.

   Psychosis means **serious mental illness; mental sickness** .

■ Companion Words

Complete each sentence with the word that fits best. Choose your answers from the words below. You may use each word more than once.

Choices: of, for, to, under

1. The unemployed patient paid the nominal sum **of** ten dollars for the test.

2. After Indonesia was placed **under** martial law, President Suharto resigned.

3. Standing on the cliffs, we saw a beautiful panorama **of** the scene far below us.

4. Blood pressure medication is vital **to (or for)** my father's health.

5. Albert Einstein became renowned **for** his work in physics.

6. The boycott **of** handguns greatly reduced sales.

7. Elleston Trevor wrote spy thrillers **under**_____ the pseudonym of Adam Hall.

8. The genesis **of**_____ the steam engine dates to the ancient Greeks.

■ *Writing with Your Words*

This exercise will give you practice in writing effective sentences that use the vocabulary words. Each sentence is started for you. Complete it with an interesting phrase that also indicates the meaning of the italicized word.

1. Your plan to redesign the city is not *viable* because _____

_____.

2. A *gargantuan* workload would _____

_____.

3. *Genocide* is _____

_____.

4. My *vivacious* friend _____

_____.

5. Her *psychosomatic* problems disappeared when _____

_____.

6. If I became a *philanthropist,* _____

_____.

7. We *boycotted* the company because _____

_____.

8. Our family suffered from *congenital* _____

_____.

9. My dream *odyssey* would consist of _____

_____ .

10. *Pandemonium* broke out when _____

_____ .

■ *Making Connections*

These questions will help you relate the words you have learned in this chapter to your own life. Answer each question by writing a paragraph or more on a separate sheet of paper.

1. Describe a person you know of who has a congenital problem.

2. Describe a time that you or someone you know has lived in spartan conditions.

3. If you could choose a pseudonym, what would it be? Why?

Passage

The Greek Myth of Winter

In modern times, science has explained the causes of storms, floods, earthquakes, and disease, but these mysterious events puzzled and awed ancient people. Perhaps to gain a sense of control, they created tales about the world around them.

Since humans tend to be **chauvinistic,** it was natural for ancient people to assume that the forces driving nature were just like themselves. They told stories of gods who ate, loved, and hated just as we do, but on a larger scale. **(1)** Because these gods had **gargantuan** powers, their smallest wish could mean disaster or good fortune for the entire world. A **misanthropic** god might send deadly storms; **(2)** a **philanthropic** one might share the secrets of fire and food.

(3) One ancient Greek tale of humanlike gods deals with the **genesis** of winter. According to the ancient Greeks, the world was once a warm, green paradise where the goddess Demeter provided summer throughout the year. But one day, **(4)** Persephone, Demeter's beautiful and **vivacious** daughter, wandered away from her friends to explore a field of flowers. Unfortunately, Hades, the god of the underworld, was visiting the Earth and enjoying a **panoramic** view of the very same place. With one look at Persephone, Hades instantly fell in love. Unable to control himself, he carried her off to the underworld and made her his bride.

Pandemonium broke out when word of Hades' crime reached the other gods. Demeter frantically tried to get her daughter back, begging Zeus, king of the gods, to order her return. **(5)** But although Zeus was **renowned** for his power, **(6)** Hades, a **maverick** among the gods, refused to return Persephone.

In her desperation, Demeter forgot to provide the world with the **(7)** warmth and sunshine **vital** to growing crops, and the earth plunged into winter. Plants began to die one by one, and when no crops were left, humans faced starvation. Demeter's grief was causing the death of the human race. Zeus appealed to Hades, who finally agreed to let Persephone return home, as long as she had not eaten anything.

What had Persephone been doing while Demeter was trying to release her? Sitting unhappily in the underworld, **(8)** she had led a **spartan** existence, refusing all the luxuries that Hades offered. She had eaten no food—except for seven pomegranate seeds. Alas! **(9)** Persephone had eaten only a **nominal** amount, but she had eaten. Hades did not have to let her go.

(10) Zeus and Demeter quickly thought of a **viable** solution. For nine months of the year, Persephone would live with her mother, and for three months she would live with Hades. Just as Persephone's life was divided, Demeter decreed that for nine months the earth would have warm weather, and for three months it would have winter.

And that is how, according to the ancient Greeks, winter began.

■ *Exercise*

Each numbered sentence below corresponds to a sentence in the Passage. Fill in the letter of the choice that makes the sentence mean the same thing as its corresponding sentence in the Passage.

1. These gods had ___**b**___ powers.
   a. important   b. huge   c. mysterious   d. mind

2. A ___**a**___ god might share the secrets of fire and food.
   a. charitable   b. lonely   c. lively   d. confused

3. One ancient Greek tale deals with the ___**d**___ of winter.
   a. hunger   b. coldness   c. problems   d. beginning

4. Persephone was Demeter's beautiful and ___**a**___ daughter.
   a. lively   b. quiet   c. rebellious   d. shy

5. Zeus was ___**c**___ for his power.
   a. feared   b. envied   c. famous   d. rewarded

6. Among the gods, Hades was a(n) ___**d**___ who resisted all control.
   a. romantic individual   b. strong individual   c. clever individual
   d. independent individual

7. Warmth and sunshine were ___**a**___ to crops.
   a. necessary   b. helpful   c. important   d. useless

8. Persephone had led a(n) ___**d**___ existence.
   a. lonely   b. unhappy   c. quiet   d. uncomfortable

9. Persephone had eaten a ___**a**___ amount.
   a. small   b. large   c. sufficient   d. healthy

10. Zeus and Demeter thought of a ___**d**___ solution.
    a. silly   b. brilliant   c. tricky   d. workable

■ *Discussion Questions*

1. Why did the Greeks think of their gods as being like humans, but on a larger scale?

2. Was Zeus's power limited? Explain your answer.

3. Describe a human situation that would bring forth the same types of emotions that Demeter felt.

◀ ENGLISH IDIOMS

Body Words

Since this chapter concerns people, the idioms presented here are all related to the human body. Many such idioms use the concept of cold. For example, to *give* (someone) *the cold shoulder* means to ignore them. When people get *cold feet,* they become nervous, and just before they plan to do something, they may refuse to do it, or *back out.* When a man becomes nervous, something *freezes his blood, makes his blood run cold,* or *makes his hair stand on end.* When people are made to wait, they *cool their heels.*

People who put forth an opinion that is completely unsupported by evidence *don't have a leg to stand on.* If you listen to another person, you *lend an ear.* If, on the other hand, you do not listen carefully, information goes *in one ear and out the other.*

To *raise eyebrows* is to shock people. When a person is embarrassed or shamed by a failure, that person *loses face.*

Long ago in China, the emperor was considered a god. To mention his body or health in any way was forbidden, since it implied that he was human. People who made this mistake had their feet pulled upward and forced into their mouths. They were forced to remain in this position for several hours. Today, to *put your foot in your mouth* means to say something that should not be said.

CHAPTER

7

Word Elements: Movement

Modern Americans are always on the move. We change our homes every few years. We hop on a jet and within hours we are on the other side of the world. This chapter presents words to describe our comings and goings. Each of the six roots and two prefixes describes an action. These word elements help to form many widely used English vocabulary words.

Chapter Strategy: Word Elements: Movement

Chapter Words:

Part 1

duc, duct	abduction	*stans, stat*	stature
	conducive		status quo
	deduction		staunch
ject	dejected	*tain, ten*	abstain
	eject		tenable
	jettison		tenacious

Part 2

tract	distraught	*circum-*	circumscribe
	extract		circumspect
	retract		circumvent
vers, vert	adversary	*trans-*	transcend
	inadvertently		transformation
	perverse		transitory

Quiz Yourself

To check your knowledge of some chapter words before you begin to study, identify these statements as true or false. Answers are on page 411.

To **jettison** is to throw out.	True	False
A **staunch** supporter would probably betray you.	True	False
Things change quickly in the **status quo.**	True	False
A **perverse** person is cooperative.	True	False

You will learn the answers as you study this chapter.

Did You Know?

How Did Inventions Get Their Names?

What would life be like if we could not switch on a light bulb, refrigerate our leftovers, or turn a faucet handle for water? If we went back in time to 1700, we would have to live without electricity, refrigeration, and running water.

Three hundred years ago, people traveled on foot or used horses, on unpaved roads with deep ruts. A twenty-mile trip took all day; today the same trip takes less than half an hour. Because there were no stoves or refrigerators, people cooked over open fires. Meat was either eaten immediately, or preserved as sausage.

In today's world, automobiles, trains, and airplanes provide rapid transportation. We use freezers and refrigerators to preserve our food and temperature-regulated stoves to cook it with precision. Many diseases have been controlled, and the average life expectancy has almost doubled.

The past one hundred years have been especially productive times for inventors. Such widely used devices as the computer, television (as well as the TV remote), vacuum cleaner, automatic washer, cell phone, zipper, paper clip, Post-it® note, digital camera, and Palm Pilot™ were all invented after 1900.

Each invention brought a new word into English. Often, scientists and inventors took names from ancient Greek and Latin word elements. This tradition started in 1611 when a Greek poet suggested a name for

Galileo's new invention, using two Greek word elements, *tele-* (far) and *scope* (look). The invention is called the *telescope*.

Modern inventors continue to create names from ancient Greek and Latin word elements. This makes a knowledge of classical word elements more useful than ever.

The inventions and discoveries listed below have made your life easier. The word for each one contains at least one classical prefix, root, or suffix. You will be studying some of the word elements in this book.

Invention	Classical Word Elements	Approximate Date of Invention
microscope	*micro-* (small) + *-scope* (look)	1665
antiseptic	*anti-* (against) + *sepsis* (rotten)	1745
anesthetic	*an-* (without) + *aisthēsis* (feeling)	1850
bicycle	*bi-* (two) + *kuklos* (wheel)	1862
phonograph	*phono-* (sound) + *-graph* (written)	1875
telephone	*tele-* (far) + *-phone* (sound)	1880
automobile	*auto-* (self) + *movēre* (to move)	1885
refrigerator	*re-* (again) + *frigus* (cold)	1890
television	*tele-* (far) + *visus* (sight)	1925
computer	*com-* (together) + *-putāre* (to reckon)	1940
microwave	*micro-* (small) + *wafian* (wave)	1963

Learning Strategy

Word Elements: Movement

The word elements in this chapter describe movements, such as leading *(duct)*, pulling *(tract)*, or turning *(vert)*. Each element forms at least fifty English words, so learning them will help you dramatically expand your vocabulary.

Element	Meaning	Origin	Function	Chapter Words
Part 1				
duc, duct	lead	Latin	root	abduction, conducive, deduction
ject	throw	Latin	root	dejected, eject, jettison
stans, stat	standing; placed	Latin; Greek	root	stature, status quo, staunch
tain, ten	hold	Latin	root	abstain, tenable, tenacious

Part 2

tract	pull	Latin	root	distraught, extract, retract
vers, vert	turn	Latin	root	adversary, inadvertently, perverse
circum-	around	Latin	prefix	circumscribe, circumspect, circumvent
trans-	across	Latin	prefix	transcend, transformation, transitory

Many of these word elements started out describing physical movement but over the years acquired related, nonphysical meanings. The word element *ject* (throw) illustrates how word elements and meanings relate. If you think about the meanings of the word elements below, you will be able to picture each word's meaning in your mind.

The word elements *de-* (down) and *ject* (throw) make *deject,* or "throw down." The word *dejected* actually means depressed, or how we feel when our mood is "thrown down."

The word elements *e-*(out of) and *ject* (throw) make *eject,* or "throw out of." When a candy bar is *ejected* from a vending machine, it is "thrown out."

Circumstance is another word in which the elements give us a mental picture. It combines the prefix *circum-* and the root *stans. Circumstances* are things that are "standing" *(stans)* "around" *(circum-)* an event; in other words, they surround it. Circumstances that might "stand around" and keep you from studying are noise in the library or a friend who wants to talk.

Word Roots

Part 1

The four word roots of movement presented in Part 1 are discussed below.

duc, duct (lead)
> This root appears in many different words. The *ducts* in a building **lead** air and water to different rooms. A *conductor* **leads** an orchestra so that all the players stay together. (*Con-* means "together.") European noblemen are called *dukes* because long ago their ancestors **led** troops into battle.

ject (throw)
> This root appears as *jet,* a stream of water or air **thrown** into space. *Ject* can also represent the idea of **throwing** rather than the physical action

itself. Although the word elements of *reject* actually mean "to **throw back**," the word itself has the related but nonphysical meaning of "not to accept."

stans, stat (standing; placed)

This root indicates a lack of movement, as in *statue*. *Stans* and *stat* can also refer to **standing** in an abstract, nonphysical way. For example, one's *status* is one's **standing** or placement in society. *Circumstance,* mentioned above, also contains this root.

tain, ten (hold)

This root can mean "hold" in a physical sense; a pan might *contain,* or **hold,** baked beans. This root can also mean **hold** in a nonphysical sense. For example, a *tenet* is a belief that somebody **holds.**

Words to Learn

Part 1

duc, duct

1. **abduction** (noun)   ăb-dŭk′shən

    From Latin: *ab-* (away) + *duct* (lead)

    kidnapping

    The **abduction** of children is a terrible crime.

    ▶ *Related Word*
       abduct (verb)   The extremist group *abducted* travelers and held them for ransom.

2. **conducive** (adjective)   kən-doo′sĭv

    From Latin: *con-* (together) + *duc* (lead)

    contributing to; leading to

    Candlelight and soft music are **conducive** to romance.

Teachers should create class environments that are **conducive** to learning.

▶ *Common Phrase*
conducive to

3. **deduction** (noun)   dĭ-dŭk′shən

From Latin: *de-* (away) + *duct* (lead)

something subtracted from a total

Josh makes $300 per week after **deductions** for taxes and insurance.

A **deduction** was made on the bill because the customer had been overcharged.

a conclusion drawn from evidence

From seeing toys on the floor, we made the **deduction** that a child lived in the house.

▶ *Related Words*
deduct (verb)   Our coach decided to *deduct* the cost of our uniforms from the prize money the team won.

deductible (adjective)   Some medical expenses are tax-*deductible*.

deduce   (verb)   (dĭ-dōōs′)   Detectives study a crime scene in order to *deduce* what took place.

deductive (adjective) Darwin used *deductive* reasoning to reach his theory of evolution.

NOTE: When *deduction* means "subtraction," it is related to *deduct* and *deductible*; when *deduction* means "conclusion," it is related to *deduce* and *deductive*.

Sherlock Holmes, a fictional English detective created by Sir Arthur Conan Doyle, is a master of *deductive* reasoning. Holmes amazes his companions by drawing brilliant conclusions from the smallest bits of evidence. The famous, but fictional, Holmes was based on a real-life Scottish doctor, Joe Bell, who was an expert in diagnosing disease from a minimum of evidence.

Sherlock Holmes is a master of *deductive* reasoning.

ject

4. **dejected** (adjective)   dĭ-jĕk'tĭd

   From Latin: *de-* (down) + *ject* (throw)

   depressed; downcast

   > Albert remained **dejected** long after the breakup of his romance.

   ▶ *Related Word*
   dejection (noun)   A mood of *dejection* hung over the defeated candidate's headquarters.

5. **eject** (verb)   ĭ-jĕkt′

From Latin: *ex-* (out) + *ject* (throw)

to force to leave; to expel

> Please **eject** the disk from the DVD player.
>
> The manager **ejected** the noisy teenagers from the restaurant.

▶ *Related Word*
> **ejection** (noun)   Seconds before the plane crashed, an automatic *ejection* device saved the pilot.

6. **jettison** (verb)   jĕt′-ĭ-sĕn

From Latin: *ject* (throw)

To throw out forcefully; to throw overboard

> During takeoff, space shuttles **jettison** empty fuel tanks into the ocean.
>
> The television network **jettisoned** the unpopular talk show.

NOTE: Jettison can also apply to nonphysical things, as in to "jettison an unworkable plan."

stans, stat

7. **stature**   stăch′ər

level of achievement and honor

> Picasso was an artist of great **stature.**

physical height

> A condition called achondroplasia prevents people from developing an average **stature.**

Two U.S. presidents demonstrated great *stature* in both senses of the word. George Washington stood six feet two inches tall, an unusual height in the 1700s. More importantly, as the first U.S. president, he unified the former colonies. He also established presidential rather than royal customs; for example, we don't bow to presidents. Abraham Lincoln stood six feet four inches tall and led the country through its worst crisis, the Civil War. He urged forgiveness after the war ended. Historians rate both Lincoln and Washington as great presidents—and presidents of great size.

---

8. **status quo** (noun)   stā′təs kwō′

From Latin: *stat* (standing, placed) + *quo* (in which), making "the condition in which"

the existing conditions; present state of things

> The increasing number of women ministers and rabbis shows a change in the **status quo.**

> Conservatives often defend the **status quo,** whereas liberals want to change it.

The French Revolution of 1789 changed the *status quo* in fundamental ways by bankrupting many of the rich, deposing a king, and even temporarily changing the names of days of the week and holidays. The Russian Revolution of 1917 changed the economic and social system of the country to Communism. In the 1980s, however, Russia's *status quo* was upset once again by a move toward capitalism. Perhaps the upcoming unification of Europe will, once again, change the *status quo*. In 1999, the creation of the euro, Europe's unified currency, became the first move toward this change.

9. **staunch** (adjective)   stônch

From Latin: *stans* (standing), through the French word *étanche* (watertight, firm) (Something *staunch* stands firm and strong.)

faithful; firmly supporting

> My **staunch** friend stood by me through my difficult divorce.

> The mayor was a **staunch** supporter of education.

healthy; strong

> My **staunch** constitution can withstand cold easily.

> A **staunch** defense saved the town from attack.

▶ *Related Word*
staunchness (noun)   Rosa Parks's *staunchness* in refusing to move to the back of a bus became important to the American civil rights movement.

tain, ten

10. **abstain** (verb)   ăb-stān′

From Latin: *abs-* (away) + *tain* (hold) ("To hold away from" is not to do something.)

not to do something by choice

> Nicotine patches help people to **abstain** from smoking.

After monks take a vow of silence, they **abstain** from speaking.

not to vote

Seven people voted yes, seven voted no, and seven **abstained.**

▶ *Common Phrase*
   abstain from

▶ *Related Words*
   abstinence (noun) (ăb′stə-nəns)   The month-long Muslim holiday of Ramadan requires *abstinence* from eating during daylight hours. (*Abstinence* usually refers to self-denial.)

   abstention (noun) (ăb-stən′shən)   China's *abstention* allowed the resolution to pass in the United Nations. (*Abstention* usually refers to not voting.)

11. **tenable** (adjective)   tən′ə-bəl

From Latin: *ten* (hold)

capable of being defended; logical

> The theory that a comet may have caused the extinction of dinosaurs is now considered **tenable.**

> The commander decided that the high hill was a **tenable** position for his troops to defend.

▶ *Related Word*
   untenable (adjective)   The theory that the world is flat is now considered *untenable*. (*Untenable* is the opposite of *tenable*.)

When the great Polish scientist Copernicus (1473–1543) proposed that the Earth revolved around the sun, many thought that his theory was *untenable*. It seemed ridiculous that the Earth, with its heavy mass, could move around the sun, which appeared so small in the sky. Most people believed the Earth to be the center of the universe. However, as more evidence accumulated, it became clear that Copernicus's theory had great *tenability*. Today, it is accepted as scientific fact.

---

12. **tenacious** (adjective)   tə-nā′shəs

From Latin: *ten* (hold)

firmly holding; gripping; retaining

> The ship's captain kept a **tenacious** grasp on the wheel throughout the storm.

> **Tenacious** protesters continued their march despite the cold wind and rain.

▶ *Related Word*

tenacity (noun)   Winston Churchill's *tenacity* in believing that Nazi Germany was a threat helped prepare England for World War II.

Sports history will applaud the *tenacity* of tennis star Venus Williams's 2003 Wimbledon performance. Despite severe pain from a pulled muscle, she was determined to play. She later said, "The people, the fans, they deserved a final. That's why I went out there." Venus won the opening set, but by the third set, she had to seek medical help. *Tenaciously,* she reentered the court for the last set, but the pain became too great. She lost—but the crowd applauded her *tenacity*. When it was over, Venus snapped a picture of the winner, her sister Serena.

Exercises

Part 1

■ *Definitions*

Match each word in the left-hand column with a definition from the right-hand column. Use each choice only once.

1. eject ___**h**___

2. status quo ___**i**___

3. staunch ___**j**___

4. tenable ___**f**___

5. conducive ___**d**___

6. dejected ___**e**___

7. deduction ___**g**___

8. tenacious ___**c**___

9. stature ___**l**___

10. abduction ___**b**___

a. to force to leave

b. kidnapping

c. gripping

d. contributing to

e. depressed

f. logical

g. something subtracted

h. to throw out

i. the present state of things

j. faithful; firmly supporting

k. not to do

l. level of achievement and honor

■ *Meanings*

Match each word root to its meaning. Use each choice only once.

1. duc, duct ___**b**___

2. stans, stat ___**d**___

3. ject ___**c**___

4. tain, ten ___**a**___

a. hold

b. lead

c. throw

d. standing; placed

■ *Words in Context*

Complete each sentence with the word that fits best. Use each choice only once.

a. abduction   e. ejection   i. staunch
b. conducive   f. jettison   j. abstain
c. deduction   g. stature   k. tenable
d. dejected   h. status quo   l. tenacious

1. After twenty years of __l, tenacious__ work, the researcher discovered a cure for the disease.

2. The Citizen of the Year award reflected his __g, stature__ in his community.

3. The __i, staunch__ Democrat always votes for every candidate the party nominates.

4. To avoid a fire, the crew of the airplane had to __f, jettison__ its fuel into the sea.

5. The congresswoman decided to __j, abstain__ because she couldn't decide whether to vote yes or no.

6. To prevent __a, abduction__ or attack, the prime minister had bodyguards who protected him at all times.

7. A dark, quiet room is __b, conducive__ to sleep.

8. There would be quite a change in the __h, status quo__ if all money were divided equally among people.

9. Putting coins into a vending machine results in the __e, ejection__ of a candy bar.

10. The man claimed a(n) __c, deduction__ for business expenses on his income taxes.

■ *Related Words*

Complete each sentence by using a word from the group of related words above it. You may need to capitalize a word when you write it in a sentence. Use each choice only once.

1. tenacious, tenacity

> Inventor Jerome Lemelson, who holds the most patents in the United States after Thomas Edison, displayed tremendous
>
> **tenacity** _____ in court battles he fought against companies who stole his ideas without getting permission. The
>
> **tenacious** _____ Lemelson was forced to fight for years to protect the rights to inventions such as the technology for automatic warehouses, video camcorders, bar code scanners, and the Hot Wheels toy. When, after a long struggle, he finally became affluent, he funded a yearly $500,000 award to help inventors who had been exploited.

2. tenable, untenable

> During the Middle Ages, people believed that attitudes and general health were controlled by four "humors" that made people choleric (angry), melancholic (sad), sanguine (happy), and phlegmatic (easygoing). Scientific evidence has shown that this theory is
>
> **untenable** _____. However, the theory that mental states
>
> can affect physical health is considered **tenable** _____ by today's physicians.

3. dejection, dejected

> Charles Gray has been developing a supercar that gets eighty miles per gallon. The project, started in the 1980s, has had a history of
>
> bureaucratic tangles. **Dejected** _____ because of its lack of success, Gray built his own car, which uses nitrogen for fuel. Although problems remain, Gray refuses to give in to
>
> **dejection** _____ and perhaps someday we will have this truly efficient vehicle.

4. abstain, abstinence

> Because the AIDS virus can spread through shared needles, the Chicago Recovery Alliance gives addicts free needles in exchange for used ones. Officials would rather that

people **abstain**_____ from heroin completely. But if

abstinence_____ is an impossible goal to meet, the Alliance at least wants to stop the spread of AIDS.

5. deductive, deduce, deduction

Identifying a person by DNA, the genetic material in cells, is becoming more common. DNA testing enables law officials to

deduce_____ who is the father of a child or who has committed a crime. By late 2003, for instance, this type of testing had freed more than 130 wrongly convicted prisoners in Florida alone. DNA analysis allowed detectives to make the

deduction_____ that these people were innocent. This

deductive_____ method will not take the place of normal police work, but will certainly add to its accuracy.

■ *Reading the Headlines*

This exercise presents four headlines that might appear in newspapers. Read each headline and then answer the questions that follow. (Remember that small words, such as *is, are, a,* and *the,* are often left out of newspaper headlines.)

LIBERALS DEJECTED BY CONTINUED STATUS QUO

1. Are the liberals happy? **no**_____

2. Are things changing? **no**_____

ACTOR JETTISONED FROM SHOW FINDS MOTHERHOOD MORE CONDUCIVE TO HAPPINESS

3. Was the star fired? **yes**_____

4. Is motherhood making her happier? **yes**_____

DETECTIVE OF GREAT STATURE SOLVES ABDUCTION THROUGH TENACIOUS INVESTIGATION

5. Is the detective well thought of? **yes**_____

6. Was the crime a robbery? **no**

7. Did the detective investigate the crime only briefly? **no**

THEORY THAT STAUNCH FRIENDS CAN HELP US ABSTAIN FROM SMOKING IS NOW THOUGHT TO BE TENABLE

8. Are these friends faithful? **yes**

9. Are we more likely to smoke if we have staunch friends? **no**

10. Is the theory capable of being defended? **yes**

Prefixes of Movement

Part 2

Part 2 continues with more word elements that show movement: first, two additional roots, *tract* (pull) and *vert* (turn); and then two prefixes, *circum-* (around) and *trans-* (across).

tract (pull)
> *Tractor,* a machine that **pulls** plows through the earth, is an example of a common word formed from this root. Like many movement roots, *tract* is used in words that no longer carry the physical meaning of **pull**. For example, when we *distract* someone's attention, we "**pull** it away" in a mental rather than a physical sense.

vers, vert (turn)
> *Vert* can mean **turn** in a direct sense. When we *invert* a cup, we **turn** it upside down. The root can also hint at a nonphysical meaning of **turn**. When we *advertise,* we "**turn** attention toward" a product.

circum- (around)
> *Circum-* is a prefix meaning **around**. The distance **around** a circle is called its *circumference*. Like other movement word elements, *circum-* can indicate the idea, rather than the action, of **around**. For example, a library book that *circulates* "goes **around**" and is used by many different people.

> *Circus* is the Latin word for "circle." A circus was originally a circular area surrounded by seats used for viewing shows. Roman emperors were said to stay in power by giving the people "bread and circuses"— that is, food and entertainment. In modern English, "three-ring circus"

is a commonly used expression. This originally was a very large circus, but it has come to mean any event that causes a great deal of excitement.

---

trans- (across)

Transcontinental jets go **across** a continent—as from New York to Los Angeles. The prefix *trans-* can also suggest the idea of **across** rather than physical movement. When we *translate* something, it goes **across** languages, or from one language to another.

Words to Learn

Part 2

tract

13. **distraught** (adjective)   dĭs-trôt′

    From Latin: *dis-* (apart) + *tract* (pull) (*Tract* changed to *traught* in Middle English.)

    crazy with worry or distress

    > The **distraught** mother searched frantically for her missing child.
    >
    > Our fear increased when we saw that the **distraught** man had a gun.
    >
    > Jasmine was **distraught** over the lost diamond bracelet.

    NOTE: Distracted, which comes from the same word elements as *distraught,* has a less extreme meaning. It can be used simply for "confused" or "not attentive."

14. **extract** (verb)   ĭk-străkt′; (verb)   ĕk′străkt (noun)

    From Latin: *ex-* (out) + *tract* (pull)

    to pull out; to draw out (verb)

    > The dentist **extracted** Eugenio's tooth.
    >
    > Computer experts can sometimes **extract** lost data from a ruined hard drive.

    something that is drawn out (noun)

    > An **extract** of the aloe plant is useful for treating burns and cuts.

► *Related Word*

> **extraction** (noun)   The *extraction* of salt from ocean water may be done by evaporation.
>
> I am of Pakistani *extraction*. (Here, *extraction* means "ancestry.")

Vanilla *extract*, a popular flavoring for baked goods, is drawn from the pods of orchids. The ancient Aztecs of Mexico used it to flavor their *xocolatl* (chocolate) drinks. The Spanish explorer Hernando Cortés drank it at the court of the Aztec ruler Montezuma and brought it to Europe, where it soon became popular. Vanilla *extract* is widely used as an ingredient in perfume. In an effort to make gasoline smell better, the French even added the odor of vanilla *extract* to it.

---

15. **retract** (verb)   rĭ-trăkt′

From Latin: *re-* (back) + *tract* (pull)

to withdraw a promise or statement; to pull something back

> The suspect **retracted** his confession.
>
> The frightened turtle **retracted** into its shell.

► *Related Word*

> **retraction** (noun)   The company issued a *retraction* of its error-filled profits statement.

vers, vert

16. **adversary** (noun)   ăd′vər-sĕr′ē; plural: adversaries

From Latin: *ad-* (toward) + *vert* (turn) (When we "turn toward" an enemy or adversary, we prepare to fight.)

opponent; foe

> After a hard-fought racquetball match, the two **adversaries** shook hands.
>
> In the Civil War, former slaves proved to be brave **adversaries** of the Confederate Army.

► *Related Word*

> **adversarial** (adjective)   Brothers and sisters close in age often have *adversarial* relationships as children.

NOTE: Adversary connotes a stubborn and determined foe.

Can you match these adversarial pairs?

1. Napoleon	a. Foxy Brown
2. Octavian	b. Luke Skywalker
3. Britney Spears	c. The Duke of Wellington
4. Darth Vader	d. Jake, Cassie, Rachel, Tobias, Marco, and Homer
5. Tweety Bird	e. Bugs Bunny
6. Lil' Kim	f. Christina Aguilera
7. Elmer Fudd	g. Sylvester
8. Yeerks	h. Mark Antony

Answers are on page 411.

---

17. **inadvertently** (adverb)   in′əd-vûr′tnt-lē

From Latin: *in-* (not) + *ad-* (toward) + *vert* (turn) (When you are "not turned toward" something, events often happen inadvertently, or accidentally.)

unintentionally; by accident

> Tom **inadvertently** locked his keys in the car.

> Greg **inadvertently** sent the e-mail to everyone in his address book.

▶ *Related Word*
   inadvertent (adjective)   We forgave Rodney's *inadvertent* insult.

18. **perverse** (adjective)   pər-vûrs′

From Latin: *per-* (completely) + *vert* (turn) (A perverse person is "completely turned away" from what is natural.)

contrary; determined not to do what is expected or right

> The **perverse** child refused to wear a coat in the freezing weather.

> Marisol takes **perverse** pleasure in her friends' problems.

▶ *Related Word*
   perversity (noun)   Out of sheer *perversity*, my mother-in-law ordered us to cook corned beef and then refused to eat it.

circum-

19. **circumscribe** (verb)   sûr′kəm-skrīb′

From Latin: *circum-* (around) + *scrib* (to write)

to limit; to restrict; to enclose

> Consumer complaints led to new laws that **circumscribe** tele-marketing calls.
>
> Paris was originally **circumscribed** by a protecting wall.

20. **circumspect** (adjective)   sûr′kəm-spĕkt′

From Latin: *circum-* (around) + *spec* (to look) (To be circumspect is "to look around" or be careful.)

cautious; careful; considering results of actions

> Since scandal has ruined many careers, public figures should be **circumspect** in their personal lives.
>
> Because e-mail can be forwarded to others, be **circumspect** about the messages you send.

▶ *Related Word*

circumspection (noun)   The senator's *circumspection* kept him from accepting any gifts.

21. **circumvent** (verb)   sûr′kəm-vĕnt′

From Latin: *circum-* (around) + venīre (to come)

to avoid; to outwit

> Ebony **circumvented** the traffic jam by taking a side street.
>
> All too often, corporations are able to **circumvent** environmental laws.

▶ *Related Word*

circumvention (noun)   *Circumvention* of child support payments continues to be a social and legal problem.

trans-

22. **transcend** (verb)   trăn-sĕnd′

From Latin: *trans-* (across) + *scandere* (to climb) (When we transcend something, we "climb across" limits and overcome them.)

to overcome; to go above limits

Marian Anderson was able to **transcend** racial prejudice to become the first African-American soloist at New York's Metropolitan Opera.

Music **transcends** cultural barriers.

Many mysteries of the universe **transcend** our understanding.

Can a person *transcend* a physical disability to become a professional athlete? Jim Abbott, born without a right hand, went on to become a major league baseball pitcher who played for the California Angels, Chicago White Sox, and Milwaukee Brewers. He used his left hand both to catch and to throw the ball. Abbott's career showed the power of the human will to *transcend* obstacles.

---

23. **transformation** (noun)   trăns′fər-mā′shən

From Latin: *trans-* (across) + *forma* (shape), making *transformāre* (to change shape)

a complete change

Makeovers sometimes produce amazing **transformations.**

We have witnessed a **transformation** of data storage from paper to computer files.

▶ *Related Words*
    transform   (verb)   (trăns-fôrm′)   Trang Le *transformed* the bankrupt company into a profit-making venture.

    transformative (adjective)   An inspiring college course can be a *transformative* experience.

24. **transitory** (adjective)   trăn′sĭ-tôr′ē

From Latin: *trans-* (across) + *īre* (to go), making *transīre* ("to go across" or to pass through quickly)

short-lived; existing briefly; passing

People hope their sorrows will be **transitory.**

The five-year-old's wish for a dog was **transitory;** the next week she wanted a pony.

Exercises

Part 2

■ *Definitions*

Match each word in the left-hand column with a definition from the right-hand column. Use each choice only once.

1. distraught __h__

2. circumvent __e__

3. inadvertently __i__

4. transformation __f__

5. transcend __b__

6. perverse __l__

7. transitory __j__

8. circumspect __g__

9. circumscribe __k__

10. adversary __d__

a. something taken out

b. to overcome

c. to withdraw

d. opponent

e. to avoid

f. complete change

g. cautious

h. crazy with worry

i. accidentally

j. short-lived

k. to limit

l. determined not to do what is right or expected

■ *Meanings*

Match each word element to its meaning. Use each choice only once.

1. tract- __b__

2. vers, vert __a__

3. circum- __c__

4. trans- __d__

a. turn

b. pull

c. around

d. across

■ *Words in Context*

Complete each sentence with the word that fits best. Use each choice only once.

a. distraught   e. inadvertently   i. circumvent
b. extract   f. perverse   j. transcend
c. retract   g. circumscribe   k. transformation
d. adversary   h. circumspect   l. transitory

1. To __g, circumscribe__ the department head's power, the CEO took some responsibilities away from her.

2. After takeoff, the wheels of a jet __c, retract__ into the plane.

3. My __f, perverse__ uncle complained constantly about his illnesses, yet refused to call a doctor.

4. My mother knows how to __b, extract__ the last bit of juice from an orange.

5. I competed with my __d, adversary__ to win the championship.

6. The government agency was __h, circumspect__ in doing business with foreign companies, and checked them carefully.

7. Some students __i, circumvent__ the long lines at school by using the telephone to register for classes.

8. The child's sadness was __l, transitory__, and he soon was smiling again.

9. Marcy was able to __j, transcend__ her poor and troubled childhood by graduating from college and getting a good job.

10. The family was __a, distraught__ when they could not locate their child after the bombing.

■ *Using Related Words*

Complete each sentence by using a word from the group of related words above it. Use each choice only once.

INVENTIONS AND DISCOVERIES

1. inadvertent, inadvertently

    In 1928, while Sir Alexander Fleming was researching bacteria, he went on vacation. During his absence, a test-tube lid **inadvertently** slipped off, and his sample was killed by an unknown mold. Fleming returned and was just about to throw the sample out when he realized that the mold might be able to kill harmful bacteria. In this **inadvertent** manner, he discovered the important antibiotic penicillin.

2. transformed, transformative, transformation

    Invented in 1901, the paper clip has been hailed as one of the world's most useful items. Yet this elegant invention can be **transformed** into something even more useful. A **transformation** of the traditional paper clip, the new Super Clip, invented by the Froehlich family, is three inches long and holds more than one hundred papers. The Super Clip may have a **transformative** effect on our lives. It can be used to hold men's ties, to attach hair curlers, to seal bags, and to decorate Christmas trees.

3. extracted, extract, extraction

    Before the invention of the washing machine, people pounded clothes on rocks and used water in streams to wash away dirt. William Blackstone, from Bluffton, Indiana, built the first washing machine as a present for his wife. Soon he began selling them. Early washing machines swished clothes around in soapy water to **extract** dirt. Then, to remove the soap, the clothes were rinsed in clean water. Finally, a separate "wringer" was used for the **extraction** of excess water. Later, John Chamberlain invented a single machine that washed, rinsed, and **extracted** water, like the washing machines of today.

4. retraction, retract

The scientist Galileo earned fame for his theories of astronomy. Convinced that his theories were not consistent with the Bible, the church forced him to **retract** them. But even after his **retraction** the Pope condemned Galileo and forced him to live alone until he died.

■ *Reading the Headlines*

This exercise presents five headlines that might appear in newspapers. Read each headline and then answer the questions that follow. (Remember that small words, such as *is, are, a,* and *the,* are often left out of newspaper headlines.)

CIRCUMSPECT WOMAN UNDERGOES TRANSFORMATION INTO GOSSIP

1. Was the woman ever cautious? **yes**

2. Has she changed? **yes**

MAN'S ABILITY TO TRANSCEND ADDICTION PROVES TRANSITORY

3. Did the person ever get rid of the addiction? **yes**

4. Did the ability to get rid of the addiction last long? **no**

ADVERSARY CIRCUMSCRIBES MAYOR'S POWER

5. Is the adversary a friend of the mayor? **no**

6. Is the mayor's power becoming greater? **no**

PERVERSE MAN INADVERTENTLY ACTS PLEASANT

7. Is the man usually pleasant? **no**

8. Did he act pleasant on purpose? **no**

DISTRAUGHT WITNESS RETRACTS EVIDENCE HE SAYS WAS EXTRACTED BY FORCE

9. Was the witness calm? __no__

10. Is the witness withdrawing his evidence? __yes__

Chapter Exercises

■ *Practicing Strategies: New Words from Word Elements*

See how your knowledge of prefixes and roots can help you understand new words. Complete each sentence with the word that seems to fit best. Use each choice only once.

a. aqueducts	e. induct	i. tenor
b. attract	f. injection	j. traction
c. circuit	g. projectile	k. translucent
d. conduct	h. subvert	l. vertigo

1. Since *pro* means "forward," a(n) __g, projectile__ is something that is being thrown forward.

2. When we get a(n) __f, injection__, medicine is "thrown into" our bodies.

3. Materials that are __k, translucent__ allow light to pass across them.

4. *Aqua* means "water"; the ancient Romans built __a, aqueducts__ to carry water to their cities.

5. *Ad-* or *at-* can mean "toward," so to __b, attract__ is to pull someone toward you.

6. To __h, subvert__ means to "turn under," or twist in an evil way.

7. When we __e, induct__ people into a club, we "lead" them "in" as new members.

8. You suffer from __l, vertigo__ when you get dizzy and things around you seem to turn and spin.

9. When your leg is broken, **j, traction**_____, or a pulling motion, may help the bones mend properly.

10. A(n) **c, circuit**_____ refers to a circular, or closed, path that carries electricity.

■ *Practicing Strategies: Combining Context Clues and Word Elements*

Combining the strategies of context clues and word elements is a good way to figure out the meanings of unknown words. In the following sentences, each italicized word contains a word element that you have studied in this chapter. Using the meaning of the word element and the context of the sentence, make an intelligent guess about the meaning of the italicized word. Your instructor may ask you to check the meaning in your dictionary when you have finished the exercise.

1. In 1522, the ships of Magellan became the first to *circumnavigate* the world.

   Circumnavigate means **circle completely; travel completely around**_____.

2. Security forces *detained* the man in the airport, refusing to let him board the plane.

   Detained means **held back; held**_____.

3. The company offered many *inducements* to attract qualified computer specialists.

   Inducements means **attractions, offers that lead to something**_____.

4. The planets are in their **circumsolar** movement around the sun.

   Circumsolar means **circling around the sun**_____.

5. Because of the blockage, blood in the artery reached a state of *stasis*.

   Stasis means **standing still**_____.

■ *Practicing Strategies: Using the Dictionary*

Read the following definition and then answer the questions below it.

suit (soot) *n*. **1a.** A set of matching outer garments, esp. one consisting of a coat with trousers or a skirt.   **b.** A costume for a special activity; *a diving suit*. **2.** A group of things used together; a set or collection.   **3.** *Games* Any of the four sets of 13 playing cards (clubs, diamonds, hearts, and spades) in a standard deck.   **4.** Attendance required of a vassal at his feudal lord's court or manor.   **5.** *Law* A court proceeding to recover a right or claim.   **6.** The act or an instance of courting a woman; courtship.   **7.** *Slang* One who wears a business suit, esp. an executive. ❖ *v*. **suit•ed, suit•ing, suits** —*tr*. **1.** To meet the requirements of; fit.   **2.** To make appropriate or suitable; adapt.   **3.** To be appropriate for; befit.   **4.** To please; satisfy.   **5.** To provide with clothing; dress. —*intr*. **1.** To be suitable or acceptable.   **2.** To be in accord; agree or match. —*phrasal verb:* **suit up** To put on clothing designed for a special activity. [ME *sute* < AN < VLat. **sequita*, act of following, fem. of **sequitus*, p. part. of **sequere*, to follow < Lat. *sequī*. See SUITOR.]

1. In which language was the word *suit* used right before it was used in Modern English? **Middle English**

2. The *ui* in *suit* is pronounced like the vowel in which word in the dictionary key? **boot**

3. What is the phrasal verb for *suit*? **suit up**

4. What is the definition number and part of speech of the definition commonly used in law? **5, noun**

5. What is the definition number and part of speech of the definition that best fits the following sentence? "She rejected his suit because she didn't love him." **6, noun**

■ Companion Words

Complete each sentence with the word that fits best. Choose your answers from the words below. You may use each word more than once.

Choices: about, from, of, to, that, over, in

1. The Queen of England is circumspect **about, in** her personal life, but her children often are not.

2. The extraction of gold **from** the mine proved expensive.

3. Freedom is conducive **to** creativity.

4. The transformation **of**_____ the old house into a beautiful residence amazed Ben.

5. She was distraught **over, about**_____ her husband's illness.

6. Circumvention **of**_____ taxes is illegal.

7. The wild horse ejected the rider **from**_____ the saddle.

8. I must abstain **from**_____ drinking alcohol if I am driving.

■ *Writing with Your Words*

This exercise will give you practice in writing effective sentences that use the vocabulary words. Each sentence is started for you. Complete it with an interesting phrase that also indicates the meaning of the italicized word.

1. One theory that is no longer *tenable* is _____

_____.

2. It has clearly become time to *jettison* _____

_____.

3. The guy was *ejected* from the nightclub when _____

_____.

4. One pair of famous *adversaries* is _____

_____.

5. People often try to *circumvent* long lines for ticket sales by _____

_____.

6. The college student felt *dejected* because _____

_____.

7. I would like to *circumscribe* the power of _____

_____.

8. The most *perverse* thing someone could do is _____

_____.

9. A protest against the *status quo* would _____

_____.

10. You must try to *transcend* the _____

_____.

■ *Making Connections*

These questions will help you relate the words you have learned in this chapter to your own life. Answer each question by writing a paragraph or more on a separate sheet of paper.

1. What brings out, or has brought out, your tenacity? Explain your answer.

2. Describe a problem, a situation, or a person you were able to circumvent.

3. If you could change the status quo, what would you do?

Passage

What Body Language Tells Us

Your posture, where you place your arms, and how you walk may reveal more to others than the words you are speaking. In fact, social psychologists tell us that body language is one of the most effective forms of communication.

A first-grade teacher stands by the door, greeting the children with friendly words. But if her smile is **transitory** and her arms are crossed, **(1)** she is **inadvertently** communicating another message. Crossed arms can indicate negative feelings, and the children will probably see her as a threat rather than as a helper.

In a nearby high school, a student sits in math class, his body straight, his hands folded, **(2)** fixing a **tenacious** stare on the teacher. Is he paying attention? Probably not! His lack of movement indicates that his thoughts are far away (perhaps on his girlfriend). If the student were

Body language sends powerful messages.

interested in the lesson, he would move and react. **(3)** Only an inexperienced teacher would **deduce** that a student who remains perfectly still is thinking about math.

In contrast to the math student's rigid posture, tilting one's head indicates friendliness and interest. A student who tilts her head and sits on the edge of her chair is paying attention to a lecture. People often bend their heads or bodies forward slightly to show interest in members of the opposite sex. Enlarged pupils in one's eyes also indicate this interest.

Smiling is a body language that may not always mean what you think. Many smiles indicate happiness. But scientists observing animals have found that **(4)** another conclusion is sometimes more **tenable:** a smile indicates apology, or the wish to avoid an attack. A gorilla often smiles when showing stronger animals that it doesn't want to fight. Similarly, a person who has accidentally poked a stranger with an elbow will give a **transitory** smile that silently requests the injured person not to become angry.

Hands communicate much body language. An open-handed gesture is **conducive** to friendliness. Perhaps this is the origin of the handshake, in which people open their hands and then join them.

In contrast, arms folded on the chest indicate defensiveness. Baseball fans have seen this behavior many times when **(5)** an umpire makes a call that a team manager wants him to **retract.** As the manager approaches, the formerly neutral **(6)** umpire undergoes a **transformation** into an **adversary** simply by folding his arms. **Abstaining** from movement, he listens to the manager's arguments. Finally, the umpire shows his rejection just by turning his back. **(7)** The **dejected** manager walks back to the dugout, shrugging his shoulders.

Walking styles can also communicate messages. **(8)** We all have seen the controlled and measured walk of a person trying to appear dignified and **circumspect. (9)** People who are **distraught** often walk with their heads down and their hands clasped behind their backs. The person with energy and willpower moves rapidly, hands swinging freely from side to side. Those who walk with their hands in their pockets may be **perverse** and critical of others. **(10)** People who look toward the ground may be trying to **circumvent** the glances of others.

Body language sends out powerful messages both to others and to ourselves. Research has shown that it helps us to think. Gesturing with hands helps people retrieve words from memory and express abstract concepts. But, of course, we also communicate messages to each other with these gestures. The next time you shake hands, tilt your head, or fold your arms, think about the messages that others may **extract** from your movements.

■ *Exercise*

Each numbered sentence below corresponds to a sentence in the Passage. Fill in the letter of the choice that makes the sentence mean the same thing as its corresponding sentence in the Passage.

1. But if her arms are crossed, she is ___**a**___ communicating another message.
    a. accidentally   b. hopefully   c. strongly   d. probably

2. The student is fixing a(n) ___**d**___ stare on the teacher.
    a. interested   b. friendly   c. hateful   d. stubborn

3. Only an inexperienced teacher would ___**c**___ that a student who remains perfectly still is thinking about math.
    a. hope   b. picture   c. conclude   d. question

4. Another conclusion is sometimes more ___**d**___.
    a. ridiculous   b. desirable   c. negative   d. logical

5. An umpire makes a call that a team manager wants him to __c__.
   a. repeat   b. make louder   c. take back   d. make public

6. The umpire undergoes a(n) __a__.
   a. change   b. reform   c. inspection   d. attitude

7. The __b__ manager walks back to the dugout.
   a. wise   b. depressed   c. helpful   d. hopeful

8. We have all seen the controlled and measured walk of a person trying

   to appear dignified and __d__.
   a. proud   b. busy   c. unfriendly   d. cautious

9. People who are __b__ walk with their heads down.
   a. sick   b. worried   c. stubborn   d. elderly

10. People who look toward the ground may be trying to __b__ the
    glances of others.
    a. capture   b. avoid   c. greet   d. notice

■ Discussion Questions

1. According to the passage, what may be the hidden message of smiling?

2. Identify two situations in which the position of a person's arms or hands indicates a particular attitude.

3. Suggest three ways in which dogs communicate by using body language.

◆ ENGLISH IDIOMS

Movement

Since this chapter concerns word elements of movement, the idioms introduced here are all related to action. Some idioms relate to negative actions. When people are *axed,* they are fired or lose their jobs. If a worker does something wrong, her boss may *call her on the carpet* or *bawl her out.* If her boss makes her feel bad, she would be *cut down to size.*

To *draw the line* means to set a limit. For example, you might help a friend to study, but *draw the line* at writing his paper for him. A professor who *covers a lot of ground* in a lecture gives much information. (Similarly, a traveler might *cover a lot of ground* by going a long distance.)

If people go to a theater to see a mystery and they are kept in suspense until the last minute, the mystery is called a *cliffhanger.* If audience members enjoy the performance, clapping and cheering loudly, they would be said to *bring the house down.*

In the hill tribes of northern India, it was the custom to bend over backwards while doing a yoga exercise that symbolized submission to God. *To bend over backwards* now means to do everything possible to please or accommodate another person. A professor might *bend over backwards* to help a student who is having difficulty in a course.

CHAPTER

Word Elements:
Together and Apart

Poet John Donne wrote, "No man is an island." All of us connect with other people in school, our jobs, our pastimes, and our personal lives. Not surprisingly, many English words describe how we come together and part from others. Chapter 8 presents word elements that mean "together" and "apart." The chapter also introduces several words that came into English from other languages. Over the years, as English speakers came in contact with people who spoke other languages, they "borrowed" non-English words.

Chapter Strategy: Word Elements: Together and Apart

Chapter Words:

Part 1

co-, com-, con-	coherent	*dis-*	discord
	collaborate		disparity
	communal		disreputable
	compatible	*sym-, syn-*	syndrome
	concur		synopsis
	contemporary		synthesis

Part 2

greg	congregate	*Borrowed Words*	bravado
	gregarious		charisma
	segregate		cliché
sperse	disperse		cuisine
	intersperse		nadir
	sparse		zenith

Quiz Yourself

To check your knowledge of some chapter words before you begin to study, identify these statements as true or false. Answers are on page 411.

Two **contemporaries** are different in age.	True	False
A **cliché** shows excellent use of language.	True	False
Discord is disagreement.	True	False
Zenith is the bottom of something.	True	False

You will learn the answers as you study this chapter.

Did You Know?

What Are Two Sources of English?

Modern English has roots in two languages, Old French and Old English. Old French was a Romance language; that is, it descended from Latin, which was spoken by ancient Romans. Old French was an ancestor of the French spoken today. Old English, spoken in England from about the beginning of the eighth century to the middle of the twelfth century, was a Germanic language, similar in many ways to the German spoken today. The two languages first came into contact in 1066 CE.

In 1066, William the Conqueror crossed the English Channel from Normandy, in northwestern France, to England. He then conquered England, and made himself king. He replaced the English nobility with his fellow Norman countrymen, who spoke a version of Old French. For many years, then, the ruling class of England spoke Old French, and the rest of the people continued to speak Old English.

Gradually the two languages merged into Middle English, which was spoken until the 1300s, when it became what we know as Modern English. But to this day, many rare, fancy English words (like the ones you find in vocabulary books) tend to be of Old French origin. In contrast, the common words of English usually come from Old English.

What does this mean to you? Perhaps you speak or have studied Spanish, Italian, French, or Portuguese. These are Romance languages, related to the Old French that William the Conqueror brought to England. If you speak a Romance language, you can easily learn many difficult

English words. All you need to do is to think of a *cognate*, a word that sounds the same and has the same meaning, from a Romance language. As an example, *furious* is an English word descended from Old French. The Spanish cognate is *furioso*.

Modern English is full of word pairs that have the same or similar meanings. One word is often derived from Old French and the other from Old English. Several of these word pairs are listed below. Notice that the words descended from Old French are often longer and less common.

Old English (Germanic Origin)	*Old French (Romance Origin)*
eat	devour
talk	converse
give	donate
earth	terrain
top	pinnacle
late	tardy

Learning Strategy

Word Elements: Together and Apart

Part 1 of this chapter presents three common prefixes that refer to being together or apart: *com-* and *syn-* mean "together"; *dis-* means "apart." These prefixes are very useful to know, since each one is used to form more than 100 English words.

Part 2 presents two roots that are related to the idea of together and apart, *greg* (flock, herd) and *sperse* (scatter).

Element	*Meaning*	*Origin*	*Function*	*Chapter Words*
Part 1				
co-, col-, com-, con-, cor-	together	Latin	prefix	coherent, collaborate, communal, compatible, concur, contemporary
dis-	apart; not	Latin; Greek	prefix	discord, disparity, disreputable
sym-, syn-	together; same	Greek	prefix	syndrome, synopsis, synthesis
Part 2				
greg	flock	Latin	root	congregate, gregarious, segregate
sperse	scatter	Latin	root	disperse, intersperse, sparse

Prefixes

Part 1

The three prefixes presented in Part 1 are discussed in more detail below.

co-, col-, com-, con-, cor- (together)

This prefix is in several hundred English words. Its five spelling variations help us pronounce it more easily when it is attached to various roots. Each of these words carries a sense of **together.** For example, a *coworker* is someone who works **together** with another worker. To *collect* means "to bring things **together.**" When people *communicate* or *correspond*, they come **together** through speech or writing. When two electrical wires establish *contact*, they come **together** by touching.

dis- (apart; not)

In most words, *dis-* means **not.** The word *distrust*, formed from the prefix *dis-* and the base word *trust*, means "**not** to trust." A person in *disgrace* is **not** in the "grace," or favor, of others. The informal word "dis" means **not** to respect, or *to show disrespect for*, as in "She dissed me." *Dis-* can also mean **apart.** Students sometimes *dissect* (cut **apart**) frogs in biology classes. A noisy student may *disrupt* (break **apart** into confusion) a class.

sym-, syn- (together; same)

The two meanings of *syn-* and *sym-* are related, making them easy to remember. For example, *sympathy* is composed from *sym-* (**same**) and the root *path* (feeling). *Synagogue*, a place where Jewish people meet to worship, is composed from *syn-* (**together**) and *agein* (to lead).

Words to Learn

Part 1

co-, col-, com-, con-, cor-

1. **coherent** (adjective)   kō-hîr′ənt

   From *co-* (together) + *haērere* (to cling or stick)

   logical; consistent; clearly reasoned

   > The Canadian government worked out a **coherent** policy for admitting refugees.

It is difficult to express yourself in a **coherent** way when you're angry.

▶ *Related Words*

coherence (noun)   Lacking any *coherence,* the student's paper was simply a disorganized collection of sentences.

cohere (verb)   In freezing weather, ice *coheres* to the surface of the road. (*Cohere* means "to stick.")

incoherent (adjective)   The English directions were *incoherent* to the Korean tourist. (*Incoherent* is the opposite of *coherent.*)

As discussed in Chapter 4, there are so many laws that people often have trouble finding out what the law in a given situation actually is. Our ancestors dealt with this problem through law codes. These *coherent* collections classified each law and made certain all were consistent. The oldest code, in Ebla (northern Syria), dates to 2400 BCE and is carved in stone. The Code of Hammurabi, assembled in Mesopotamia in approximately 1750 BCE, was publicly displayed. The Napoleonic Code applied to territory under that French emperor. The state of Louisiana, once controlled by the French, still operates partially under Napoleonic Code. In general, however, English civil law is the basis for the laws in the United States.

---

2. **collaborate** (verb)   kə-lăb′ə-rāt′

From Latin: *col-* (together) + *labōrāre* (to work)

to work together

The United States must **collaborate** with other nations to catch terrorists.

Scientists J. D. Watson and F. H. C. Crick **collaborated** on a project to determine the structure of DNA.

▶ *Related Words*

collaboration (noun)   Building a high-rise requires the *collaboration* of architects, engineers, and construction crews.

collaborator (noun, person)   Traitor Benedict Arnold became a collaborator with the English enemy during the Revolutionary War.

NOTE: The word *collaborator* can have the negative meaning of "one who aids an enemy occupying one's country."

▶ *Common Phrases*

collaborate with (others); collaborate on (a project)

3. **communal** (adjective)   kə-myoo′nəl

From Latin: *com-* (together) (*Communis* meant "shared," "public.")

referring to a community or to joint ownership

> A single rude cell-phone user can disturb a large **communal** space.

> The swimming pool was **communal** property, so everybody in the condo association paid dues to keep it clean.

▶ *Related Word*

commune (noun)   (kŏm′yoon′)   In a *commune,* people live together, sharing housing and incomes.

4. **compatible** (adjective)   kəm-păt′ə-bəl

From Latin: *com-* (together) + *path* (feeling)

harmonious; living in harmony

> Zoning laws in the suburb required that the outsides of new homes be **compatible** with those of existing homes.

> My **compatible** cat and dog play happily with each other.

▶ *Common Phrase*
compatible with

▶ *Related Words*

compatibility (noun)   *Compatibility* is an important factor in a happy marriage.

incompatible (adjective)   My TV was *incompatible* with my DVD player. (*Incompatible* means *not* compatible.)

5. **concur** (verb)   kən-kûr′

From Latin: *con-* (together) + *currere* (to run)

to agree

> Experts **concur** that the sun's rays can cause skin cancer.

> In a 1998 pact, forty-four nations **concurred** on principles for restoring stolen art to survivors of the Holocaust.

> The second report **concurred** with the first.

▶ *Common Phrases*
concur with (agree with) a person; concur on (agree on or about) something

▶ *Related Words*

concurrence (noun)   The U.S. president needs the *concurrence* of Congress to declare war.

concurrent (adjective)   If you want to see two *concurrent* TV programs, you must tape one. (*Concurrent* means "at the same time.")

6. **contemporary** (noun, person; adjective)   kən-tĕm′pə-rĕr′ē   (plural: *contemporaries*)

From Latin: *com-* (together) + *tempus* (time)

a person about the same age as another person (noun)

> **Contemporaries** Albert Einstein and Joseph Stalin were both born in 1879.

a person living at the same time as another person (noun, person)

> Great artists are sometimes not appreciated by their **contemporaries.**

existing at the same time (adjective)

> The expansion of railroads and the migration to the West were **contemporary** developments in U.S. history.

current; modern (adjective)

> **Contemporary** fashion trends include body piercing and tattooing.

▶ *Related Word*
> **contemporaneous** (adjective)   Diaries from the American Civil War give a *contemporaneous* view of the conflict.

dis-

7. **discord** (noun)   dĭs′kôrd′

From Latin: *dis-* (apart) + *cor* (heart, mind)

strife; lack of agreement

> Loud arguments revealed the **discord** in our neighbors' household.

▶ *Related Word*
> **discordant** (adjective)   (dĭ-skôr′dnt)   The beginning violin student filled the room with *discordant* sounds.

A Greek legend tells the story of the apple of *discord*. The goddess of discord, Eris, had not been invited to a wedding at which all the other gods were to be present. Enraged, she arrived at the party and threw onto the table a golden apple intended "for the most beautiful." Three goddesses, Hera, Athena, and Aphrodite, all claimed it. Paris, prince of Troy, was asked to settle the dispute. He chose Aphrodite because she promised him the world's most beautiful woman, Helen of Troy. Unfortunately, Helen was already married to the Greek king Menelaus. When Paris abducted her, a Greek army went to Troy to get her back. This was the start of the Trojan War, the subject of Homer's *Iliad*.

8. **disparity** (noun)   dĭ-spăr′ĭ-tē   (plural: *disparities*)

From Latin: *dis-* (not) + *par* (equal)

inequality; difference

> Despite the **disparity** in their ages, the boy and his grandfather enjoyed fishing together.
>
> The **disparity** between my boss's promises and my actual working conditions soon became clear.

Research indicates that a college degree increases income. The 1990 census found a considerable *disparity* in the earning power of college graduates and nongraduates. On average, the difference amounted to $600,000 over a working life. An advanced degree can increase earning power by as much as $2 million over a lifetime.

▶ *Related Word*
  disparate (adjective) (dĭs′pər-ĭt) Lyle Lovett's music reflects the *disparate* influences of country, Tin Pan Alley, swing, and jazz.

9. **disreputable** (adjective)   dĭs-rĕp′yə-tə-bəl

From Latin: *dis-* (not) + *re-* (again) + *putāre* (to think) (Literally, *disreputable* means "not worth a second thought.")

not respectable; having a bad reputation

> It was rumored that the **disreputable** businessman sent gangsters to collect unpaid debts.

▶ *Related Word*
  disrepute (noun) (dĭs′rĭ-pyoot′) The chemist who had reported false results fell into *disrepute*.

sym-, syn-

10. **syndrome** (noun)   sĭn′drōm′

From Greek: *syn-* (together) + *dramein* (to run)

a group of symptoms that indicates a disease or disorder

> Carpal tunnel **syndrome** can include pain, tingling, weakness, and numbness in the hands and fingers.

> In the late 1800s, the U.S. economy suffered from a **syndrome** of alternating growth and sudden declines.

11. **synopsis** (noun)   sĭ-nŏp′sĭs   plural: synopses

From Greek: *syn-* (together) + *opsis* (view) (In a synopsis, something is viewed "all together.")

a short summary

> Movie reviews often give a short **synopsis** of the film.

12. **synthesis** (noun)   sĭn′thĭ-sĭs   plural: syntheses

From Greek: *syn-* (together) + *tithenai* (to put)

something made from combined parts; the making of something by combining parts

> Guitarist Carlos Santana has created a **synthesis** of his Latin roots and new music styles.

> This artist's work is a **synthesis** of many traditions.

▶ *Related Words*

synthesize (verb)   Plants *synthesize* oxygen through photosynthesis.

synthetic (adjective)   (sĭn-thĕt′ĭk)   Nylon and polyester are examples of *synthetic* materials made from petroleum.

NOTE: Synthetic refers to products, such as nylon, produced chemically, or by other artificial means, rather than those of natural origin.

Exercises

Part 1

■ Definitions

Match each word in the left-hand column with a definition from the right-hand column. Use each choice only once.

1. disparity ___f___   a. strife; lack of agreement

2. syndrome ___c___   b. something made from combined parts

3. synopsis ___i___   c. symptoms that make up a disease

4. discord ___a___   d. logical; consistent

5. synthesis ___b___   e. existing at the same time

6. communal ___g___   f. inequality

7. concur ___k___   g. jointly owned

8. disreputable ___l___   h. harmonious

9. coherent ___d___   i. summary

10. collaborate ___j___   j. to work together

                                            k. to agree

                                            l. not respectable

■ Meanings

Match each prefix to its meaning. Use each choice only once.

1. con-___a___   a. together

2. dis-___c___   b. together; same

3. syn-___b___   c. apart; not together

■ Words in Context

Complete each sentence with the word that fits best. Use each choice only once.

a. coherent   e. concur   i. disreputable
b. collaborate   f. contemporary   j. syndrome
c. communal   g. discordant   k. synopsis
d. compatible   h. disparity   l. synthesis

1. Students who read a **k, synopsis** _____ of a book, rather than the book itself, will miss the richness of the original language.

2. Although we understood parts of her speech, it was not
a, coherent _____ enough for us to understand her main points.

3. There is a great **h, disparity** _____ of power between a master and a slave.

4. Since we are the same age, Juan is my **f, contemporary** _____.

5. I was annoyed by the **g, discordant** _____ noise from five radios playing different music on the bus.

6. The **d, compatible** _____ flavors of ice cream and hot fudge combine to make a delicious hot-fudge sundae.

7. In Swiss villages, all the people in town baked bread in one
c, communal _____ oven.

8. All eight doctors **e, concur** _____ that the patient suffered a mild stroke.

9. Veterans who suffer from Gulf War **j, syndrome** _____ experience memory loss, tiredness, headaches, and pain in their joints.

10. The neighbors felt that the **i, disreputable** _____ lawyer cheated his clients.

■ Using Related Words

Complete each sentence by using a word from the group of related words above it. You may need to capitalize a word when you write it in a sentence. Use each choice only once.

1. compatibility, compatible

> Kidney donors can often save the life of a person whose kidneys no longer function. Of course, the donor's kidney must be **compatible** with the body of the receiver. The American Transplant Society helps sick people locate a donor and establish the **compatibility** of the donor kidney and its recipient.

2. synthetic, synthesize, synthesized, synthetically

> Although the human body can produce many substances, vitamin C cannot be **synthesized** by humans. Now, however, Nicholas Smirnoff has discovered how plants **synthesize** this chemical, and may be able to produce plants that contain more of the vitamin. Currently, people must eat many foods such as oranges and grapefruits or take pills containing **synthetic** vitamin C. In the future, there may well be less reliance on **synthetically** produced vitamin C, as smaller amounts of food will supply more of the vitamin.

3. collaboration, collaborated

> Several Peruvian women have **collaborated** to form a radio station that presents programs on women's health and welfare. A **collaboration** has also been formed between women's groups in Mexico and in Boston. Latinas (Latin American women) are leading the world in this type of networking.

4. contemporaries, contemporaneous, contemporary

> Wolfgang Amadeus Mozart, who lived from 1756 to 1791, was a musical **contemporary** of composer Franz Joseph Haydn. Mozart was a child prodigy who performed throughout Europe at the age of six. However, as an adult, his **contemporaries** often ignored his best music. **Contemporaneous** reports tell us that he lost the sponsorship of royalty. He died in poverty when he was thirty-six years old, but his great music lives on today.

■ *Reading the Headlines*

This exercise presents five headlines that might appear in newspapers. Read each headline and then answer the questions that follow. (Remember that small words, such as *is, are, a,* and *the,* are often left out of newspaper headlines.)

CRITIC WRITES THAT INCOMPATIBLE INSTRUMENTS PRODUCE DISCORD IN CONTEMPORARY MUSIC

1. Was the music written recently? **yes**

2. Do the instruments sound good together? **no**

ONLY SPARSE RESEARCH DONE ON SYNDROME THAT MAKES SPEECH INCOHERENT

3. Has there been much research on the syndrome? **no**

4. Can the speech be understood? **no**

CHEFS COLLABORATE TO PRODUCE SYNTHESIS OF FRENCH AND MEXICAN FOOD

5. Are the chefs working on different projects? **no**

6. Is a combination being produced? **yes**

JUDGES CONCUR THAT COMMUNAL PARK SHOULD BE USED ONLY BY CHILDREN

7. Do the judges agree? **yes**

8. Is the park jointly owned? **yes**

DISREPUTABLE STUDY-GUIDE WRITER PRODUCES SYNOPSIS THAT HAS DISPARITIES WITH BOOK

9. Does the study-guide writer have a good reputation? **no**

10. Do the book and synopsis agree? **no**

Word Roots

Part 2

Part 2 presents two word roots that are concerned with coming together and moving apart, but do not carry these meanings directly. These roots are *greg* and *sperse*.

This part also presents some words that were borrowed from other languages when English speakers came into contact with them.

greg (flock; herd)

Greg once referred to a flock of sheep or a herd of cattle. By extension, *greg* is now used as a word element meaning the action of **flocking** or coming together. One word you will learn, *gregarious,* describes people who like to **come together** with other people.

sperse (scatter)

When we **scatter** things, we move them apart. Thus, the root *sperse* is concerned with being apart. *Disperse,* one of the words in this chapter, means "to **scatter** widely."

Words to Learn

Part 2

greg

13. **congregate** (verb)   kŏng′grĭ-gāt′

    From Latin: *con-* (together) + *greg* (flock, herd)

    to meet; to assemble

    > Fifty thousand people **congregated** to hear the Dalai Lama speak in Central Park.

    > Elephants **congregated** at the water hole.

    ▶ *Related Word*

    congregation (noun)   The *congregation* listened intently to the minister's sermon.

Congregation is a religious word, meaning the members of a religious organization, such as a church or synagogue. Many other religious words have interesting origins.

Catholic, from the meaning *universal.* When spelled with a small *c,* *catholic* still means "universal," rather than the religion.

Protestant, from *protest.* In the early 1500s, Martin Luther and his followers protested against certain Catholic practices. They formed a new set of *protesting* religions.

Jewish, from the Hebrew word *Judah,* the ancient Jewish Kingdom.

Muslim, from the Arabic word *aslama,* meaning *he surrendered,* referring to people who are obedient to Allah's will.

Hindu, from the Persian word for India, *Hind.*

14. **gregarious** (adjective)   grĭ-gâr′ē-əs

From Latin: *greg* (flock; herd)

sociable; fond of company

Gregarious college students may spend too much time at parties and too little time studying.

▶ *Related Word*

gregariousness (noun)   Because of his *gregariousness,* George hated to work at home alone.

15. **segregate** (verb)   sĕg′rĭ-gāt′

From Latin: *sē-* (apart) + *greg* (flock; herd) (*Sēgregāre* meant "to separate from the flock.")

to separate

In some religious traditions, men are **segregated** from women during prayer services.

Although laws do not **segregate** them, Turkish immigrants often choose to live separately from others in Germany.

▶ *Related Word*

segregation (noun)   The civil rights movement made racial *segregation* illegal in the United States.

sperse

16. **disperse** (verb)   dĭ-spûrs′

From Latin: *dis-* (apart) + *sperse* (scatter)

to scatter; to distribute widely

Class ended, so the students **dispersed**.

Refinishing furniture outdoors allows harmful chemical fumes to **disperse** into the open air.

▶ *Related Word*
dispersion (noun)   (dĭ-spûr′zhən)   The students observed the *dispersion* of light through a prism.

17. **intersperse** (verb)   ĭn′tər-spûrs′

From Latin: *inter-* (between) + *sperse* (scatter)

to scatter here and there; to distribute among other things

The text in this chapter is **interspersed** with interesting photos.

Most people **intersperse** their speech with expressions like "hmmm" and "uh."

▶ *Common Phrase*
intersperse with

Parents and teachers become annoyed with teenagers who *intersperse* their speech with the word *like*: "It's like, did you see her?" "She's got, like, an attitude." But linguist Muffy E. A. Siegel found that this word can work as a mighty communicator. It can be used instead of *said*: "She's like, 'I'm going.'" It can show exaggeration: "She has like a million sweaters." It can be used when the speaker is not sure: "He's like seventeen." And it can be used to emphasize: "That's so, like, last week" (or out of date).

18. **sparse** (adjective)   spärs

From Latin: *sperse* (scatter)

thinly scattered or distributed; meager

Rain has been so **sparse** in western Nebraska that ruts of wagon wheels made over 100 years ago can still be seen.

Borrowed Words

19. **bravado** (noun)   brə-vä′dō

From Spanish

false bravery; showy display of courage

In a show of **bravado,** the teenager challenged the famous gunslinger to a shootout.

20. **charisma** (noun)   kə-rĭz′mə

From Greek

quality of leadership that attracts other people

> The **charisma** of the professor attracted crowds of adoring students.

▶ *Related Word*

charismatic (adjective)   (kăr′ĭz-măt′ĭk)   Winston Churchill's *charismatic* leadership was a source of strength to England during the dark days of World War II.

Although the special quality of *charisma* is hard to define, history records many *charismatic* leaders. Emiliano Zapata, powerful leader of the 1910 Mexican Revolution, struggled for *tierra y liberdad*—land and liberty—for Mexican peasants. So powerful was his *charisma* that modern-day Mexican reformers are still known as *Los Zapatistas*.

Napoleon Bonaparte rose from a relatively poor Corsican family to become emperor of France. It is said that Napoleon's *charisma* was so great that anybody who met him would be captured by his personality. Uniting the French behind him, he managed to conquer half of Europe before England and Austria defeated him in 1815.

In his powerful speeches, the modern civil rights leader Martin Luther King Jr. inspired all who heard him with the justice of his great cause. King employed nonviolent peace marches to win rights for African Americans.

21. **cliché** (noun)   klē-shā′

From French

an overused, trite expression

> The official's speech was full of **clichés** and promises, but it gave no plan of action.

> A **cliché** often used in sports is "No pain, no gain."

> Love songs, romance novels, and greeting cards are filled with **clichés.**

Many clichés are more than a century old. In 1878, W. S. Gilbert and Arthur Sullivan wrote a song featuring clichés in their operetta *H.M.S. Pinafore*. Many are still in use today, including, "All that glitters is not gold," "Only brave deserve the fair," "Who spares the rod spoils the child," and "Here today and gone tomorrow."

---

22. **cuisine** (noun)   kwĭ-zēn′

From French

a style of food or cooking

> Puerto Rican **cuisine** features delicious pasteles, which are made of cornmeal and stuffed with meat, raisins, olives, capers, and almonds.

> The elegant restaurant featured Northern Chinese **cuisine.**

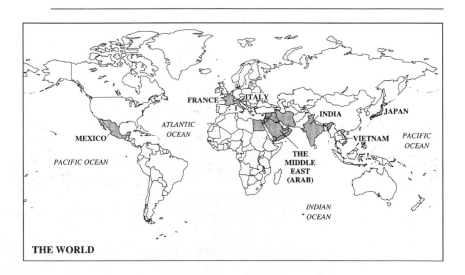

Cuisines of different regions feature various specialties. Can you match each food item with its country or group of origin?

1. hummus   a. Middle Eastern
2. fajitas   b. Japanese
3. bulogi   c. Mexican
4. phò tai   d. Korean
5. sushi   e. Vietnamese
6. curry   f. Indian

Answers are on page 411.

NOTE: Generally, a *cuisine* refers to food prepared by skilled cooks or chefs.

23. **nadir** (noun)   nā′dər

From Arabic: *nazīr as-samt* (the lowest point; opposite the zenith)

the lowest point

> At the **nadir** of his fortunes, he was broke and alone.
>
> Human behavior reaches its **nadir** in the act of genocide.

24. **zenith** (noun)   zē′nĭth

From Arabic: *samt ar-ra's* (the path overhead; the highest point in the heavens)

the highest point

> Centered in present-day Iraq, the Assyrian empire reached the **zenith** of its power from 900 to 650 BCE.

Arabic and early Middle Eastern cultures made many important contributions to astronomy. As early as 800 BCE, Babylonians and Assyrians calculated new moons and composed a seasonal calendar. The Chaldeans (about 500 BCE) had a table of lunar eclipses and knew the cycles of five planets around the sun. The work of Abū Ma'shar (born in 787 CE), who calculated the length of the year and catalogued the stars, was translated from Arabic into Latin. This work became one of the first books printed in Germany.

NOTE: *Zenith* is not used to refer to such physical things as the top of a mountain. In that case, we refer to the *pinnacle* of a mountain.

Exercises

Part 2

■ Definitions

Match each word in the left-hand column with a definition from the right-hand column. Use each choice only once.

1. bravado ___j___
2. nadir ___h___
3. cuisine ___a___
4. congregate ___l___
5. gregarious ___g___
6. zenith ___i___
7. intersperse ___e___
8. sparse ___b___
9. segregate ___c___
10. cliché ___d___

a. style of cooking
b. thinly scattered
c. to separate
d. overused expression
e. to distribute among other things
f. a quality that attracts others
g. sociable
h. lowest point
i. highest point
j. showy display of bravery
k. to scatter; to distribute widely
l. to gather together

■ Meanings

Match each word root to its meaning. Use each choice only once.

1. sperse ___b___
2. greg ___a___

a. flock; herd
b. scatter

■ Words in Context

Complete each sentence with the word that fits best. Use each choice only once.

a. congregate e. intersperse i. cliché
b. gregarious f. sparse j. cuisine
c. segregate g. bravado k. nadir
d. disperse h. charisma l. zenith

1. The __b, gregarious__ hairstylist loved to talk to her clients as she worked.

2. Because of his __h, charisma__, the rock star attracted fans and imitators.

3. The presenter wanted to __e, intersperse__ his presentation with several short breaks.

4. The expression "Every cloud has a silver lining" is a(n) __i, cliché__ that most of us have heard many times.

5. The new boxer displayed true __g, bravado__ when he publicly dared the champion to a fight.

6. The crowd will __d, disperse__ after the concert ends.

7. Child abuse shows the __k, nadir__ of human nature.

8. Because their team kept losing, only a __f, sparse__ crowd came to watch the football game.

9. At the __l, zenith__ of his power, Genghis Khan ruled a vast Asian empire.

10. Indian __j, cuisine__ uses vegetables in many dishes.

■ Using Related Words

Complete each sentence by using a word from the group of related words above it. Use each choice only once.

1. segregated, segregation
   At one time, victims of contagious diseases such as smallpox and whooping cough were "quarantined." This meant they were

segregated_____ from healthy people and allowed no

contact with them. Doctors hoped that this **segregation**_____ would control the spread of disease. Quarantine is still used today, but not very often.

2. dispersion, disperse

Small, fast-moving hummingbirds **disperse**_____ the pollen that fertilizes flowers. The birds' long bills gather nectar, and as hummingbirds move, they carry pollen from flower to flower.

In this way, **dispersion**_____ allows flowers to be fertilized. Hummingbirds are especially attracted to red and orange flowers. If you wear these colors, they will be attracted to you too!

3. charisma, charismatic

His riveting blue eyes and mysterious manner made the Russian spiritual adviser Rasputin (1872–1916) extremely

charismatic_____. His **charisma**_____ attracted many followers, including Czarina Alexandra. Her devotion to Rasputin, deeply resented by the Russian people, may have been a factor leading to the revolution of 1917.

4. congregated, congregation

Aretha Franklin, described by many as the Queen of Soul, began her career as a gospel singer in Detroit, where her father led the

congregation_____ of New Bethel Baptist Church. Later, Aretha switched to rock and soul music. But in 1987, fans

congregated_____ at New Bethel when she returned to record a gospel album.

■ *Reading the Headlines*

This exercise presents five headlines that might appear in newspapers. Read each one carefully and then answer the questions that follow. (Remember that little words, such as *is, are, a,* and *the,* are often left out of headlines.)

CLOUDS TOO DISPERSED TO FORM RAIN IN AREA WITH SPARSE CROP GROWTH

    1. Are the clouds gathered together? __no__

    2. Are there many crops? __no__

GREGARIOUS GROUP INTERSPERSES BUSINESS TALK WITH SOCIALIZING

    3. Do the members of the group prefer to be alone? __no__

    4. Do the members socialize as well as talk business? __yes__

REBELS DISPLAY BRAVADO AT NADIR OF THEIR FORTUNES

    5. Do the rebels seem courageous? __yes__

    6. Are they enjoying good luck? __no__

VIETNAMESE CUISINE CALLED ZENITH OF TASTE

    7. Does the headline refer to food? __yes__

    8. Is it good? __yes__

PEOPLE CONGREGATE TO HEAR CHARISMATIC SPEAKER TALK IN CLICHÉS

    9. Does the speaker appeal to people? __yes__

    10. Is the speaker saying new things? __no__

Chapter Exercises

■ *Practicing Strategies: New Words from Word Elements*

See how your knowledge of word elements can help you understand new words. Complete each sentence with the word that seems to fit best. Use each choice only once.

a. aggregate	e. compress	i. dislocate
b. coexist	f. conform	j. disuse
c. collide	g. disassociate	k. sympathize
d. compact	h. discourteous	l. synchronized

1. You can **i, dislocate**_____ your shoulder when an accident pushes it out of its correct location.

2. Something that is not used has fallen into **j, disuse**_____.

3. *Chronos* means "time," so two things that happen at the same time are **l, synchronized**_____.

4. When all of something is herded or gathered together, the total is called the **a, aggregate**_____.

5. When we pack something together, we **d, compact**_____ it.

6. Groups of people or animals that live together are said to **b, coexist**_____.

7. Someone who is not courteous is **h, discourteous**_____.

8. When a person acts and dresses like others, we say he or she is trying to take the same form, or **f, conform**_____.

9. When we break apart from people we have been associated with, we **g, disassociate**_____ ourselves from them.

10. *Path* means "feeling," so when we feel the same as someone who suffers, we **k, sympathize**_____.

■ *Practicing Strategies: Combining Context Clues and Word Elements*

Combining the strategies of context clues and word elements is a good way to figure out the meanings of unknown words. In the following sentences, each italicized word contains a word element that you have studied in this chapter. Using the meaning of the word element and the context of the sentence, make an intelligent guess about the meaning of the italicized word. Your instructor may ask you to check the meaning in your dictionary when you have finished the exercise.

1. At the *confluence* of the Green River and the Colorado River, the color of the water is a mix of both sources.

   Confluence means **flowing together; joining together**.

2. In many movie musicals, stars *lip-synch* lyrics that are actually sung by other people.

   Lip-synch means **mouthing the words at the same time that someone else is singing them**.

3. After seven active children played in the house all day, it was in a state of *disarray*.

   Disarray means **disorder; messiness**.

4. The man grew so *disheartened* by his failure to find a job that he stopped his search.

   Disheartened means **upset; discouraged**.

5. After reaching total *concordance* among the delegates, they declared the meeting a complete success.

   Concordance means **agreement; togetherness**.

■ *Companion Words*

Complete each sentence with the word that fits best. Choose your answers from the words below. You may use each word more than once.

Choices: with, on, of, in, between, from

1. The student read a five-page synopsis **of** _____ *Romeo and Juliet*.

2. I collaborated **with** _____ other students on the presentation.

3. The collaboration **of** _____ artists resulted in a beautiful installation.

4. This style is a synthesis **of** _____ many different fashion trends.

5. Good speakers often intersperse their presentations **with** _____ jokes.

6. The taste of ketchup is not compatible **with** _____ that of ice cream.

7. My adviser concurred **with** _____ me.

■ *Writing with Your Words*

This exercise will give you practice in writing effective sentences that use the vocabulary words. Each sentence is started for you. Complete it with an interesting phrase that also indicates the meaning of the italicized word.

1. I hate the *cliché* _____
   _____.

2. A *communal* dormitory _____
   _____.

3. His *charismatic* personality _____
   _____.

4. It might be necessary to *segregate* _____
   _____.

5. My favorite *cuisine* is _____
   _____.

6. Because people are *sparse* in the wilderness, ___
   _____.

7. At the *zenith* of his career, the athlete _____
   _____.

8. The directions were *incoherent,* so _____
   _____.

9. If two people are *incompatible,* _____
   _____.

10. When people *congregate* at a club, _____
    _____.

■ *Making Connections*

These questions will help you relate the words you have learned in this chapter to your own life. Answer each question by writing a paragraph or more on a separate sheet of paper.

1. Describe a person you know or know about who has charisma.

2. If you could disperse as much money as you wanted, what would you do?

3. Do you think you are a gregarious person? Why or why not?

Passage

Intelligence Under Fire: The Story of the Navajo Code Talkers

When Marines raised the U.S. flag on the island of Iwo Jima in 1945, the picture of Ira Hayes, a Navajo Indian, became world famous. A statue modeled from this picture stands in Arlington National Cemetery as a tribute to one of the hardest-fought battles of World War II. But unlike Hayes's picture, the heroic role of the Navajo code talkers in the battle has only recently become known. This is their story.

In many ways, the **(1) nadir** of United States justice could be the country's treatment of Native Americans. In 1863, for example, the U.S. Army destroyed crops and animals of the Navajos and forced them onto reservations. There Navajo children attended Bureau of Indian Affairs schools, where they were forbidden to use their own language. One man remembers being chained in a basement for daring to speak his native tongue! Navajos were **(2) segregated** in restaurants and movie theaters.

But the language that the schoolmasters disdained would prove to be a powerful weapon in World War II. When the United States entered the war in 1941, over 100 Navajos, some as young as fifteen, volunteered to fight. In a show of **bravado,** some even brought their own rifles, which would have been useless against the powerful weaponry of Japan and Germany. As it turned out, however, Navajos themselves were one of the most precious resources of the war.

(3) Experts **concur** that communication becomes extremely difficult during warfare. Fighting units can be miles apart, yet they must **collaborate** in making decisions so that attacks can be coordinated. Messages may be put into code, but the enemy always has "code breakers" specially designed to decode them. What could the U.S. Army do?

Philip Johnston, an army engineer, had lived on a Navajo reservation as a child. He understood some Navajo and recognized what a complex,

Ira Hayes, a Navajo, helps to plant a flag celebrating victory at Iwo Jima.

sophisticated, and precise language it was. Because it had no written symbols, it was almost impossible for the Japanese enemy to study. He asked the armed forces to gather Navajo enlistees and have them create a code for their native language.

In response, twenty-nine Navajos gathered in San Diego and began a **communal** effort to write the code. Messages could not simply be given in Navajo, for a captured Navajo soldier might be forced to decode them for an enemy. **(4)** So, the coders **synthesized** symbols and spelling. Some words got symbols, such as *bird* for *airplane* and *fish* for *ship*. In addition, each letter of the alphabet was given a Navajo word, so that other words could be spelled. *A*, for example, was given the Navajo word for *ant*, which is *wol-la-chee*. **(5)** Since symbols for words were **interspersed** with symbols for letters, the code could not be understood, even by those who spoke Navajo. One had to speak Navajo, speak English, and know the code for a message to be **coherent.**

After composing the code, **(6)** the code writers were **dispersed** into Marine battalions fighting the Japanese in the Pacific. Within a few weeks, they had proved their worth. At one point, one American force accidentally attacked another. When the people under attack radioed their fellow Americans, the attackers refused to stop unless they heard the message in Navajo code. A code talker was located and, within minutes, the firing was over.

But the value of code talking reached its **(7) zenith** during the attack on Iwo Jima, one of the most dangerous missions of the war. U.S. Marines had to land on the Japanese island and then cross loose volcanic ash. **(8)** With their movements slowed and only **sparse** tree growth to hide them, Americans became easy targets. In contrast, the Japanese were hidden in deep trenches. Under terrible fire, the Marines painfully made their way to Mount Suribachi. During the assault, the code talkers sent more than 800 messages, all without error. Six men worked without sleep for forty-eight hours. When the Marines got to the peak of Suribachi, Ira Hayes planted the U.S. flag. Another Navajo sent the message of victory: "Sheep-Uncle-Ram-Ice-Bear-Ant-Cat-Horse-Itch." The first letters of each word spell "Suribachi." **(9)** The language that was too **disreputable** to use in school had enabled the United States to take Iwo Jima. One official referred to the Navajos as "walking, talking weapons."

When World War II ended, the code talkers were released with no honors or awards. In fact, the armed forces cautioned them not to talk about their experiences, in case the code had to be used again. **(10)** There was a shameful **disparity** between the priceless service the men had given and their lack of recognition. Even worse, the men who had served their country so well went back to states where they were not permitted to vote!

Today, most of the Navajo code talkers and their **contemporaries** are gone, but their story is becoming widely known. Their intelligence under fire serves as a reminder of a nation's shameful past, a war's most heroic moments, and the enduring value of different cultures to the United States.

■ *Exercise*

Each sentence below corresponds to a sentence in the Passage. Fill in the letter of the choice that makes the sentence mean the same thing as its corresponding sentence in the Passage.

1. The ____**b**____ of U.S. justice may be the treatment of Native Americans.
   a. hope   b. lowest point   c. test   d. best example

2. Navajos were ____**a**____ in restaurants and movie theaters.
   a. separated   b. picked on   c. helped   d. crowded

3. Experts ____**d**____ that communication is a difficult problem during warfare.
   a. discover   b. know   c. feel   d. agree

4. The coders __**b**__ symbols and spelling.
   a. commonly used   b. put together   c. found out about   d. left alone

5. Symbols for words were __**d**__ symbols for letters.
   a. replaced   b. confused   c. given for   d. scattered among

6. The twenty-nine Navajos were __**d**__ into Marine battalions.
   a. shipped   b. forced   c. trapped   d. scattered

7. Code talking reached its __**c**__ during the attack on Iwo Jima.
   a. busiest point   b. most interesting point   c. highest point   d. most famous point

8. They had only __**c**__ tree growth to hide them.
   a. one type of   b. short   c. thinly scattered   d. green

9. The language too __**b**__ to use in school enabled the United States to take Iwo Jima.
   a. lacking in easiness   b. lacking in reputation   c. lacking in translation   d. lacking in speakers

10. There was a shameful __**b**__.
    a. discrimination   b. difference   c. response   d. hopelessness

■ *Discussion Questions*

1. Name two ways in which Navajos were deprived of their rights.

2. In what way was the Navajo code a synthesis?

3. Would you have been a code talker if given the opportunity? Why or why not?

◆ ENGLISH IDIOMS

Agreement and Anger

English has many idioms that express agreement, which brings us together with others, and anger, which sets us apart. People who become angry are said to *lose their heads, blow their tops,* or *lose their cool.* Such individuals *let off steam* through harsh words or actions.

Other idioms concern negative reactions that are weaker than outbursts. *To speak one's piece* is to speak frankly, and usually with some anger, but without losing one's temper. Somebody who annoys you *rubs you the wrong way.*

People calm their anger and make peace, or *make up* with others. When people realize they have been wrong and want to regain friendship or influence, they *mend fences,* perhaps by apologizing. Similarly, when people find that they are in agreement or have interests in common, they are said to have *common ground.*

If you are angry with people, you might *read them the riot act,* or give a strong warning or scolding. The original riot act was passed in 1774 to stop protests against King George III of England. When more than a dozen people gathered, a riot act was read, ordering them to disperse. If they did not obey, they were imprisoned or shot.

REVIEW

Chapters 5–8

■ Reviewing Words in Context

Complete each sentence with the word or term that fits best. You may have to capitalize some words.

A JOURNEY FROM VIETNAM TO THE UNITED STATES

a. abducted	e. congregated	i. reconcile	m. tenacity
b. antipathy	f. interminable	j. status quo	n. transcend
c. circumvent	g. jettison	k. staunch	o. transformations
d. communal	h. odyssey	l. transitory	p. vital

Background: Viem, a student in the author's class, was born in Vietnam. This is the story of his life there and his escape to the United States.

1. I was born in Saigon, Vietnam. My father had fought for the U.S. allies against the Communists. The Communists felt much **b, antipathy** for people like him. They even put him in jail for six months.

2. I too felt some discrimination, and had to **n, transcend** many difficulties. To get into college, I needed a higher exam score than children of people who had fought for the Communists.

3. I knew that unless the **j, status quo** changed, I would have a hard time in Vietnam.

4. Since I could not **i, reconcile** myself to such a life, I decided to escape.

5. **m, Tenacity** was very important, because ten of my efforts failed. In 1982, I finally succeeded.

6. I made my way to the seacoast, carefully trying to **c, circumvent** the police, who would have arrested me.

7. Forty-three people **e, congregated** on a beach to board the small, open fishing boat that would take us from Vietnam to Malaysia.

8. The sea grew so rough that at times we had to bail water out of the boat and even **g, jettison**_____ some of our belongings.

9. We ran short of food, water, and other **p, vital**_____ supplies.

10. Although the trip seemed **f, interminable**_____, it was actually only four days.

11. In fact, we were very lucky. The boat before us was lost at sea for fifty-two days and many died. The boat after us was captured by the Vietnamese police. Other boats were stopped by pirates who **a, abducted**_____ passengers and held them for ransom. Some pirates even killed the passengers.

12. Once I arrived in Malaysia, I was put in a refugee camp with **d, communal**_____ living quarters that I shared with several men.

13. My **h, odyssey**_____ to the United States included transfers to two other refugee camps.

14. When I came to the United States, my **k, staunch**_____ health enabled me to quickly adapt to the cold weather and the snow in Chicago, the city where I live.

15. In the fifteen years that I have been here, I have made many **o, transformations**_____ in my lifestyle, my language, and my career. I have now graduated from college and am working in the field of computers.

■ *Passage for Word Review*

Complete each blank in the passage with the word that makes the best sense. The choices include words from the vocabulary lists along with related words. Use each choice only once.

RUNNING TRACK

a. abstained   e. dejected   i. renowned   m. synopsis
b. compatible   f. gregarious   j. spartan   n. tenaciously
c. conducive   g. psyche   k. stature   o. viable
d. congregated   h. reconcile   l. subdue   p. vital

Background: William, a student in the author's class, describes what competitive running did for him—and to him. Currently, he is serving his country in Afghanistan.

When I started high school, I was only about five feet two inches in

(1) <u>k, stature</u> and weighed about ninety-five pounds. As you can imagine, I was very small. I wanted to play a sport, and I didn't have much of a choice of which one. I didn't have the size for football, the height for basketball, or an interest in baseball. But I could run fast, so joining the

track team seemed to be my only **(2)** <u>o, viable</u> option. I was afraid of the coach, but I decided to go ahead. After a week of tryouts, I finally made it.

Being in good shape is **(3)** <u>p, vital</u> to an athlete. I worked out every day, including weekends. After a boring job, I remember going home to do yet another workout. I also trained

(4) <u>n, tenaciously</u>, practicing my running whenever I could. I was so tired that I would sometimes fall asleep while eating my dinner.

I **(5)** <u>a, abstained</u> from doing anything unhealthy, like

smoking. I lived a(n) **(6)** <u>j, spartan</u> existence, concentrating on school, work, and running.

My **(7)** <u>f, gregarious</u> teammates liked to socialize. I found

their interests to be **(8)** <u>b, compatible</u> with my own, and I enjoyed spending time with them. This atmosphere was

(9) <u>c, conducive</u> to developing a winning team spirit.

By my senior year, I became captain of a(n) **(10)** <u>i, renowned</u> track team that had set records throughout the state. Supporters

(11) <u>d, congregated</u> to see our races. I even had a personal fan or two!

Then, during the indoor track season of my senior year, a terrible thing happened. I pulled both my hamstrings! I went through two months of physical therapy before I could walk normally. You can imagine that

I felt extremely **(12)** <u>e, dejected</u> when I heard I would never compete again.

But I could not **(13)** <u>l, subdue</u> my desire to run. After therapy, I began working out again and told my coach I wanted to run in the city meets. He let me run, although I now had to

(14) <u>h, reconcile</u> myself to the fact that it would hurt. Despite this, I qualified for the city meet. But the following week I had to quit running in the middle of my race—the race I was favored to win. As I walked across the finish line, I heard the crowd cheer! You can imagine that this

helped my **(15)** <u>g, psyche</u>.

I have not given up on my dream of competing. At the moment, I am training to run track later in my college years.

■ *Reviewing Learning Strategies*

New Words from Word Elements.   Below are words you have not studied that are formed from ancient Greek and Latin word elements. Using your knowledge of these elements, write in the word that best completes each sentence. You may have to capitalize some words. Use each choice only once.

a. anthropogenesis	e. inequity	i. regenerates
b. coreligionist	f. impermanent	j. symposium
c. distaste	g. intractable	k. synonym
d. exoskeleton	h. introvert	l. vivid

1. A(n) <u>h, introvert</u> is a person "turned in" upon himself, or not sociable.

2. A word with the "same name," or same meaning, as another is a(n) <u>k, synonym</u>.

3. If you do not like a particular food, you may have a(n) <u>c, distaste</u> for it.

4. My <u>b, coreligionist</u> and I go to church together.

5. __a, Anthropogenesis__ refers to the origins of human beings.

6. When two things are not fair, or equal, there is a(n) **e, inequity** .

7. Something **f, impermanent** does not last a long time.

8. When a plant grows new leaves or is "born again" after appearing to be dead, it **i, regenerates** .

9. A(n) **g, intractable** person is stubborn or "cannot be pulled."

10. A(n) **d, exoskeleton** is a hard structure on the outside of an animal that supports it the way our bones support us.

Word Elements:
Numbers and Measures

Ever since human beings learned numbers, we have been trying to count and measure our world. We measure time using clocks and calendars. We use scales to weigh things, and we count our money. This chapter presents Latin and ancient Greek word elements, related to numbers and measures, that will help you with the meanings of thousands of words.

Chapter Strategy: Word Elements: Numbers and Measures

Chapter Words:

Part 1

uni-	unanimity	*di-, du-*	dilemma
	unilateral		duplicity
mono-	monarchy	*tri-*	trilogy
	monopoly		trivial
bi-	bilingual	*dec-*	decade
	bipartisan		decimate

Part 2

cent-	centennial	*integer*	disintegrate
	centigrade		integrity
ambi-, amphi-	ambiguous	*magn-, mega-*	magnanimous
	ambivalence		magnitude
ann, enn	annals	*meter, -meter*	metric
	perennial		symmetrical

Quiz Yourself

To check your knowledge of some chapter words before you begin to study, identify these statements as true or false. Answers are on page 411.

The **metric** system includes inches.	True	False
Integrity is dishonor.	True	False
Ambiguous directions are clear.	True	False
A **dilemma** is a problem.	True	False

You will learn the answers as you study this chapter.

Did You Know?

How Were the Months of the Year Named?

Did you ever wonder how the months got their names? Ancient calendars were so inaccurate that people often found themselves planting crops when the calendar claimed that winter was approaching. The Roman leader Julius Caesar ordered the calendar reformed about 2,000 years ago, and hence, the months bear Latin names. There have been other changes since then, but even now the calendar is not perfect. We must adjust the length of our years by adding an extra day (February 29) in every fourth, or leap, year.

January gets its name from the god Janus, the doorkeeper of the gate of heaven and the god of doors. Since doors are used to enter, Janus represented beginnings, and the first month of the year is dedicated to him. Janus is pictured with two faces; one looks back to the past year, and one looks forward to the new year.

February comes from Februa, the Roman festival of purification. *March* is named for Mars, the Roman god of war. *April* has an uncertain origin. It may be from *apero,* which means "second," for at one time it was the second month of the year, or from *aperīre* (to open) since it is the month when flowers and trees open out in bloom. *May* comes from the goddess of fertility, Maia. It was natural to name a spring month for the goddess who was thought to control the crops.

June was named either for the Junius family of Roman nobles or for the goddess Juno, wife of Jupiter. Julius Caesar named the month of July after himself. *August* is named for Augustus Caesar, the nephew of Julius and the first emperor of Rome. His actual name was Octavian, but he took the title of *Augustus* because it meant "distinguished." The word *august* still means "distinguished" when the second syllable of the word is stressed.

The last four months all contain number prefixes: *September, sept* (seven); *October, oct* (eight); *November, nov* (nine); *December, dec* (ten). As you can see, the number roots are wrong! How did the ninth, tenth, eleventh, and twelfth months get the elements of seven, eight, nine, and ten?

Until 153 BCE the new year was celebrated in March, so the months corresponded to the correct numbers. Then a change in the calendar left these months with the wrong meanings.

Learning Strategy

Word Elements: Numbers and Measures

Every word element in this chapter has a meaning of number or measurement. A list of the prefixes for the first ten numbers is given below. Although you won't be studying all of them in this chapter, you will find this list a handy reference for textbooks and everyday reading. English uses these number prefixes frequently; in fact, we are still making new words from them.

Prefix	Meaning	Example Word
uni-	one	unidirectional (in one direction)
mono-	one	monologue (speech by one person)
bi-	two	bidirectional (in two directions)
di-, du-	two	diatomic (made up of two atoms)
tri-	three	trio (a musical group of three)
quad-, quar-	four	quartet (a musical group of four)
quint-, quin-	five	quintet (a musical group of five)
sex-	six	sextet (a musical group of six)
sept-	seven	septet (a musical group of seven)
oct-	eight	octet (a musical group of eight)
nov-	nine	novena (a prayer offered for nine days)
dec-	ten	decade (ten years)

*You will study these word elements intensively in this chapter.

To test your understanding of these number word prefixes, fill in the blanks in the following sentences.

a. A duplex is an apartment with **two**_____ floors.

b. A trilingual person speaks **three**_____ languages.

c. A quadruped is an animal that walks on **four**_____ feet.

d. When a mother has quintuplets, **five**_____ children are born.

e. Sextuple means to multiply by **six**_____.

f. A septennial occurs once every **seven**_____ years.

Answers are on page 411.

All the word elements you will study in this chapter are either number prefixes *(uni-, mono-, bi-, di-, tri-, dec-, cent-)* or measurement roots and prefixes *(ambi-, ann, integer, magn-, meter)*.

Element	Meaning	Origin	Function	Chapter Words
Part 1				
uni-	one	Latin	prefix	unanimity, unilateral
mono-	one; single	Greek	prefix	monarchy, monopoly
bi-	two	Latin	prefix	bilingual, bipartisan
di-, du-	two	Greek; Latin	prefix	dilemma, duplicity
tri-	three	Greek; Latin	prefix	trilogy, trivial
dec-	ten	Greek; Latin	prefix	decade, decimate
Part 2				
cent-, centi-	hundred	Latin	prefix	centennial, centigrade
ambi-, amphi-	both; around	Latin; Greek	prefix	ambiguous, ambivalence
ann, enn	year	Latin	root	annals, perennial
integer	whole; complete	Latin	root	disintegrate, integrity
magn-, mega-	large	Latin; Greek	prefix	magnanimous, magnitude
meter, -meter	measure	Greek; Latin	root suffix	metric, symmetrical

This chapter presents a large number of word elements for study, twelve in all. However, the number prefixes follow a clear pattern. They are arranged in order of the numbers they represent, rather than in alphabetical order. The first six are discussed below.

Prefixes

Part 1

uni- (one)

The Latin prefix for one, *uni-*, is used in many English words. To *unite*, for example, is to make several things into **one**. *Unisex* clothing uses **one** design that is suitable for both men and women.

The *unicorn* was a mythical animal of great grace and beauty. Named for its **one** horn, it was supposed to have the legs of a deer, the tail of a lion, and the body of a horse. A speedy runner, it was almost impossible to catch. Since those who drank from its horn were thought to be protected from poison, cups supposedly made from unicorn horns were prized during the Middle Ages. Legends of the unicorn appear in ancient Greece, medieval Europe, India, and the Muslim world.

mono- (one, single)

The Greek prefix for one, *mono-,* is usually joined to Greek combining roots. For example, *monogamy* is marriage to **one** person. A *monologue* is a speech given by **one** person. *Mono-* is also used to form many technical words used in scientific fields.

bi- (two)

The Latin prefix for two, *bi-,* forms words such as *bifocals,* glasses that contain **two** visual corrections. When the *bicycle* was invented in the 1860s, it was named for its **two** wheels.

di-, du- (two)

This Greek prefix for two is often used in scientific and technical words, so you will find it useful in your college courses. For example, the word *dichromatic* refers to animals that change their colors in different seasons and, therefore, have **two** colors.

tri- (three)

A *triangle* is a **three**-sided figure. A *tricornered* hat has a brim turned up on **three** sides. A *tricycle* has **three** wheels.

dec- (ten)

The *decimal* system uses the base **ten.** The common word *dime,* a **tenth** part of a dollar, is also taken from the prefix *dec-.*

Words to Learn

Part 1

uni-

1. **unanimity** (noun)   yōo′nə-nĭm′ĭ-tē

   From Latin: *uni-* (one) + *animus* (soul) (When people agree, they seem to have one soul.)

   complete agreement

   > If jurors in a criminal trial cannot reach **unanimity,** the case must be tried again.

   > In a surprising display of **unanimity,** every city council member voted to ban parking on Main Street.

   ▶ *Related Word*
   unanimous (adjective)   Europeans were not *unanimous* in their decision to adopt the euro.

2. **unilateral** (adjective)   yōo′nə-lăt′ər-əl

   From Latin: *uni-* (one) + *latus* (side)

arbitrary; one sided; relating to only one side or part

> Students and faculty became angry when the dean of student services made a **unilateral** decision to ban cell phone use on campus.

> **Unilateral** contracts require that only one side take action.

mono-

3. **monarchy** (noun)   mŏn'ər-kē   (plural: monarchies)

From Greek: *mono-* (one) + *arkein* (rule)

a state ruled by a king, queen, or emperor

> In 1215, the Magna Carta limited the power of the English **monarchy.**

Monarchs are often shown wearing crowns.

▶ *Related Word*

   monarch (noun)   The official title of the Malaysian *monarch* is "Paramount Ruler."

Although *monarchs* once held absolute power, there are now many constitutional *monarchies,* or governments that limit the power of kings. Bhumibol Adulyadej, constitutional monarch of Thailand (formerly Siam), has provided stable leadership by supporting democratic institutions. He is the world's longest-reigning *monarch.* His ancestors led the way for strong leadership. His grandfather, Chulalongkorn (or Rama V, 1869–1910), abolished slavery and maintained independence from English and French colonialism. His father, Mongkut (1804–1868), had prepared for modernization by welcoming foreigners. The famous play and movie *The King and I* tells the story of an English governess who worked in Mongkut's court.

---

4. **monopoly** (noun)   mə-nŏp′ə-lē

From Greek: *mono-* (single) + *pōlein* (to sell) (When only one company or person can sell something, a monopoly exists.)

exclusive possession or control

   England once held a **monopoly** over the sale of salt in India.

   At the end of World War II, the United States had a **monopoly** on the atomic bomb.

▶ *Related Words*

   monopolistic (adjective)   *Monopolistic* control of an industry generally leads to high prices for the consumer.

   monopolize (verb)   The teenager *monopolized* the family telephone.

bi-

5. **bilingual** (adjective)   bī-lĭng′gwəl

From Latin: *bi-* (two) + *lingua* (tongue, language)

having or speaking two languages

   Children can easily become **bilingual,** but adults have more difficulty learning a second language.

   The **bilingual** prayer book was printed in Hebrew and English.

▶ *Related Word*

   bilingualism (noun)   The growing numbers of Hispanics in the United States make *bilingualism* essential in many professions.

Many people in both Canada and the United States are *bilingual*. Both French and English are official language of Canada. In the United States, the most widely spoken languages, after English, are Spanish, Mandarin Chinese, French, German, Tagalog, Vietnamese, Italian, Korean, Russian, and Polish.

6. **bipartisan** (adjective)   bī-pär′tĭ-zən

From Latin: *bi-* (two) + *pars* (part)

supported by members of two parties

> A hate-crimes bill gained **bipartisan** support from both Democrats and Republicans in the Senate.

di-, du-

7. **dilemma** (noun)   dĭ-lĕm′ə

From Greek: *di-* (two) + *lēmma* (proposition) (A choice between two propositions or alternatives puts us in a *dilemma*.)

problem; difficult choice between equally bad things

> Dorothy faced the **dilemma** of having to drop the course or to flunk it.

8. **duplicity** (noun)   dōō-plĭs′ĭ-tē

From Latin: *du-* (two) + *plicāre* (to fold or complicate) (A person who is involved in duplicity is not straightforward but is "folded in two ways.")

betrayal; deceit; double-dealing

> The spy's **duplicity** was revealed to a shocked nation.
>
> In an act of **duplicity,** Mona's friend taped their private conversations and passed them on to her boyfriend.

▶ *Related Word*
duplicitous (adjective)   The *duplicitous* leader betrayed his allies.

tri-

9. **trilogy** (noun)   trĭl′ə-jē

From Greek: *tri-* (three) + *log* (word; to speak)

a group of three works, such as books, plays, movies, or stories

> The famous book **trilogy** *Lord of the Rings* led to a successful film **trilogy.**

10. **trivial** (adjective)   trĭv′ē-əl

From Latin: *tri-* (three) + *via* (road) (In Latin, *trivium* meant "where three roads meet," the public square where people would gossip.)

unimportant; silly

> Fashion is a **trivial** topic when compared to world peace.
>
> The teenager's fight with a friend upset her, but seemed **trivial** to her parents.

ordinary; commonplace;

> Changing a car's oil is a **trivial** task for most car mechanics.
>
> Dusting the shelves seemed a **trivial** task to the bored waitress.

▶ *Related Words*

   trivia (noun)   Many TV game shows require contestants to know a lot of *trivia*. (*Trivia* is unimportant information.)

   trivialize (verb)   A focus on gifts and parties can *trivialize* the religious meaning of Christmas.

NOTE: The "ordinary, commonplace" meaning of *trivial,* often also connotes "easy": "It is *trivial* for a Ph.D. in math to add two numbers in her head."

dec-

11. **decade** (noun)   dĕk′ād′

From Greek: *dec-* (ten) (*Dekas* meant "group of ten.")

a ten-year period

> The **decade** of the 1960s is known for social and political protest.
>
> Because he had to support a family, it took Mr. Markman almost a **decade** to complete his college degree.

12. **decimate** (verb)   dĕs′ə-māt′

From Latin: *dec-* (ten) (*Decimāre* meant "to take the tenth." This was the severe practice of killing every tenth soldier, chosen by lot, in order to punish a mutiny.)

to destroy or kill a large part of

> Introduced accidentally through imports, the Asian longhorn beetle has **decimated** trees in some U.S. urban areas.
>
> Hailstones **decimated** the farmer's crop.

▶ *Related Word*

   decimation (noun)   The Japanese rebuilt Hiroshima after its *decimation* by an atomic bomb in World War II.

Exercises

Part 1

■ Definitions

Match each word in the left-hand column with a definition from the right-hand column. Use each choice only once.

1. bipartisan __e__

2. duplicity __b__

3. bilingual __d__

4. unanimity __g__

5. decimate __i__

6. trilogy __h__

7. trivial __c__

8. unilateral __a__

9. monarchy __l__

10. dilemma __k__

a. arbitrary

b. deceit

c. unimportant

d. speaking two languages

e. supported by both sides

f. ten-year period

g. complete agreement

h. three books or plays

i. to destroy most of something

j. control by one person or company

k. problem

l. a state ruled by a king or queen

■ Meanings

Match each word element to its meaning. Two of the choices in the right-hand column should be used twice.

1. bi- __d__

2. mono- __c__

3. dec- __a__

4. uni- __c__

5. tri- __b__

6. di- __d__

a. ten

b. three

c. one

d. two

■ *Words in Context*

Complete each sentence with the word that fits best. Use each choice only once.

a. unanimity   e. bilingual   i. trilogy
b. unilateral   f. bipartisan   j. trivial
c. monarch   g. dilemma   k. decade
d. monopoly   h. duplicity   l. decimate

1. One famous film **i, trilogy** _____ consists of *Star Wars, The Empire Strikes Back,* and *Return of the Jedi.*

2. Since people are different, things that seem **j, trivial** _____ to some may be important to others.

3. One **c, monarch** _____, Henry VIII, who ruled England in the 1500s, declared himself head of the church.

4. The government of Japan once had a(n) **d, monopoly** _____ on tobacco and, thus, full control of cigarette sales.

5. The **k, decade** _____ between 1970 and 1980 has been called the "Me Decade."

6. The **e, bilingual** _____ book is printed in English on one side and Spanish on the other.

7. By their 9–0 vote, the Supreme Court members showed their **a, unanimity** _____ in declaring school segregation unconstitutional in the 1954 case *Brown* v. *Board of Education.*

8. Lubna faced the **g, dilemma** _____ of living in poverty or going to an unfamiliar country.

9. Without asking for advice, the general made a(n) **b, unilateral** _____ decision to attack.

10. Betraying a good friend is an act of **h, duplicity** _____.

■ *Using Related Words*

Complete each sentence by using a word from the group of related words above it. Use each choice only once.

THE LIFE OF JULIUS CAESAR

1. unanimity, unanimous

   Historians are **unanimous**　　　　　in considering Julius Caesar one of the towering figures of history. His conquests, his reforms in government, his intelligence, and his wonderful writing all

   contribute to this **unanimity**　　　　　of opinion.

2. decimation, decimated

   Born in about 100 BCE, Caesar came from a poor but noble family. As he rose in leadership, he conquered other lands. He attacked

   and **decimated**　　　　　forces in Gaul (now Belgium and France). He also invaded England and, although his forces did not

   inflict the same **decimation**　　　　　there, they established a Roman base that lasted hundreds of years.

3. monopolize, monopoly

   A decade of conquest gained Caesar considerable political power. He formed a ruling triumvirate with Crassus and Pompey. When Crassus died, despite the fact that Pompey had married Caesar's daughter, Caesar and Pompey became rivals. It seemed that one of

   them was destined to **monopolize**　　　　　power. After some hesitation, Caesar attacked Pompey. Caesar's victory gave him a

   monopoly　　　　　on Roman power.

4. trivialize, trivial

   As ruler, Caesar made many reforms. He extended Roman citizenship to everyone in Italy. He improved the conditions of Roman farmers. He even replaced an inaccurate calendar with the "Julian" calendar, still used today. In a somewhat more

   trivial　　　　　action, he named the month of July after

himself. However, his romance with the Egyptian queen Cleopatra angered Romans. While this may seem unimportant, we should

not **trivialize**_____ Cleopatra's influence on historical events.

5. monarch, monarchy

As Caesar became ever more powerful, Romans feared that he

would declare himself a **monarch**_____. With their tradition of noblemen ruling in the Senate, Romans resented the idea of a

monarchy_____. Led by Cassius, several senators plotted to murder Caesar on the ides of March. When Caesar entered the Senate, they attacked him. Caesar resisted until he realized that his friend Brutus had turned against him. "Et tu, Brute?" (You too, Brutus?), he cried as he died. A few years later, Caesar's nephew Octavian became the first Roman emperor.

■ *Reading the Headlines*

This exercise presents five headlines that might appear in newspapers. Read each headline and then answer the questions that follow. (Remember that small words, such as *is, are, a,* and *the,* are often left out of newspaper headlines.)

DUPLICITY OF GENERAL LEADS TO DECIMATION OF TROOPS

1. Was the general an honorable man? **no**_____

2. Did troops die? **yes**_____

BIPARTISAN SUPPORT SHOWN FOR BREAKING UP A DECADE OF GOVERNMENT MONOPOLY ON SALES OF LIQUOR

3. Did only one party support this? **no**_____

4. Did many businesses control the sale of liquor? **no**_____

IN UNILATERAL DECISION, DEPARTMENT HEAD CUTS BILINGUAL PROGRAMS

5. Did the department head consult others? **no**_____

6. Will there be more education in two languages? **no**_____

**LOCAL GOVERNMENTS DISPLAY UNANIMITY ON METHODS
OF DEALING WITH DILEMMA OF ILLEGAL DRUG SALES**

7. Do the local governments agree? **yes**

8. Is the problem easy to solve? **no**

**WELL-KNOWN AUTHOR'S TRILOGY REQUIRED DECADE
OF EFFORT**

9. Did the author write four works? **no**

10. Did the trilogy take twenty years to write? **no**

Word Elements

Part 2

Part 2 presents the last number prefix, *cent-,* as well as five roots and prefixes that refer to quantities.

cent- (one hundred)
   The prefix *cent-* is used in many common words. A *century* is a period of **one hundred** years. A *cent* is a coin worth **one-hundredth** of a dollar.

Thanks to medical advances, more than 60,000 people in the United States are *centenarians,* or people **one hundred** years old or older. By 2060, the number of *centenarians* is expected to increase to 2.5 million.

---

ambi-, amphi- (both; around)
   These prefixes have two meanings. The meaning of "both" occurs in the word *ambidextrous,* meaning "able to use **both** hands." The meaning of "around" is found in *amphitheater,* a theater with seats on all sides of, or **around,** the stage. This prefix comes from ancient Greek and Latin: *amphi-* is the Greek form; *ambi-* is the Latin form.

The common word *ambitious* is derived from the Latin verb *ambīre* (to go around). In ancient Rome, an ambitious person was a candidate who "went around" asking people to vote for him. Now, of course, an ambitious person is one who desires achievement.

ann, enn (year)

An *annual* event occurs every **year.** At times, *ann* is spelled *enn,* as in the word *perennial.*

integer (whole; complete)

This root can refer to numbers, as in the English word *integer,* which means a **whole** number without a fraction value. Thus, 3 is an integer, but 3.5 is not. In Latin, *integer* also describes a "**whole**" person, who does not have serious character flaws. Such a person is said to have *integrity.*

magn-, mega- (large)

To *magnify* something is to make it **larger.** Books have been written about *megatrends,* meaning **large** trends in society. A *megalopolis* is a region including several **large** cities. *Magn-* is the Latin spelling; *mega-* is the Greek spelling.

meter, -meter (measure)

This element often appears as a root but can also be used as a suffix. One word using *meter* as a root is *metronome,* an instrument for **measuring** musical time. The element *-meter* is used as a suffix in the words *thermometer,* an instrument for **measuring** heat, and *speedometer,* an instrument for **measuring** speed.

Words to Learn

Part 2

cent-

13. **centennial** (noun)   sĕn-tĕn′e-əl

    From Latin: *cent-* (one hundred) + *ann* (year)

    one-hundred-year anniversary; a period of one hundred years

    > The year 2003 marked the **centennial** of the first airplane flight by Orville and Wilbur Wright.

The Roman numeral C meant one hundred. Today, the cent sign—¢—
and the abbreviation for century—C—remind us that the root *cent*
means one hundred.

---

14. **centigrade** (adjective)   sĕn′tĭ-grād′

From Latin: *centi-* (one hundred) + *gradus* (step)

referring to a temperature scale based on one hundred degrees

> In the **centigrade** scale, 0 degrees marks the freezing point of
> water and 100 degrees marks its boiling point.

> Many signs now display outdoor temperatures in both the **centi-
> grade** and Fahrenheit scales.

The *centigrade scale* is also referred to as *Celsius* in honor of its origina-
tor, Anders Celsius. The Fahrenheit scale was named for its inventor,
Daniel Fahrenheit.

---

ambi-, amphi-

15. **ambiguous** (adjective)   ăm-bĭg′yōo-əs

From Latin: *ambi-* (around) + *agere* (to lead) (When something is
ambiguous, two meanings are equally possible, and a person is led
around rather than "straight toward" the meaning.)

not clear; having two or more meanings

> The **ambiguous** test item was difficult to answer.

▶ *Related Word*
  ambiguity   (noun)   (ăm′bĭ-gyōo′ĭ-tē)   The   *ambiguities*
  in U.S. copyright laws make them difficult to follow
  precisely.

16. **ambivalence** (noun)   ăm-bĭv′ə-ləns

From Latin: *ambi-* (both) + *valēre* (to be strong) (A person who is
ambivalent about something has two equally strong feelings about it.)

existence of mixed or conflicting feelings

> The child felt **ambivalence** toward the roller-coaster ride, which
> inspired both excitement and fear.

► *Common Phrases*
    feel ambivalent toward; feel ambivalent about

► *Related Word*
    ambivalent (adjective)   Sonya and Herman felt *ambivalent* about having children.

ann, enn

17. **annals** (noun)   ăn'əlz

From Latin: *ann* (year) (*Annālis* meant "yearly." Written *annals* are often divided by years.)

a written record of events

> Inspiring speeches are recorded in the **annals** of the U.S. Congress.

general records

> Italian explorers famous in the **annals** of American history include Christopher Columbus, Giovanni Caboto (John Cabot), Giovanni da Verrazano, and Giacomo Beltrami.

> Will any of today's political leaders be considered great in the **annals** of history?

18. **perennial** (adjective)   pə-rĕn'ē-əl

From Latin: *per-* (through) + *ann* (year)

occurring again and again; constant; lasting for a long time

> Homelessness persists as a **perennial** problem in urban areas.
> Dr. Seuss's *The Cat in the Hat* is a **perennial** children's favorite.
> **Perennial** flowers bloom year after year without having to be replanted.

integer

19. **disintegrate** (verb)   dĭs-ĭn'tĭ-grāt'

From Latin: *dis-* (apart) + *integer* (whole) (When something disintegrates, it becomes "not whole," or falls apart.)

to separate into small parts

> In a terrible tragedy, the space shuttle *Columbia*, with astronauts on board, **disintegrated** when it reentered Earth's atmosphere.
> Paper will **disintegrate** into powder if it becomes too dry.

to become worse; to go wrong

> The happy family party **disintegrated** into an argument.

▶ *Common Phrase*
disintegrate into

▶ *Related Word*
disintegration (noun)   My grandmother blames computers and TV for the *disintegration* of family life.

More than 4,600 years ago, a man froze to death in the Alps. His remains were saved from *disintegration* by the cold, and they mummified. Warmed by furs stuffed with grass, the Otzi, as he was named, had tattoos and may have worn an earring.

---

20. **integrity** (noun)   ĭn-tĕg′rĭ-tē

From Latin: *integer* (whole)

honesty; good moral character

> A person of **integrity** would not cheat on an exam.

> We expect that judges will act with **integrity.**

wholeness; completeness

> Earthquakes can cause cracks in foundations and affect a building's **integrity.**

A passenger left a bag in the trunk of Mohammed Hussain's taxi. A few days later, Hussain found the bag while cleaning the car. To his amazement, it contained a collection of precious jewels. As a man of *integrity*, Hussain notified the police, and they returned the jewels to their owner, who rewarded Hussain with a check and a pair of earrings for his mother.

---

magn-, mega-

21. **magnanimous** (adjective)   măg-năn′əm-məs

From Latin: *magn-* (great) + *animus* (soul)

noble; above revenge or resentment; forgiving of insults

> **Magnanimous** New York detective Stephen MacDonald publicly forgave the man who shot and paralyzed him in 1986.

The victor in the presidential race was **magnanimous** toward his defeated rival.

▶ *Common Phrase*
magnanimous toward

▶ *Related Word*
magnanimity (noun)   (măg′nə-nĭm′ĭ-tē)   Nelson Mandela demonstrated *magnanimity* by cooperating with the white South Africans who had imprisoned him.

22. **magnitude** (noun)   măg′nĭ-tōōd′

From Latin: *magn-* (great)   (*Magnitūdō* meant "greatness.")

greatness of size or importance

It is impossible to imagine the **magnitude** of the universe.

The problem of AIDS has grown in **magnitude.**

▶ *Common Phrase*
magnitude of

NOTE: Magnitude can also refer to the brightness of stars.

meter, -meter

23. **metric** (adjective, noun)   mĕt′rĭk

From Greek: *meter* (measure)

referring to a measurement system based on grams and meters (adjective)

The **metric** system measures distance in kilometers rather than miles.

The *metric* system is easier to use than the U.S. system of pounds and feet. Whereas the U.S. system is based on numbers like 16 (number of ounces in a pound) and 5,280 (number of feet in a mile), the metric system is a decimal system based on multiples of 10. Most countries use the metric system, but the United States has delayed conversion several times. Common metric measures include centimeters, meters, kilometers, grams, and kilograms. (Kilo means 1,000.) There are also *metric* tons.

---

24. **symmetrical** (adjective)   sĭ-mĕt′rĭ-kəl

From Greek: *sym* (same) + *meter* (measure) (Things that "measure the same" are balanced, or symmetrical.)

balanced in physical size or form

> Because there are slight differences between the left and right sides of the human body, it is not perfectly **symmetrical.**

▶ *Related Word*
symmetry (noun)   (sĭm′ə-trē)   The Japanese breed the koi fish for the *symmetry* of patterns decorating their bodies.

When something is **symmetrical,** you can put a line through the center of it and both halves will be just the same. However, the ancient Greeks believed a rectangle of certain proportions to be more beautifully *symmetrical* than other shapes. The shape, called the "Golden Section," looked like this:

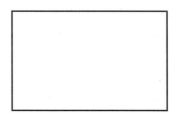

Exercises

Part 2

■ *Definitions*

Match each word in the left-hand column with a definition from the right-hand column. Use each choice only once.

1. metric ___**g**___

2. magnitude ___**d**___

3. integrity ___**i**___

4. annals ___**c**___

a. hundred-year anniversary

b. existence of mixed feelings

c. written records

d. greatness of size or importance

5. centigrade __f__   e. not clear

6. perennial __j__   f. referring to a temperature scale

7. disintegrate __k__   g. a system of measurement
                              using grams
8. magnanimous __l__
                           h. balanced
9. centennial __a__
                           i. honesty
10. ambiguous __e__
                           j. lasting a long time

                           k. to fall apart

                           l. noble

■ Meanings

Match each word element to its meaning. Use each choice only once.

1. cent-__b__   a. measure

2. integer __f__   b. hundred

3. ambi-, amphi-__c__   c. both; around

4. meter, -meter __a__   d. large

5. ann, enn __e__   e. year

6. magn-, mega-__d__   f. whole

■ Words in Context

Complete each sentence with the word that fits best. Use each choice only once.

a. centennial   e. annals   i. magnanimous
b. centigrade   f. perennial   j. magnitude
c. ambiguous   g. disintegrate k. metric
d. ambivalent   h. integrity   l. symmetrical

1. Because of the __j, magnitude__ of his achievements in medicine, the physician was awarded the Nobel Prize.

2. The __e, annals__ of history record Julius Caesar as a great
   ruler.

3. Since Anne parted her hair in the middle and kept both sides the same length, her haircut was **l, symmetrical** _____.

4. Arizona was admitted to the United States in 1912 and will celebrate its **a, centennial** _____ in 2012.

5. Countries that use the metric system measure temperature with the **b, centigrade** _____ scale.

6. An aspirin that is left in a glass of water will soon **g, disintegrate** _____.

7. Because of **c, ambiguous** _____ instructions, we could not tell exactly how to install the software.

8. A person of great **h, integrity** _____ can be easily trusted.

9. Since weeds are a(n) **f, perennial** _____ problem, people must constantly care for their gardens.

10. Doris felt **d, ambivalent** _____ toward her difficult yet helpful mother-in-law.

■ *Using Related Words*

Complete each sentence by using a word from the group of related words above it. Use each choice only once.

1. disintegration, disintegrate, disintegrates

   Would you like to keep your great-grandmother's precious letters from **disintegration** _____? If they were written after 1850, it may be difficult. Before 1850, paper was made of rags. After that time, it has been made of free pulp that **disintegrates** _____ rapidly. The acidity of paper makes it **disintegrate** _____, but an alkaline spray can stop further damage.

2. ambivalent, ambivalence

The U.S. public remains **ambivalent**＿＿＿ about the death penalty. People are increasingly disturbed about wrongful convictions. Witnesses who withdrew their testimony and DNA analysis have resulted in freedom for hundreds of prisoners awaiting

execution. This **ambivalence**＿＿＿ toward the death penalty has often been reflected in U.S. polls.

3. ambiguity, ambiguous

The use of plants, natural light, and glass walls and ceilings in public spaces such as hotels and office buildings creates visual

ambiguity＿＿＿ between the indoors and outdoors. Such

ambiguous＿＿＿ visual clues may create an odd perception of being both indoors and outdoors at the same time.

4. symmetry, symmetrically

The ancient Greeks produced some of the world's greatest architects. In Athens, the Parthenon, a temple dedicated to the goddess Athena, stands as a great architectural achievement. The temple features a series of decorated columns that are arranged

symmetrically＿＿＿. Greek architects often used such

symmetry＿＿＿ in their designs.

5. magnanimous, magnanimity

The great baseball player Lou Gehrig remained

magnanimous＿＿＿ even when illness forced him to retire at age thirty-five. In a farewell speech at Yankee Stadium, he

displayed **magnanimity**＿＿＿ rather than bitterness when he said, "Today I am the luckiest man in the world." He died two years later of ALS, now also called Lou Gehrig's disease.

■ *Reading the Headlines*

This exercise presents five headlines that might appear in newspapers. Read each headline and then answer the questions that follow. (Remember that small words, such as *is, are, a,* and *the,* are often left out of newspaper headlines.)

ALLIANCE DISINTEGRATES AFTER INTEGRITY OF LEADER IS QUESTIONED

1. Is there still an alliance? __no__

2. Is the honesty of the leader being questioned? __yes__

MAGNANIMOUS LEADER FORGIVES INSULT OF CONSIDERABLE MAGNITUDE

3. Is the leader noble? __yes__

4. Was the insult small? __no__

AFTER TAKING METRIC MEASUREMENTS, ARCHITECTURAL PANEL GIVES AMBIGUOUS RULING ON BUILDING'S LACK OF SYMMETRY

5. Were the measurements taken in inches and feet?

   __no__

6. Does the ruling concern the balance of the building?

   __yes__

CONVERSION TO CENTIGRADE SCALE A PERENNIAL ISSUE FOR AMBIVALENT U.S. PUBLIC

7. Is the issue a long-term one? __yes__

8. Is the U.S. public undecided? __yes__

STATE ANNALS REVEAL NO CELEBRATION OF CALIFORNIA CENTENNIAL

9. Does the state keep records? __yes__

10. Did the period of time concern ten years? __no__

Chapter Exercises

■ *Practicing Strategies: New Words from Word Elements*

See how your knowledge of word elements can help you understand new words. Complete each sentence with the word that seems to fit best. Use each choice only once.

a. amphibious   e. dioxide   i. monorail
b. bipolar   f. integrate   j. photometer
c. centimeter   g. magnify   k. trimester
d. decalogue   h. monodrama   l. uniform

1. A play performed by one person is called a(n) **h, monodrama** .

2. A(n) **e, dioxide** molecule has two oxygen molecules.

3. A(n) **a, amphibious** aircraft can land on both land and water.

4. The Ten Commandments are often called the **d, decalogue** .

5. A(n) **k, trimester** system divides the academic year into three terms.

6. Since "photo" means light, a(n) **j, photometer** measures light.

7. If you **g, magnify** something, you make it bigger.

8. In a(n) **b, bipolar** disorder, people swing between two different mood states.

9. If you **f, integrate** one thing with another, you form them into a whole.

10. Things that are **l, uniform** all have the same, or one, appearance.

■ *Practicing Strategies: Combining Context Clues and Word Elements*

Combining the strategies of context clues and word elements is a good way to figure out the meaning of unknown words. In the following sentences, each italicized word contains a word element that you have studied in this chapter. Using the meaning of the word element and the context of the sentence, make an intelligent guess about the meaning of the italicized word. Your instructor may ask you to check the meaning in your dictionary when you have finished.

1. The Jewish religion became the first to practice *monotheism* and reject the worship of many gods.

   Monotheism means <u>**the worship of one god**</u>.

2. My mother now wears *trifocals* to help adjust her vision to different distances.

   Trifocals means <u>**glasses with three separate corrections**</u>.

3. After we counted the sides of the figure, we determined that it was a *decagon*.

   Decagon means <u>**figure with ten sides**</u>.

4. The gracious room, beautiful furniture, and pleasant music all contributed to the *ambience* of the restaurant.

   Ambience means <u>**atmosphere; surroundings**</u>.

5. The *megahit* movie was in first place for six months.

   Megahit means <u>**huge success; huge hit**</u>.

■ *Practicing Strategies: Using the Dictionary*

Read the following definition and then answer the questions below it.

> **crunch** (krŭnch) *v.* **crunched, crunch•ing, crunch•es** —*tr.*
> **1.** To chew with a noisy crackling sound.   **2.** To crush, grind, or tread noisily.   **3.** *Slang* To perform operations on; manipulate or process (numerical or mathematical data). —*intr.* **1.** To chew noisily with a crackling sound.   **2.** To move with a crushing sound.   **3.** To produce or emit a crushing sound. ❖ *n.* **1.** The act or sound of crunching.   **2a.** A decisive confrontation.   **b.** A critical moment or situation.   **3.** A sit-up having a small range of motion that reduces back strain. [Alteration of *craunch*, poss. of imit. orig.] —**crunch′a•ble** *adj.*

1. What is the adjective form of *crunch*? <u>**crunchable**</u>

   What is the part of speech and definition number that best fits each of the following sentences?

2. I did fifty *crunches* each morning after running two miles.
   noun, 3 _____

3. Because our state has a deficit we have a *crunch* in finances.
   noun, 2b _____

4. The machine *crunched* the stone to sand. **transitive verb, 2** _____

5. I *crunched* across the gravel-covered road. **intransitive verb, 2** _____

■ *Companion Words*

Complete each sentence with the word that fits best. Choose your answers from the words below. You may use each word more than once.

Choices: of, toward, into, about

1. Raj felt ambivalent **toward, about** _____ the difficult but worthwhile course.

2. The winners were magnanimous **toward, about** _____ the losers.

3. We were amazed by the magnitude **of** _____ the state of Texas.

4. The meeting disintegrated **into** _____ a shouting match.

■ *Writing with Your Words*

This exercise will give you practice in writing effective sentences that use the vocabulary words. Each sentence is started for you. Complete it with an interesting phrase that indicates the meaning of the italicized word.

1. One example of a *trivial* problem is _____

   _____.

2. He showed his *duplicity* by _____

   _____.

3. A *bilingual* person _____

   _____.

4. The *magnanimous* champion _____

_____.

5. One issue needing *bipartisan* support is _____

_____.

6. If I ever celebrate the *centennial* of my birth, _____

_____.

7. One *perennial* concern of society is _____

_____.

8. There is *unanimous* agreement that _____

_____.

9. A *bipartisan* organization differs from a nonpartisan one in that

_____.

10. Converting to the *metric* system would _____

_____.

■ *Making Connections*

These questions will help you relate the words you have learned in this chapter to your own life. Answer each question by writing a paragraph or more on a separate sheet of paper.

1. Describe a *dilemma* you have faced.

2. Describe an issue you feel *ambivalent* about.

3. What are your hopes and dreams for the next *decade*?

Passage

Cleopatra—The Last Pharaoh

This fascinating Egyptian queen has captured our imagination for thousands of years. Who was she? A beautiful temptress who fascinated men? A tragic victim of war? A brilliant ruler playing greater powers off against each other?

(1) The great Egyptian **monarch** Cleopatra is a source of endless fascination. The **annals** of history record her great romances, her personal triumphs, and her final tragedy. At a time when few women held public power, she ruled Egypt for more than two **decades.**

(2) Cleopatra's appearance is a topic of **perennial** debate. Love affairs with two of the era's most powerful men suggest she was a great beauty. **(3)** Certainly she did not consider her appearance a **trivial** matter.

Meticulous about her looks, she carefully chose jewelry and makeup, and indulged in daily goat milk baths. So it surprises history lovers to learn that Cleopatra was rather ordinary looking. She attracted men with two qualities more important than appearance: intelligence and charm.

Cleopatra grew up as one of many children of Ptolemy XII, pharaoh of Egypt. Although the family had ruled Egypt for hundreds of years, they were Macedonian and had not one drop of Egyptian blood! **(4)** More than **bilingual,** the highly intelligent Cleopatra spoke nine different languages. In fact, she was the first Ptolemy to speak Egyptian. She also excelled at mathematics and business.

When Ptolemy XII died, he willed the throne to Cleopatra and her younger brother, Ptolemy XIII. Egyptian custom required the brother and sister to marry, although historians doubt that they shared a typical marriage. Soon after becoming queen at age seventeen, Cleopatra **(5)** began to make **unilateral** decisions. Ignoring her brother, she signed documents alone and issued coins with her image, but not his. Her taste for ruling alone soon caused open conflict with him.

In Cleopatra's times, the power of Rome was increasing in **magnitude** as the Romans conquered more and more lands. **(6)** The status of independent countries such as Egypt was **disintegrating.** In order for independent **monarchs** to stay in power, they had to please the Romans. When newly victorious Roman Julius Caesar landed on the shores of Egypt, Cleopatra wanted desperately to win his favor.

Legend has it that Cleopatra had herself rolled into a carpet and delivered to Caesar. She charmed him so thoroughly that by the time her brother visited Caesar the next day, Cleopatra and Caesar were already lovers. Not surprisingly, Caesar allowed Cleopatra a **monopoly** on power in Egypt. The romance continued, and they had a son. When Cleopatra visited Rome, Caesar had a golden statue built to honor her. However, the Romans hated Cleopatra's hold over Caesar, and after Roman leaders assassinated Caesar, Cleopatra withdrew to Egypt.

What would she do now? Cleopatra bet on Mark Antony, the new ruler of the eastern third of the Roman territory. When he sent for the Egyptian queen, she saw a second chance for control over a powerful Roman. To make him desire her, she delayed her visit. Then, when he sent for her again, she came in a luxurious boat loaded with gifts. Soon the two were lovers.

But Antony had to contend with his fellow rulers. He met with young Octavian and concluded a treaty. According to the agreement, Antony had to marry Octavian's beautiful sister Octavia and rule from Greece. However, Antony soon divorced Octavia, returned to Egypt, and married Cleopatra. She hoped that their three children would one day rule Rome.

Some have said that the ambitious **(7)** Cleopatra had **ambivalent** feelings toward Antony. She recognized his instability and idleness. To keep a hold on him, she encouraged his bad habits, but perhaps she grew disgusted. Although the historical record is **ambiguous,** Cleopatra may have made important mistakes. She may even have betrayed her lover.

Enraged by Antony's rejection of his sister, Octavian revealed to the Roman people that Antony intended to make Cleopatra and her children rulers. The horrified Romans encouraged Octavian to attack Antony and Cleopatra. At Actium, near Greece, 400 of Antony and Cleopatra's ships met an equal fleet of Octavian's. As the battle raged, it seems Cleopatra and Antony fled to Egypt. Or perhaps Cleopatra fled first, betraying Antony, and he followed her. In any case, **(8)** their forces were **decimated.**

Octavian pursued the couple, and **(9)** Cleopatra may have performed a terrible act of **duplicity** to bring about Antony's death. Enclosing herself in a tomb, it is said that she spread word that she was dead. In grief, Antony ran a sword through his body. Then, learning that she still lived, he asked to be taken to Cleopatra. He is said to have died in her arms, advising her to make peace with Octavian.

(10) With an unsurprising lack of **integrity,** Cleopatra then offered herself to Octavian. But he rejected her and told her she would be treated as a captive. Despairing, Cleopatra killed herself by holding an asp—an Egyptian cobra—to her body.

Historians disagree about Cleopatra. Was she beautiful or ordinary? Did she betray Antony? How did she die? But there seems to be **unanimity** on one thing: this last pharaoh and her tragic end have given history one of its most extraordinary figures.

■ *Exercise*

Each numbered sentence below corresponds to a sentence in the Passage. Fill in the letter of the choice that makes the sentence mean the same thing as its corresponding sentence in the Passage.

1. The great Egyptian __**b**__, Cleopatra, is a source of fascination.
   a. woman   b. queen   c. president   d. betrayer

2. Cleopatra's beauty is a topic of __**c**__ debate.
   a. very bitter   b. not very interesting   c. long-lasting   d. historical

3. Physical appearance was not a(n) __**d**__ matter.
   a. interesting   b. time-consuming   c. worthy   d. unimportant

4. Cleopatra was more than __**b**__.
   a. a speaker of one language   b. a speaker of two languages
   c. a speaker of three languages   d. a speaker of four languages

5. She began to make __**a**__ decisions.
   a. one-sided   b. kingly   c. unified   d. constant

6. The status of independent countries was ___c___.
   a. improving quickly   b. becoming dependent   c. getting worse
   d. becoming dangerous

7. Cleopatra may have had ___c___ feelings toward Antony.
   a. powerful   b. deceitful   c. conflicting   d. dying

8. Antony and Cleopatra's forces were ___d___.
   a. aided   b. victorious   c. abandoned   d. defeated

9. Cleopatra may have performed an act of ___b___.
   a. power   b. betrayal   c. despair   d. defeat

10. Cleopatra had a lack of ___a___.
    a. honor   b. charm   c. hope   d. options

■ *Discussion Questions*

1. It is said that Cleopatra backed two losers. Explain why this is true.

2. What attractions apart from beauty, charm, and intelligence did Cleopatra have for men?

3. Do you think that Cleopatra was justified in doing what she did in order to protect her monarchy? Why or why not?

◆ ENGLISH IDIOMS

Money

Since numbers and measures are used to describe money, the idioms for this chapter concern wealth and poverty. A person without any money is referred to as *broke*. To lose all your money is to *lose your shirt*. Not to have enough money is to be *caught short*. People who have been cheated out of money have been *taken to the cleaners* or *ripped off*. Such people may be forced to *live from hand to mouth,* with just enough to cover only their immediate needs.

When a person quickly goes from poverty to wealth, he or she goes *from rags to riches*. That person has a lot of money, or is *in the money*. A rich person might *live high on the hog* spending money freely and buying the best of everything. We might say that the person is *on easy street*.

A rich man or woman who refuses to spend money is often called a *cheapskate*. Kate Robinson inherited $5 million from her parents but spent only about $80 per year. When she died in 1920, her furniture was stuffed with money. Since then, anybody who has money, but will not spend it, has been called *Cheap Kate* or, in more modern English, a *cheapskate*.

CHAPTER

10

Word Elements: Thought and Belief

Our ability to think and our system of beliefs help to define us as human beings. Not surprisingly, English has many words for these mental activities. Part 1 of this chapter presents word elements related to thought and belief. Part 2 presents prefixes we use when we do *not* believe something; these are prefixes of negation. Finally, several idioms will be discussed in this chapter. An idiom carries a different meaning from what we believe it to have when we first hear it.

Chapter Strategy: Word Elements: Thought and Belief

Chapter Words

Part 1

cred	credibility	*ver*	veracity
	creed		verify
	incredulity		veritable
fid	defiant	*-phobia*	acrophobia
	fidelity		claustrophobia
	fiduciary		xenophobia

Part 2

de-	delude	*Idioms*	behind the eight ball
	destitute		give carte blanche
	deviate		hold out an olive branch
non-	nonchalant		leave no stone unturned
	nondenominational		star-crossed
	nondescript		tongue-in-cheek

314

Quiz Yourself

To check your knowledge of some chapter words before you begin to study, identify these statements as true or false. Answers are on page 411.

Veracity is truth.	True	False
A **defiant** person obeys orders.	True	False
A **claustrophobic** person fears closed-in spaces.	True	False
Star-crossed people are lucky	True	False

You will learn the answers as you study this chapter.

Did You Know?

Animal Words of Thought and Belief

For thousands of years, animals have played an important part in human beliefs. Primitive human beings tried to give themselves the powers of the animal world. To acquire the speed of a jaguar or the power of a lion, humans dressed up in the animals' skins and imitated their cries and movements. These customs have contributed words to modern English. The feared ancient warriors of what is now Norway covered themselves in bear *(ber)* skin shirts *(serkr)* and rushed madly into battle, attacking all in sight. From this custom, we derive the phrase *to go berserk,* or crazy.

Many great civilizations worshiped animal gods. In ancient Egypt, the goddess Taurt was thought to have the head of a hippo, the back and tail of a crocodile, and the claws of a lioness. In some parts of Egypt, people worshiped cats, crocodiles, and baboons. These animals have been found carefully preserved as mummies in special cemeteries.

Some animals retain important positions in modern religions. Traditional Hindus hold one type of cow, the East Indian humped zebu, to be sacred. Since these cows symbolize riches given by the gods, Hindus are forbidden to kill these animals or even control them. The cow has come to be identified as a national symbol of India. Such beliefs have resulted in the English expression *sacred cow,* meaning a belief that is so well established that it cannot be challenged.

More than 2,000 years ago, the ancient Jews chose one goat to symbolize people's sins against God. This goat was released into the desert wilderness, symbolically carrying sins away with it. Although this custom has vanished, the English word *scapegoat* still means someone who takes the blame for another.

The creation of animal idioms remains a strong trend in modern English. Many modern expressions use animal actions for human behavior. For example, to *parrot* means to repeat, as a parrot repeats familiar words. To *horse around* means to play, as horses do in a field. A man who is nagged by his wife is called *henpecked,* recalling the behavior of female chickens. When we do something wonderful, we may *crow* about it. We may *eat like pigs* (greedily) or disappoint our host by *eating like birds* (eating little). The generally bad reputation of the rat has given us the phrase *to rat on,* meaning to turn someone in, or "squeal" on someone.

Can you identify the human meanings given to these common animal expressions?

1. catty

2. birdbrain

3. lionize

4. a dinosaur

5. a can of worms

6. puppy love

7. hogwash

Answers are on page 411.

Learning Strategy

Word Elements: Thought and Belief

The first part of this chapter concentrates on word elements relating to thought and belief. Three roots are presented: *cred* (believe), *fid* (faith), and *ver* (truth). Part 1 also introduces the suffix *-phobia* (fear of). Part 2 of this chapter presents two important prefixes with negative meanings. We use them when we do *not* believe in something. *Non* means "not." *De-* also has a negative sense, indicating "to remove from" or "down."

Element	Meaning	Origin	Function	Chapter Words
Part 1				
cred	believe	Latin	root	credibility, creed, incredulity
fid	faith	Latin	root	defiant, fidelity, fiduciary
ver	truth	Latin	root	veracity, verify, veritable
-phobia	fear of	Greek	suffix	acrophobia, claustrophobia, xenophobia
Part 2				
de-	to remove from; down	Latin	prefix	delude, destitute, deviate
non-	not	Latin	prefix	nonchalant, nondenominational, nondescript

Word Elements

Part 1

Information on the roots and the suffix for Part 1 is presented below.

cred (believe)

The root *cred* is used in many English words. When we do not **believe** something, we may call it *incredible. Credit* is granted to a customer because merchants **believe** that they will be paid. The concept of a *credit card* is also based upon **belief.**

fid (faith)

The English word *faith* is taken from this root. Because dogs are thought to be **faithful** companions to human beings, they have traditionally been given the name of *Fido,* meaning **faithful.**

ver (truth)

The root *ver* means "truth." A *verdict,* the judgment of a jury, is made up from the root *ver* **(truth)** and the root *dict* (say). Even that much-used word *very,* meaning "**truly**" or "really," comes from *ver.*

-phobia (fear of)

As a suffix, *-phobia* describes a strong or illogical **fear** of something and often forms words that are used in psychology. For example, *nyctophobia* is a **fear** of the dark. The base word *phobia* also means "**fear.**" In a popular TV show, *Fear Factor,* people are shown facing their *phobias.*

According to Greek mythology, Phobos was the son of Ares, the god of war who was similar to the Roman god Mars. Greek warriors sometimes painted the likeness of Phobos on their shields, hoping that the enemy would run merely at the terrifying sight of his picture.

Words to Learn

Part 1

cred

1. **credibility** (noun)   krĕd′ə-bĭl′ĭ-tē

   From Latin: *cred* (believe)

   believability; ability to be trusted

   > The witness's **credibility** vanished when he admitted he had not been at the scene of the crime.

   > She had undermined her **credibility** by lying too often.

   ▶ *Common Phrase*
   undermine (her/his/our/my/your/their) credibility

   ▶ *Related Word*
   credible (adjective)   (krĕd′ə-bəl)   Rodney's handsomeness and sex appeal made him a *credible* Romeo in the play.

2. **creed** (noun)   krēd

   From Latin: *cred* (believe) (*Crēdo* meant "I believe.")

   set of beliefs or principles

   > The **creed** of the United Methodist Church includes belief in God, dedication to helping those in need, and commitment to world peace.

   > The **creed** of the Muslim religion included five central duties: reciting the words of witness, prayer, charity, fasting, and pilgrimage.

   NOTE: Creed often refers to a formal system of religious or moral beliefs.

3. **incredulity** (noun)   ĭn′krĭ-dōō′lĭ-tē

   From Latin: *in-* (not) + *cred* (believe)

disbelief; amazement

> Spanish explorers of the 1500s expressed **incredulity** at the excellent health and sanitation of the Incas and Aztecs.

> Enforcement of the rules for downloading music was met with **incredulity** by the teenagers.

▶ *Related Word*
incredulous (adjective)   (ĭn-krĕj′ə-ləs)   Neighbors were *incredulous* when they heard that the respected citizen had abused his daughter.

fid

4. **defiant** (adjective)   dĭ-fī′ənt

From Latin: *dis-* (not) + *fid* (faith)

refusing to follow orders or rules; resisting boldly

> **Defiant** Venezuelans gathered in the streets to protest government policies.

NOTE: Since this word begins with *de,* we might expect it to have the sense of "down." However, the Latin word had a *dis-* prefix, which became *de-* as the word *defiant* went through the French language.

▶ *Related Words*
defiance (noun)   The man drank alcohol in *defiance* of his doctor's orders.

defy (verb)   (dĭ-fī′)   The twelve-year-old *defied* his mother's orders and visited a forbidden Web site at his friend's house.

5. **fidelity** (noun)   fĭ-dĕl′ĭ-tē

From Latin: *fid* (faith)

faithfulness to obligation or duty

> Mamet showed his **fidelity** to his mother by caring for her in her old age.

> Sexual **fidelity** is important to a marriage.

exactness, accuracy

> New technology enables scanners to reproduce pictures with great **fidelity.**

▶ *Common Phrase*
fidelity to

6. **fiduciary** (adjective, noun)   fĭ-dōō′shē-ĕr′ē

From Latin: *fid* (faith) (You need to have faith in the person who handles your money.)

Referring to money or property held for one person (or several people) by others (adjective)

A condominium board has a **fiduciary** responsibility to manage money in the interest of unit owners.

a person holding money for another (noun)

The inheritance grew under the guidance of the **fiduciary.**

ver

7. **veracity** (noun)   və-răs′ĭ-tē

From Latin: *ver*   (truth)

truth; accuracy

It is difficult to determine the **veracity** of young children's testimony.

Birth records confirmed the **veracity** of the man's claim to be one hundred years old.

▶ *Common Phrase*
veracity of

8. **verify** (verb)   vĕr′ə-fī

From Latin: *ver* (truth) + *facere* (to make)

to determine the truth or accuracy of; to confirm

Weapons inspectors **verified** that the country had dismantled its nuclear weapons.

After she yelled out "Bingo!," her winning numbers were **verified.**

People often use a dictionary to **verify** a word's meaning.

▶ *Related Word*
verification (noun) Scientists obtain *verification* of their results by repeating experiments.

9. **veritable** (adjective)   vĕr′ĭ-tə-bəl

From Latin: *ver*   (truth)

unquestionable; being truly so

The food show was a **veritable** gold mine of ideas for the student chef.

almost; nearly; very similar to

> Our 500 satellite channels provide a **veritable** feast of TV programs.

▶ *Common Phrases*
a veritable; the veritable

-phobia

10. **acrophobia** (noun)   ăk′rə-fō′bē-ə

From Greek: *acros* (highest) + *-phobia* (fear)

fear of heights

> Marek's **acrophobia** prevented him from looking out the airplane window.

▶ *Related Word*
acrophobic (adjective)   Carolyn became *acrophobic* after falling off a playground slide.

11. **claustrophobia** (noun)   klô′strə-fō′bē-ə

From Latin: *claustrum* (enclosed space) + Greek: *-phobia* (fear)

fear of closed or small spaces

> Mr. Kim's **claustrophobia** made him panic when the elevator would not move.

▶ *Related Word*
claustrophobic (adjective)   Denice felt *claustrophobic* in her small office.

12. **xenophobia** (noun)   zĕn′ə-fōb′ē-ə

From Greek: *xenos* (stranger) + *-phobia* (fear)

fear or hatred of foreigners or foreign things

> The fear that foreign workers would take away jobs sparked **xenophobia** in France.

> Because of his **xenophobia,** the senator wanted to pass laws that would prohibit immigration into the country.

▶ *Related Word*
xenophobic (adjective)   It would be difficult for a *xenophobic* person to enjoy living in Los Angeles, New York, or any other city with a diverse population.

Match these phobias to their meanings.

1. ailurophobia   a. fear of cats

2. zoophobia   b. fear of being alone

3. toxiphobia   c. fear of poison

4. monophobia   d. fear of animals

Answers are on page 411.

Exercises

Part 1

■ Definitions

Match each word in the left-hand column with a definition from the right-hand column. Use each choice only once.

1. defiant ___e___   a. set of beliefs

2. fiduciary ___k___   b. unquestionable

3. credibility ___d___   c. faithfulness

4. acrophobia ___j___   d. ability to be believed

5. claustrophobia ___i___   e. resisting boldly

6. creed ___a___   f. disbelief

7. xenophobia ___g___   g. fear of foreigners

8. veritable ___b___   h. to determine truth or accuracy

9. fidelity ___c___   i. fear of small spaces

10. verify ___h___   j. fear of heights

k. a person holding money for another

l. truth

■ Meanings

Match each word element to its meaning. Use each choice only once.

1. fid ___a___
2. -phobia ___b___
3. cred ___d___
4. ver ___c___

a. faith
b. fear
c. truth
d. believe

■ Words in Context

Complete each sentence with the word that fits best. Use each choice only once.

a. credible e. fidelity i. veritable
b. creed f. fiduciary j. acrophobia
c. incredulity g. veracity k. claustrophobia
d. defiant h. verify l. xenophobic

1. The printer did not reproduce colors with **e, fidelity**____, so the bride's white dress looked green in the digital photograph.

2. A(n) **l, xenophobic**____ person would be suspicious of foreign visitors.

3. Because of his **k, claustrophobia**____, he would probably not bear to be in the small, dark phone booth.

4. The board of a company has a(n) **f, fiduciary**____ responsibility to manage the money of stockholders.

5. Charity and forgiveness lie at the heart of the Christian

   b, creed____.

6. The paintings in Irena's attic proved to be a(n) **i, veritable**____ treasure of old family portraits.

7. Birth records confirm the **g, veracity**____ of my great-grandfather's claim to be a century old.

8. People expressed **c, incredulity**____ that Maya had named her daughter Huckleberry.

9. The **d, defiant** _____ athlete refused to follow the directions of the team captain.

10. The art dealer tried to **h, verify** _____ that the painting was really the work of the famous artist.

■ *Using Related Words*

Complete each sentence by using a word from the group of related words above it. You may need to capitalize a word when you write it in a sentence. Use each choice only once.

1. defied, defiance

   A man of great conscience who **defied** _____ his own government, Sempo Sugihara is credited with saving more than 2,000 Jews from murder during the Holocaust. Because he was the Japanese diplomat to Lithuania, people begged him for visas that would allow them to escape the Nazis by going to Japan. In

   defiance _____ of government orders and at risk to his own life, Sugihara signed the visas as fast as he could write. His memory is revered by humanitarians.

2. incredulity, incredulous

   In February, Chicago temperatures usually average about twenty-five degrees Fahrenheit. So imagine Chicagoans'

   incredulity _____ when, on one day, temperatures reached

   seventy-one degrees. **Incredulous** _____ residents rushed outdoors to play golf and tennis.

3. acrophobia, acrophobic

   The 200-foot-high Mackinac Bridge, in Michigan, inspires

   acrophobia _____ in many people, who cannot bear to look down into the water. Some burst into tears or have attacks of dizziness. Fortunately, officials are available to drive the cars

   of **acrophobic** _____ people, who usually shut their eyes during the journey.

4. verification, verified

Some reports have **verified**＿＿＿＿＿＿ that falls from great heights need not be fatal. In 1998, a British soldier survived a 4,600-foot fall from an airplane after his parachute failed to open. There

has also been **verification**＿＿＿＿＿＿ of an incident in which a flight attendant fell six miles to the ground—and lived.

5. credibility, credible

Reporters who falsify information undermine the

credibility＿＿＿＿＿＿ of the press. In 2003, the *New York Times* fired a reporter for publishing untrue information and copying, or plagiarizing, the stories of others. In another incident, the Pulitzer board withdrew its famous prize from another reporter. Her

seemingly **credible**＿＿＿＿＿＿ star witness, supposedly an addict, never existed.

■ *True or False?*

Each of the following statements contains one or more words from this section. Read each sentence carefully and then indicate whether you think it is probably true or probably false. Your instructor may ask you to reword false statements to make them true.

T   1. A man who could multiply seventeen numbers in his head would be a veritable genius at math.

T   2. Credibility is important to a fiduciary agent.

T   3. We would express incredulity about the veracity of the statement "The moon is made of green cheese."

F   4. A defiant person follows orders.

F   5. When you betray a friend, you are demonstrating fidelity.

F   6. Claustrophobic people hate being up high.

F   7. Religious creeds usually include acrophobia.

<u>T</u>   8. Fidelity is important to friendship.

<u>T</u>   9. When you ask for a loan, a bank would be expected to verify your employment.

<u>F</u>   10. A xenophobic person would enjoy meeting people from many other countries.

Prefixes

Part 2

Part 2 of this chapter presents two very common prefixes with negative meanings: *de-* means "to remove from" or "down"; *non-* means "not." Both prefixes are used in thousands of English words.

This Words to Learn section also presents several idioms. These phrases involve our thoughts and beliefs, for an idiom does not carry the meaning we believe it to have when we first hear it.

de- (removal from; down)

The common prefix *de-* has a few meanings. In some English words it has the sense of "to remove from." For example, when we *decontaminate* something, we **remove** the contamination or impurities **from** it. When people *deforest* land, they **remove** trees **from** it. *De-* can also mean "down." When we *depress* a button, we push it **down.** When something *declines,* it goes **down.**

non- (not)

The prefix *non-* simply means "not." *Nonsense* is something that does **not** make sense. A *nonjudgmental* person is one who does **not** make judgments. *Non-* often combines with base words (roots that can stand alone as English words).

Words to Learn

Part 2

de-

13. **delude** (verb)   dĭ-lo͞od′

From Latin: *de-* (away from) and *lūdere* (to play) (*Delūdere* meant "to deceive, to mock.")

to cause someone to think something that is false; to mislead

> The man **deluded** himself into thinking that he would make a fortune by gambling.
>
> Can a lawyer **delude** a jury into thinking an innocent man committed the crime?

▶ *Common Phrase*
delude himself/herself/myself/yourself into

▶ *Related Words*
delusion (noun)   (dǐ-loō′zhən)   The mentally ill person suffered from the *delusion* that aliens were sending her messages.

delusional (adjective)   The *delusional* man thought the police were always watching him.

For years, people have searched for the monster Bigfoot in the Pacific Northwest. In 1993 Roy L. Wallace, a resident of Toledo, Washington, presented photos of its giant footprint. But in 2002, he admitted that he had faked giant footprints and film footage of the beast. His falsified evidence was meant to *delude* people into believing the monster exists.

---

14. **destitute** (adjective)   děs′tǐ-toōt′

From Latin: *de-* (down) + *stat* (placed)

without money; poor

> The **destitute** parents could not afford the medication their child needed.

NOTE: Destitute is a very strong word that means "entirely without resources; broke."

▶ *Related Word*
destitution (noun)   Many people in rural Afghanistan live in *destitution*.

The saintly Mother Teresa, a nun who died in 1998, opened the Nirmal Hriday (Pure Heart) home for the dying and *destitute* in Calcutta, India. Treating the very poorest, those who had been abandoned because they were dying of AIDS or leprosy, Mother Teresa provided help to those who needed it most.

Mother Teresa earned the Nobel Peace Prize in 1979.

15. **deviate** (verb)   dē′vē-āt′

From Latin: *de-* (to remove from) + *via* (road) (*Dēviāre* meant "to go away from the road.")

to vary from a path, course, or norm

> Airplane pilots must not **deviate** from their flight plan.
>
> Topol **deviated** from tradition when he refused to let his family arrange a marriage for him.

▶ *Common Phrases*
deviate from; deviation from

▶ *Related Words*
deviant (adjective)   (dē′vē-ənt)   Many mentally ill people may show *deviant* behavior. (*Deviant* means "odd in a negative way.")

deviation (noun)   The chef's *deviation* from the recipe made the soufflé flop.

non-

16. **nonchalant** (adjective)   nŏn′shə-länt′

From Latin: *non-* (not) + *calēre* (to be warm) (Many people feel physically warm when they get angry. Therefore, someone who is nonchalant, "not warm," does not feel angry or concerned.)

unconcerned; carefree

> The high school student had a **nonchalant** attitude toward school, barely opening a book.
>
> With a **nonchalant** toss of the covers, John declared that he had made the bed.

▶ *Related Word*
> **nonchalance** (noun)   The resistance fighter displayed *nonchalance* in the face of danger.

NOTE: Nonchalant can be a somewhat negative word, indicating that someone should care but does not.

17. **nondenominational** (adjective)   nŏn′dĭ-nŏm′ə-nā′shə-nəl

From Latin: *non* (not) + *nomen* (name) (Something "not named" is not associated with any one "group," or religion.)

not associated with one specific religion

> The **nondenominational** chapel in the hospital provided a place of peace for the families of all patients.

18. **nondescript** (adjective)   nŏn′dĭ-skrĭpt′

From Latin: *non-* (not) + *de-* (down) + *script* (write) (Something nondescript is hard to describe in writing because it is plain and lacks specific distinguishing features.)

not distinct; difficult to describe because it lacks individuality

> In an area of **nondescript** office buildings, the green-tiled library attracted much attention.
>
> Amy abandoned her **nondescript** clothing in favor of red high-heel sandals, a leather miniskirt, and fishnet stockings.

Idioms

19. **behind the eight ball**

at a disadvantage; in a hopeless situation

After losing the president, provost, and two deans, the college felt it was **behind the eight ball** for the upcoming certification visit.

With a record of nineteen losses and three wins, the soccer team entered the second half of the season **behind the eight ball.**

In eight ball, a pocket billiards game also known as pool, the object is to hit all the balls into the pockets on the edges of the table before sinking the eight ball. Since the eight ball must go in last, you will lose if a ball you want to shoot at is blocked by the eight ball, or if you are *behind the eight ball*.

20. **give carte blanche**   kärt blänsh′

From French: a blank document

to give full, unrestricted power

The president **gave** the secretary of state **carte blanche** to negotiate a peace agreement.

A *carte blanche* was originally a piece of paper with nothing but a signature on it, used when an army surrendered. The defeated leader would sign his name, and the victor could then write in the terms of surrender. In French, *carte blanche* means "blank document."

21. **hold out (or extend) an olive branch**

to make an offer of peace

Mrs. Garcia **held out an olive branch** to her ex-husband so that they could both attend Federico's graduation.

According to the Bible, God punished the wicked world by sending a flood. However, God chose to save one good man, Noah, along with his family and one pair of each type of animal on Earth. Noah floated in an ark for the forty days of the flood. When the waters went down at last, a dove flew from the boat and brought back an *olive branch* as a symbol of God's peace. Today, both the dove and the *olive branch* have come to symbolize peace.

▶ *Common Phrases*
offer an olive branch; extend an olive branch; hold out an olive branch

22. **leave no stone unturned**

to search thoroughly; to investigate thoroughly

The police **left no stone unturned** in their search for the murderer.

In 477 BC, a Greek commander of the city of Thebes won a victory. However, he failed to locate a treasure that he was seeking in the defeated enemy's camp. So the commander consulted the Delphic Oracle (sort of a mythical question-and-answer service). The Oracle advised him to "**leave no stone unturned,**" and he finally found the treasure.

---

23. **star-crossed**

doomed to a bad fate; unlucky

The **star-crossed** Chicago Cubs have not won a World Series since 1908.

For centuries, people of many cultures have believed that the astrological position, or placement, of the stars at a person's birth determined the person's future. A *star-crossed* person was born under unfavorable astrological influences. Shakespeare described the famous lovers Romeo and Juliet as *star-crossed,* or destined to a bad fate.

---

24. **tongue-in-cheek**

joking; insincere; without really meaning something

When mom made a **tongue-in-cheek** comment that she planned to get a nose ring, her kids burst out laughing.

A popular series of manuals carries such **tongue-in-cheek** titles as *Windows for Dummies* and *eBay for Dummies.*

At one time, people indicated that they didn't mean what they said by pushing one of their cheeks out with their tongue. Several actions have even longer histories. The "OK" sign, a circle made with the thumb and forefinger, is used as a *mudra,* or sacred sign, by Buddhists and Hindus to indicate perfection. Crossing one's fingers for good luck is thought to be a gesture early Christians used to indicate the cross.

Exercises

Part 2

■ *Definitions*

Match each word or phrase in the left-hand column with a definition from the right-hand column. Use each choice only once.

1. star-crossed __a__

2. tongue-in-cheek __l__

3. hold out an olive branch

   __h__

4. nondescript __b__

5. leave no stone unturned

   __g__

6. behind the eight ball __e__

7. give carte blanche __f__

8. nonchalant __k__

9. deviate __d__

10. nondenominational __j__

a. unlucky

b. not distinct

c. to mislead

d. to vary from a path

e. at a disadvantage

f. to give full power

g. search thoroughly

h. to make a peace offer

i. without money

j. not limited to one religion

k. unconcerned

l. joking; insincere

■ *Meanings*

Match each prefix to its meaning. Use each choice only once.

1. non-__b__

2. de-__a__

a. to remove from; down

b. not

■ *Words in Context*

Complete each sentence with the word or phrase that fits best. Use each choice only once.

a. delude
b. destitute
c. deviate
d. nonchalant

e. nondenominational
f. nondescript
g. behind the eight ball
h. left no stone unturned

i. give carte blanche
j. held out an olive branch
k. star-crossed
l. tongue-in-cheek

1. The wealthy owner could __i, give carte blanche__ to the decorator to spend whatever money he needed to redo the penthouse.

2. The __e, nondenominational__ charity helped people of all faiths.

3. Don't __a, delude__ yourself into thinking that your child is perfect.

4. After she lost her job and savings, the woman was left __b, destitute__.

5. Because the football player had missed so much practice, he felt he was __g, behind the eight ball__.

6. Fate seemed to be against the __k, star-crossed__ lovers.

7. The valuable documents were hidden in a __f, nondescript__ brown briefcase that looked like hundreds of others.

8. The department store personnel __h, left no stone unturned__ in their efforts to find the lost child.

9. To make peace, the parents finally __j, held out an olive branch__ to the son they had not spoken to in years.

10. "Don't get there first!" was the __l, tongue-in-cheek__ comment the driver shouted to the man who was walking.

■ Using Related Words

Complete each sentence by using a word from the group of related words above it. Use each choice only once.

1. destitute, destitution

Homeless and __destitute__, Joe Long was spending another lonely day when he spied a car on fire. Rushing to the scene, he heroically pulled two people from the flames, saving their lives. A grateful public has now saved Joe from

destitution_____ by gifts of money and the offer of a job.

2. nonchalance, nonchalant

In the mid 1970s, forty-seven states required motorcyclists to wear helmets. However, these laws have since been weakened in twenty-seven states. Tragically, motorcycle accidents have risen sharply. Safety advocates accuse motorcyclists who oppose helmet rules of

nonchalance_____ about their safety. Motorcyclists answer that they oppose helmet rules, not because they are

nonchalant_____, but because they value personal freedom.

3. deviant, deviates

Cultures differ from each other in their social conventions. In the Middle East, people stand close together when they talk. In North America and Europe, people stand farther apart. If someone

deviates_____ from this distance and stands too close, the other speaker becomes uncomfortable. In Japan, one speaker does not look directly at the other. To look directly at someone is

considered **deviant**_____ and offensive.

4. delusions, deluding, delusional

When Andrea Yates was on trial for drowning her five children, her lawyers entered a plea of insanity. They argued that Yates was

delusional_____ at the time of the crime and that these

delusions_____ made her commit crimes. Typically, the test for sanity is "knowing right from wrong." Are such criminals simply

deluding_____ judges and juries, or should the plea of insanity be allowed?

■ *True or False?*

Each of the following statements contains one or more words or phrases from this section. Read each statement carefully and then indicate whether you think it is probably true or probably false. Your instructor may ask you to reword false statements to make them true.

_F_   1. A destitute father would be able to give his daughter a carte blanche to buy anything she wanted.

_F_   2. If you deviate from instructions, you follow them exactly.

_F_   3. A student who has to maintain a B+ average would be nonchalant if he felt he was behind the eight ball in class.

_T_   4. To leave no stone unturned is to do a very thorough search.

_F_   5. Star-crossed people are lucky.

_F_   6. A tongue-in-cheek comment is serious.

_T_   7. Extending an olive branch indicates that someone wants to make peace.

_F_   8. A Catholic church is nondenominational.

_F_   9. A delusion is real.

_F_   10. Something nondescript is very noticeable.

Chapter Exercises

■ Practicing Strategies: New Words from Word Elements

See how your knowledge of prefixes, roots, and suffixes can help you understand new words. Complete each sentence with the word that seems to fit best. Use each choice only once.

a. anthrophobia   e. demilitarize   i. noninvasive
b. bona fide   f. demote   j. phobic
c. credentials   g. discredited   k. verify
d. degrease   h. nonappearance   l. very

1. In a(n) __i, noninvasive_____ medical procedure, the physician does not cut into the human body.

2. To *promote* is to move upward, and to **f, demote**_____ is to move down.

3. In legal terms, a(n) **h, nonappearance**_____ occurs when a defendant does not show up for court.

4. Physicians and other professionals often hang diplomas and other

   c, credentials_____ in their offices so that you will "believe" they are qualified.

5. To remove the oil from machinery is to **d, degrease**_____ it.

6. Fear of other human beings is **a, anthrophobia**_____.

7. If you can no longer believe in somebody, that person has been

   g, discredited_____.

8. Somebody who is fearful is **j, phobic**_____.

9. *Bona* means "good," so something presented in good faith is

   b, bona fide_____.

10. Because they wanted to **e, demilitarize**_____ the area, soldiers removed all the weapons.

■ *Practicing Strategies: Combining Context Clues and Word Elements*

Combining the strategies of context clues and word elements is a good way to figure out the meaning of unknown words. In the following sentences, each italicized word contains a word element that you have studied in this chapter. Using the meaning of the word element and the context of the sentence, make an intelligent guess about the meaning of the italicized word. Your instructor may ask you to check the meaning in your dictionary when you have finished.

1. Because of *musophobia*, the woman panicked when she saw a mouse.

   Musophobia means **fear of mice**_____.

2. Physicians give *credence* to a new treatment for a disease only after it has been tested.

   Credence means **belief; credibility** .

3. Disposing of garbage is a *nontrivial* problem.

   Nontrivial means **important; difficult** .

4. The *deciduous* trees were bare of leaves in winter.

   Deciduous means **not having leaves in winter** .

5. We *debarked* from the plane and stepped into the airport terminal.

   Debarked means **got off** .

■ Companion Words

Complete each sentence with the word that fits best. Choose your answers from the words below. You may use each word more than once.

Choices: from, undermine, into, of, a, in, to, toward, extend

1. Because the man had lied before, we doubted the veracity **of** his words.

2. My friend seemed claustrophobic **in** the cave.

3. The athlete deluded herself **into** thinking she could compete successfully without practicing.

4. The daughter's deviation **from** her parents' traditional beliefs alienated her from them.

5. Try to **extend** an olive branch and make peace with your in-laws.

6. If you cheat, you will **undermine** your credibility.

7. The creed **of** a U.S. juror states, "I am a seeker of truth."

8. Dogs display fidelity **to, toward** their owners.

■ *Writing with Your Words*

This exercise will give you practice in writing effective sentences that use the vocabulary words. Each sentence is started for you. Complete it with an interesting phrase that also indicates the meaning of the italicized word or words.

1. Despite her *nondescript* appearance, _____

    _____ .

2. When caught in the elevator, the *claustrophobic* man _____

    _____ .

3. An example of *xenophobia* I have seen is _____

    _____ .

4. I would like to have *carte blanche* to _____

    _____ .

5. I would *leave no stone unturned* to find _____

    _____ .

6. My *destitute* brother _____

    _____ .

7. My *fiduciary* responsibilities include _____

    _____ .

8. I was surprised that he remained *nonchalant* when _____

    _____ .

9. My day became a *veritable* disaster when _____

    _____ .

10. I would doubt the *veracity* of _____

    _____ .

■ *Making Connections*

These questions will help you relate the words you have learned in this chapter to your own life. Answer each question by writing a paragraph or more on a separate sheet of paper.

1. Choose a person you know with a phobia, and describe his or her fear and coping behavior.

2. Describe something or someone you know who has a nondescript appearance but an unusual personality.

3. Describe a time when you, or someone you know, seemed to be star-crossed.

Passage

The Origins of Superstitions

Just about everyone holds one superstition or another. Read this passage to find out about the origins of your favorites, or should we say your least favorites?

Is the number thirteen unlucky? Why do people who spill salt throw some over their shoulder? Are black cats evil? Can a mirror steal your soul? No scientist has **verified** these superstitions, yet people once believed them without question. How did they originate?

The number thirteen has long been considered unlucky. **(1)** Thirteen was believed to be a central number in the **creed** of witches. These supposedly evil souls were thought to **defy** God by **(2)** swearing **fidelity** to the devil. Thirteen was the ideal number for a witches' coven, or meeting.

Many people considered Friday an unlucky day of the week because it was the day on which Christ was crucified. As a result of the bad reputation of the number thirteen, some buildings do not have a thirteenth floor; the floor numbers skip from twelve to fourteen. When Friday coincides with the thirteenth of the month, we get a particularly unlucky day. However, other Fridays have also been known to bring misfortune. On Friday, May 10, 1886, **(3)** a financial panic in London, known as Black Friday, left many people **destitute.**

Unlike the number thirteen and Friday, salt was considered lucky. Because salt was used to preserve food, people believed that it would drive away bad spirits. However, spilling salt was thought to invite evil. **(4)** In fact, dropping a salt container could make **nonchalant** diners suddenly frantic. To avoid disaster, they had to take salt into their right hands (the side for one's lucky spirit) and throw it over their left shoulders. **(5)** Any **deviation** from this procedure would invite the invasion of the evil spirit, who was always lurking on the left.

Cats have held a special place in our superstitions. Their mysterious ability to survive falls from high places led the Egyptians to believe that they had nine lives. In fact, the Egyptians worshiped cats. **(6)** In contrast, cats have had a rather **star-crossed** fate in Europe. The fact that cats' eyes reflect light in the dark caused Europeans of the Middle Ages to think that the animals were evil spirits. Cats were often pictured as witches' companions, and some people believed that, after seven years' service, a cat might even become a witch. Since black was the color of the devil, black cats inspired especially intense fear. God-fearing people walking at night might see a black cat cross their path. **(7)** Certain that they had met the devil, they would break into a **veritable** panic. A cat that crossed from left to right was particularly frightening.

People often made ridiculous claims about cats. For example, in 1718 a man named William Montgomery claimed that two elderly women had been found dead in their beds on the morning after he had killed two noisy cats. **(8)** Montgomery **deluded** himself into thinking that the cats had been these women in disguise.

A less harmful, though no less silly, superstition revolved around mirrors. The ancients believed that breaking a mirror would bring seven

Cats have a special place in our superstitions.

years of bad luck, avoidable only if the pieces were quickly buried. The length of the bad luck stemmed from the Roman belief that the human body renewed itself every seven years. Throughout history, people have feared that a mirror would steal the weak soul of a sick person or a newborn. **(9)** Of course, this idea had no **veracity,** yet some people would not allow infants to see a mirror until their first birthdays.

Although most modern people are **incredulous** when told of these superstitions, some of us still believe that they have **credibility.** An occasional high-rise still lacks a thirteenth floor. **(10)** Some people throw salt over their left shoulders, even if it is a **tongue-in-cheek** gesture or they no longer know why they are doing it. Perhaps you know people who shiver with fright when a black cat crosses their paths at night and flashes its fiery eyes. Whatever the origin of superstitions, it's clear that some haunt us even today.

■ *Exercise*

Each numbered sentence below corresponds to a sentence in the Passage. Fill in the letter of the choice that makes the sentence mean the same thing as its corresponding sentence in the Passage.

1. Thirteen was believed to be central to the witches' ___**b**___.
   a. truths   b. beliefs   c. poverty   d. faithfulness

2. Witches were supposed to have sworn ___**d**___ to the devil.
   a. belief   b. truth   c. service   d. faithfulness

3. A financial panic known as Black Friday left many people ___**c**___.
   a. unhappy   b. insane   c. poor   d. fearful

4. In fact, dropping a salt container could make a ___**a**___ diner suddenly become frantic.
   a. calm   b. pleasant   c. hungry   d. horrified

5. Any ___**d**___ from this procedure would invite the invasion of the evil spirit.
   a. rumor   b. benefit   c. noise   d. change

6. In contrast, cats have had a rather ___**a**___ fate in Europe.
   a. unlucky   b. fortunate   c. unusual   d. religious

7. Certain that they had seen a devil, they would break into a ___**d**___ panic.
   a. slight   b. sudden   c. dreadful   d. true

8. Montgomery ____d____ himself into thinking that the cats had been these women in disguise.
   a. frightened   b. helped   c. advised   d. fooled

9. This idea has no ____b____.
   a. believability   b. truth   c. excitability   d. faithfulness

10. People throw salt over their left shoulders, even if it is a ____d____ gesture.
    a. foolish   b. frightened   c. believing   d. joking

■ *Discussion Questions*

1. Why were infants not allowed to see mirrors?

2. Why do you think so many people think cats have supernatural powers?

3. Would you be comfortable living on a thirteenth floor? Why or why not?

ENGLISH IDIOMS

Animals

This feature presents more idioms dealing with animals. An *ugly duckling* is a child who is physically unappealing. The phrase comes from a Hans Christian Andersen fairy tale in which an ugly duckling becomes a beautiful swan. A *lame duck* is a political official who is completing a term after someone else has been elected.

People who are nervous often *have butterflies in their stomachs,* perhaps because of the movement we often feel in a churning stomach. When we tell people to *hold your horses,* we want them to slow down. An unknown political candidate, or one that is not favored to win, is called a *dark horse.*

Dogs and wolves appear in other idioms. People who are out of favor because of wrongdoing are *in the doghouse.* When a situation gets very bad, we say it has *gone to the dogs.* When we refer to the brutality of life, we say, *"It's a dog-eat-dog world."* A *wolf in sheep's clothing* is a bad person who pretends to be good. To *keep the wolf from the door* is to keep out hunger.

In the 1890s, cartoonist Francis "Red" Tulane, a radical, wrote a comic strip featuring overworked, exploited mice and a fat, unsympathetic cat who was their boss. Today a rich, unsympathetic person is known as a *fat cat.*

CHAPTER

11

Word Elements: The Body and Health

Since 1900, life expectancy in the United States has risen from forty-seven years to almost eighty. Some researchers feel that the human body can last up to 150 years. In the past century, medical science has learned how to treat and even prevent scores of diseases. Polio, measles, chicken pox, smallpox, and tetanus have almost been eliminated. Refrigeration and plumbing have also contributed to healthier lives. The word elements in this chapter are related to the human body and health. Part 1 presents four roots; Part 2 presents four prefixes. These word elements are common in the sciences and health professions and also form words you will meet in reading.

Chapter Strategy: Word Elements: The Body and Health

Chapter Words:

Part 1

audi	audit	*ped*	expedite
	auditory		impede
	inaudible		pedigree
patho, -pathy	empathy	*spec, spic*	auspicious
	pathetic		conspicuous
	pathology		introspection

Part 2

a-, an-	anarchy	*bio-, bio*	biodegradable
	anonymous		biopsy
	apathy		symbiotic
bene-	benefactor	*mal-*	malady
	beneficial		malevolent
	benign		malpractice

Quiz Yourself

To check your knowledge of some chapter words before you begin to study, identify these statements as true or false. Answers are on page 411.

Apathetic people care deeply.	True	False
A **malady** is a disease.	True	False
Benign things are harmful.	True	False
When we **expedite** something, we slow it down.	True	False

You will learn the answers as you study this chapter.

Did You Know?

How Did Snacks Originate?

Modern life is filled with food that may not be as healthy as spinach but tastes better and is easily available in packaged form. Such snacks are often called "junk food," and despite this negative label, most of us are far more likely to snack on a package of potato chips or nachos than on a raw carrot. Junk food is likely to be with us for a long time, so let's see how some snacks got their names.

The potato chip originated in the 1860s. According to one story, Chef George Crum had an annoying customer who kept complaining that his french fries were too thick. Finally, Mr. Crum cut the potatoes into very thin slices and created the potato chip. In another story, settlers of Spanish descent who lived on large haciendas in California invented the potato chip. In any event, the first potato chip factory opened in 1925.

In 1896, Leo Hirschfield, an Austrian immigrant, invented a chewy candy and gave it the nickname of his childhood sweetheart, Tootsie. This became the Tootsie Roll. In the 1940s, the daughter of Charles Lubin gave her name to Sara Lee cakes and desserts.

The ice cream cone was invented in 1904 at the St. Louis World's Fair. Ernest A. Hamwi, a Syrian immigrant, was selling *zalabias*, wafers that could be rolled up. When a person at the ice cream booth next to him ran out of plates, Hamwi substituted his rolled-up wafers, and the ice cream cone was born.

In the early 1900s, eleven-year-old Frank Epperson accidentally invented a snack food by leaving a sweet drink out overnight in the cold. The liquid froze around a stick. Epperson originally called his invention the "epsicle," but the name later changed to the more appealing "popsicle."

Enjoyed by children and adults throughout the world, the Twinkie was named for the Twinkle Toe shoe. In 1930, the inventor, Jimmy Dewar, passed a billboard advertising the shoe and decided it would be a fitting name for a snack. How do they get the filling into the Twinkie? The manufacturers bake the surrounding cake, and then inject the cream.

M & M's got their name from the initial letters of the last names of inventors Forrest Mars and Bruce Murrie. The candies first became popular during World War II because soldiers could eat them without making their trigger fingers sticky.

Match the food to the origin of its name.

1. ketchup

2. marshmallow

3. Baby Ruth bar

4. Pez

a. the Chinese word for pickled fish

b. a plant with a sticky root

c. the first, middle, and last letters of the word for *peppermint* in German

d. the daughter of President Grover Cleveland

Answers are on page 411.

Learning Strategy

Word Elements: The Body and Health

With the many advances in medicine and the life sciences during the past century, more and more scientific words have been made from the word elements in this chapter. Part 1 presents four common roots; Part 2 presents four common prefixes.

Element	Meaning	Origin	Function	Chapter Words
Part 1				
audi	hear	Latin	root	audit, auditory, inaudible
patho, -pathy	feeling, suffering; disease	Greek	root; suffix	empathy, pathetic, pathology
ped	foot	Latin	root	expedite, impede, pedigree
spec, spic	look	Latin	root	auspicious, conspicuous, introspection
Part 2				
a-, an-	without	Greek	prefix	anarchy, anonymous, apathy
bene-	good, well	Latin	prefix	benefactor, beneficial, benign
bio-, bio	life	Greek	prefix; root	biodegradable, biopsy, symbiotic
mal-	bad, harmful	Latin	prefix	malady, malevolent, malpractice

Word Elements

Part 1

The four roots in Part 1 are explained in more detail below.

audi (hear)

Our *auditory* nerves enable us to **hear.** The word root *audi* is used also in such words as *audience,* a group of people who **hear** a performance, and *auditorium,* a place where crowds gather to **hear** something.

patho, -pathy (feeling, suffering; disease)

The root *patho* has two meanings, both stemming from ancient Greek. First, *patho* can mean "feeling, suffering," as in the word *pathos,* meaning "a **feeling** of pity." A second meaning of *patho* is "disease," as in *pathologist,* a doctor who diagnoses **disease,** and *psychopath,* a person with a **diseased** mind. The spelling *-pathy* is used for the suffix form. For example, *sympathy* means "**suffering** along with the sorrows of another."

ped (foot)

Ped is found in such words as *pedal,* a control operated by the **foot,** and *quadruped,* an animal with four **feet.** Some words made from *ped* reflect society's scorn for the lowly **foot.** *Pedestrian,* which refers to people who travel by **foot,** is also used to describe something that is dull or ordinary.

spec, spic (look)

The root *spec* is used in such words as *inspect,* "to **look** at carefully," and *despise,* to "**look** down on" or "scorn" someone. *Spectators* **look** at movies and sports events. Finally, the word *spy,* a person who secretly **looks** at the actions of others, may also be derived from *spec.*

Words to Learn

Part 1

audi

1. **audit** (noun, verb)   ô'dĭt

   From Latin: *audit* (hear)   At one time, examinations of finances were held in public so that all could hear.

   examination of financial accounts by an outside agency (noun)

   > Companies registered on public stock exchanges must submit their accounts for a yearly **audit.**

   to examine accounts (verb)

   > When the accountant **audited** the records, he found evidence of theft.

   to attend a class without receiving credit (verb)

   > I **audited** Spanish 103 so that I could practice the language.

   ▶ *Related Word*
   auditor (noun)   The *auditor* found the company's financial records to be sound. (An *auditor* is a financial analyst.)

   NOTE: Audit is also used in a more general, nonfinancial sense: "An *audit* of student records revealed that many people had overpaid tuition."

2. **auditory** (adjective)   ô′dĭ-tôr′ē

From Latin: *audi* (hear)

referring to hearing

> Damage to the **auditory** nerve can cause deafness.
>
> Lectures require students to process **auditory** information.

Animals often have well-developed and sensitive *auditory* systems. In 1994, an okapi (a relative of the giraffe) collapsed and died from stress caused by unusual noise. Three hundred yards away, an opera company was rehearsing Wagner's heroically loud *Tannhäuser*.

---

3. **inaudible** (adjective)   ĭn-ô′də-bəl

From Latin: *in-* (not) + *audi* (hear)

not able to be heard

> Noise from the crowd made the announcer's remarks **inaudible.**

▶ Related Word
> **audible** (adjective)   The microphones made the announcer *audible* to the large crowd. (Audible means "capable of being heard" and is the opposite of *inaudible*.)

patho, -pathy

4. **empathy** (noun)   ĕm′pə-thē

From Greek: *em-* (in) + *-pathy* (feeling, suffering)

understanding of or identification with another person's feelings

> When we raise our own children, we develop **empathy** for our parents.
>
> When children identify with characters in books, they experience **empathy** for others.

▶ *Common Phrase*
> empathy for

▶ *Related Words*
> **empathic/empathetic** (adjective)   (ĕm-păth′ĭk)   (ĕm′pə-thĕt′ĭc)
> Alcoholics Anonymous offers support groups where *empathic* (or *empathetic*) members help each other address their addictions.

empathize (verb)   Northwestern University students laughed and groaned as they *empathized* with the characters on *University Place,* a student-produced TV soap opera about campus life.

NOTE: How do *empathy* and *sympathy* differ? Sympathy means feeling sorry for another person. However, if we have empathy, we identify with or experience the feelings of another human being.

5. **pathetic** (adjective)   pə-thĕt′ĭk

From Greek: *patho* (feeling, suffering)

pitiful; arousing pity

The injured bird made a **pathetic** attempt to fly.

6. **pathology** (noun)   pă-thŏl′ə-jē

From Greek: *patho* (disease) + *-logy* (study of)

the study of disease

The science of **pathology** advanced greatly through the general use of the microscope.

signs of disease; something that is not normal

Tumors are part of the **pathology** of cancer.

Progress in the study of gene 72 is revealing the **pathology** of severe mental illness.

Continued joblessness sometimes leads to family **pathology.**

▶ *Related Words*

pathological (adjective)   (păth′ə-lŏj′ĭ-kəl)   He was a *pathological* liar. (*Pathological* can mean mentally ill.)

pathologist (noun, person)   Tissue samples go to the *pathologist* for evaluation. (A pathologist is a medical doctor who investigates body tissue samples (biopsies) for disease. Pathologists also do autopsies, or examinations of bodies, to determine the cause of death. Forensic pathologists help establish clues to criminal activities.)

ped

7. **expedite** (verb)   ĕk′spĭ-dīt′

From Latin: *ex-* (out) + *ped* (foot) (*Expedīre* meant "to free a person's feet from fetters or chains.")

to speed up; to accomplish quickly

> Instant messaging **expedites** communication even more than e-mail does.

> We can **expedite** this emergency order by moving it ahead of other requests.

NOTE: Don't confuse *expedite* with *expedient*, which means "convenient."

▶ *Related Words*

expeditious (adjective) (ĕk′spĭ-dĭsh′əs) Emergency rooms must give *expeditious* service.

expedition (noun) (ĕk′spĭ-dĭsh′ən) The Lewis and Clark *expedition* (1804–1806) became the first U.S. exploratory trip to the Pacific. (*Expedition* means "journey.")

8. **impede** (verb) ĭm-pēd′

From Latin: *im-* (in) + *ped* (foot) (*Impedīre* meant "to entangle," as one's foot becomes caught.)

to hinder; to slow down; to block

> Lack of funding **impedes** progress on research.

> Heavy snow **impeded** the bus trip.

▶ *Related Word*

impediment (noun) (ĭm-pĕd′ə-mənt) Many public buildings need ramps because stairs present an *impediment* to wheelchairs.

9. **pedigree** (noun) pĕd′ĭ-grē′

From Latin (*ped*) through Old French: *pie* (foot) + *de* (of) + *grue* (crane) (In a pedigree, or family tree, an outline shaped like a crane's foot was used to show the different generations.)

ancestry; certificate of ancestry

> The **pedigree** of English royalty includes many German ancestors.

> My cat may not have a distinguished **pedigree,** but I love her anyway.

The names of race horses often reflect their *pedigrees* by referring somehow to their parents' names. The great champion Seabiscuit's sire was named Hard Tack—another name for biscuit. His father's mother was named Tea Biscuit, and her mother was Tea's Over. His mother was named Swing On, his mother's mother was Whisk Broom, and her father was Broomstick.

---

spec, spic

10. **auspicious** (adjective)   ô-spĭsh′əs

From Latin: *avis* (bird) + *spic* (look, watch)

favorable; promising success

> Decreasing unemployment rates are an **auspicious** sign for our economy.
>
> Some people view four-leaf clovers and rainbows as **auspicious.**

> The ancient Romans believed that since the flight of birds was close to the heavens, it could easily be guided by the gods. Thus, birds were watched as signs or omens. A man trained to observe flight patterns was an *auspex*. When an important matter was being considered, the *auspex* decided whether the signs given by birds were *auspicious*.

---

11. **conspicuous** (adjective)   kən-spĭk′yoo-əs

From Latin: *con-* (closely) + *spec* (look)

easy to notice; attracting attention

> The **conspicuous** presence of the police helped lower the crime rate.
>
> Pam's flaming red hair made her **conspicuous** among her brown-haired cousins.

▶ *Related Word*
   conspicuousness (noun)   The *conspicuousness* of my sister's bright pink car embarrassed me.

12. **introspection** (noun)   ĭn′trə-spĕk′shən

From Latin: *intro-* (within) + *spec* (look)

examination of one's own thoughts and feelings

> Journal writing can work as a tool for **introspection.**

▶ *Related Words*

introspect (verb)   A person should *introspect* for a time before deciding to marry.

introspective (adjective)   During *introspective* moments, the man recognized that he was responsible for the problems in his own life.

Exercises

Part 1

■ Definitions

Match each word in the left-hand column with a definition from the right-hand column. Use each choice only once.

1. empathy __a__

2. introspection __j__

3. audit __h__

4. inaudible __i__

5. auditory __e__

6. auspicious __d__

7. pedigree __l__

8. pathetic __f__

9. impede __b__

10. conspicuous __c__

a. identification with another person's feelings

b. to hinder

c. noticeable

d. favorable

e. referring to hearing

f. pitiful

g. to speed up

h. examination of financial accounts

i. not able to be heard

j. examination of one's own thoughts

k. study of disease

l. record of ancestry

■ *Meanings*

Match each word element to its meaning. Use each choice only once.

1. audi ___d___

2. patho, -pathy ___c___

3. ped ___a___

4. spec, spic ___b___

a. foot

b. look

c. feeling, suffering; illness

d. hear

■ *Words in Context*

Complete each sentence with the word that fits best. Use each choice only once.

a. audit
b. auditory
c. inaudible
d. empathy

e. pathetic
f. pathology
g. expedite
h. impede

i. pedigree
j. auspicious
k. conspicuous
l. introspection

1. The dog's __i, pedigree__ included many prize-winning ancestors.

2. Because dogs have very sensitive hearing, they can hear many sounds that are __c, inaudible__ to humans.

3. I put the note in a very __k, conspicuous__ place so my dad would be sure to see it.

4. I would like to __a, audit__ the course rather than take it for credit.

5. Carrying a heavy load will __h, impede__ your ability to run.

6. The ear is the outermost part of the body's __b, auditory__ system.

7. We nearly wept at the __e, pathetic__ sight of starving people begging on the street.

8. To __g, expedite__ answers to consumer questions, the company has installed a hot line that operates twenty-four hours a day.

9. Anne's perfect score on her first test seemed a(n) **j, auspicious** sign for her performance in the course.

10. Psychological counseling encourages **l, introspection**.

■ Using Related Words

Complete each sentence by using a word from the group of related words above it. Use each choice only once.

1. empathy, empathic, empathize

   Do men and women differ in their management skills? One study

   found that women managers were **empathic** to employees. They served as role models and fostered creativity.

   Women could **empathize** with their subordinates and

   encourage them. In contrast to the **empathy** shown by women, male managers tended to appeal to the self-interest of the subordinate, explaining, for example, how taking on an extra project could lead to a promotion.

2. pathological, pathologist

   Physicians can freeze some cancerous tumors that cannot be

   removed by surgery. After a **pathologist** determines that a tumor is malignant, the doctor locates it through ultrasound techniques. The tumor is then injected with liquid nitrogen that freezes it. This destroys the **pathological** tissue without harming healthy organs.

3. impede, impediment

   Lance Armstrong, world champion cyclist, refused to allow

   anything to **impede** his progress. After a few years as an award-winning racer, Armstrong was diagnosed with cancer in 1996. He bravely faced difficult chemotherapy but

   did not allow cancer to become an **impediment** to his

career. Within a year, he was back cycling. He was the Tour de France winner for five consecutive years. He also became a major philanthropist, donating money to cancer-related causes.

4. expedite, expedition, expeditious

In 1911, two teams set out to reach the South Pole first. Battling through the frozen land, each man fought to **expedite** his team's progress. Norwegian Roald Amundsen's **expedition** reached the pole first and then made a reasonably **expeditious** return. The British explorer Robert Falcon Scott reached it a month afterward, but on the return journey perished in the cold.

■ *Reading the Headlines*

This exercise presents five headlines that might appear in newspapers. Read each headline and then answer the questions that follow. (Remember that small words, such as *is, are, a,* and *the,* are often left out of newspaper headlines.)

ONCE POOR, BILLIONAIRE DEMONSTRATES EMPATHY FOR PATHETIC STARVING CHILDREN

1. Does the billionaire understand how the children feel? **yes**

2. Are the children in a bad state? **yes**

PATHOLOGIST FINDS THAT NEW DRUG IMPEDES DEVELOPMENT OF PATHOLOGY IN CELLS

3. Does the new drug speed the development of pathology? **no**

4. Is sickness impeded? **yes**

IN AUSPICIOUS SIGN, EXPEDITED AUDIT OF DEPARTMENT FINDS NO WRONGDOING

5. Is the sign favorable? **yes**

6. Was the audit slowed down? **no**

**INTROSPECTION IS A CONSPICUOUS ELEMENT
IN ATHLETE'S BOOK**

7. Does the athlete write about his thoughts? __**yes**__

8. Is introspection a small part of the book? __**no**__

**AUDITORY PROBLEMS OFTEN CAUSE HIGH SOUNDS
TO BE INAUDIBLE**

9. Are the problems related to sight? __**no**__

10. Can high sounds be heard? __**no**__

Word Elements

Part 2

Part 2 concentrates on four prefixes that are often used in words about the body and in the health sciences.

a-, an- (without)
The words *amoral* and *immoral* help us understand the prefix *a-, an-* by contrasting it with *im-* (meaning "not"). An *immoral* person is *not* moral: this person has a sense of right and wrong, yet chooses to do wrong. An *amoral* person is **without** morals: such a person has no sense of right and wrong. The prefix *a-* is used in many medical words, such as *aphasia* (loss of speech) and *anesthetic* ("**without** feeling," referring to chemicals that make patients unconscious or unable to experience pain during a medical procedure).

bene- (good; well; helpful)
Bene- is used in such words as *benefit* (something that is **helpful**) and *beneficiary* (one who receives **help** or money from another).

bio-, bio (life)
The prefix *bio-* is used in the word *biology,* "the study of **living** things." You may have taken a biology course in school. *Biochemistry* deals with the chemistry of **living** things. A word you have already studied in this book, *autobiography,* includes *bio* as a root.

mal- (bad; badly; harmful)
The prefixes *mal-* and *bene-* are opposites. *Mal-* is used in the word *malpractice,* or "**bad** practice." Doctors and lawyers may be sued for malpractice. In 1775, the playwright Richard Sheridan coined the word *malaprop* as a name for his character Mrs. Malaprop, who used words that were not appropriate (or **badly** appropriate). One of her malapropisms is "He's the very *pineapple* of politeness." (She should have used the word *pinnacle.*)

Words to Learn

Part 2

a-, an-

13. **anarchy** (noun)   ăn'ər-kē

    From Greek: *an-* (without) + *arkhos* (ruler)

    political confusion; disorder; lack of government

    > **Anarchy** resulted when the ruler fled the country.

    > The rioting and looting showed that the country had reached a state of **anarchy.**

    > Without an adult present, **anarchy** soon took over in the fourth-grade classroom.

    ▶ *Related Words*
    > **anarchist** (noun)   The *anarchist* hoped to bring about the fall of the government.

    > **anarchic** (adjective)   ăn-är'kĭk   The streets of Baghdad became *anarchic* after the 2003 war.

14. **anonymous** (adjective)   ə-nŏn'ə-məs

    From Greek: *an-* (without) + *onoma* (name)

    not revealing one's name; of unknown identity

    > An **anonymous** composer wrote the famous tune "Greensleeves."

    > Thanks to caller ID, people who telephone us can no longer remain **anonymous.**

    ▶ *Related Word*
    > **anonymity** (noun)   ăn'ə-nĭm'ĭ-tē   Police have assured the *anonymity* of the witness.

15. **apathy** (noun)   ăp'ə-thē

    From Greek: *a-* (without) + *-pathy* (feeling)

    lack of emotion, feeling, or interest

    > The students' bored faces showed their **apathy.**

    > The city's **apathy** toward soccer turned to enthusiasm when the hometown team started winning.

The great physicist Albert Einstein said of *apathy,* "The world is a dangerous place to live; not because of the people who are evil, but because of the people who don't do anything about it."

▶ *Related Word*
apathetic (adjective)   (ăp′ə-thĕt′ĭk)   The teenager loved hip-hop but was *apathetic* toward school.

bene-

16. **benefactor** (noun)   bĕn′ə-făk′tər

From Latin: *bene-* (well) + *facere* (to do)

a person who gives financial or other aid; a donor

Pope Julius II became a great **benefactor** when he commissioned Michelangelo to paint the Sistine Chapel.

Ms. Oseola McCarthy was an unlikely *benefactor*. Born in Mississippi, she quit school in the sixth grade and worked most of her life doing laundry. But her frugal nature allowed her to save several hundred thousand dollars. In 1995, she donated $150,000 to fund scholarships for needy African Americans. That endowment stood as the single largest endowment ever given to the University of Southern Mississippi.

17. **beneficial** (adjective)   bĕn′ə-fĭsh′əl

From Latin: *bene-* (well) + *facere* (to do)

helpful; producing benefits

Tourism is **beneficial** to the economy of Costa Rica.
Moderate exercise is **beneficial** to one's health.

▶ *Related Word*
benefit (noun)   May's job provided her with health *benefits*.

18. **benign** (adjective)   bĭ-nīn′

From Latin: *bene-* (well) + *genus* (birth) (*Benignus* meant "well-born, gentle.")

kind; gentle

Santa Claus is a **benign,** fatherly figure.

not containing cancer cells

Fortunately, my grandfather's **benign** tumor did not require surgery.

NOTE: The antonym, or opposite, of *benign* is *malignant.*

bio-, bio

19. **biodegradable** (adjective)   bī′ō-dĭ-grā′də-bəl

From Greek: *bio-* (life) + Latin: *de-* (down) + *gradus* (step)

capable of being chemically broken down by natural biological processes

> Most plastic bags are not **biodegradable,** but paper bags are.
>
> Manufacturers now make golf tees from **biodegradable** cornstarch.

NOTE: Biodegradable substances break down into natural elements.

Even a *biodegradable* substance will not decompose, or break down, if it lies in an anaerobic landfill—one that lacks oxygen. This is because the organisms that break down *biodegradable* materials do not have the oxygen they need to live there. Newspapers from more than forty years ago have been found in old landfills in their original state, still readable!

---

20. **biopsy** (noun)   bī′ŏp′sē

From Greek: *bio-* (life) + *opsis* (sight)

the study of living tissue to diagnose disease

> A **biopsy** showed that the mole on my arm was not cancerous.

The words *biopsy, benign,* and *pathology* are often used together. If a doctor suspects cancer, he or she will take a small sample of cell tissue for a *biopsy.* A pathologist will then examine it, usually under a microscope, for *pathology,* or cancer. If the tumor is *benign,* it is usually harmless. If the tumor is *malignant* (note the *mal-* prefix), it must be treated.

---

21. **symbiotic** (adjective)   sĭm′bē-ŏt′ĭk

From Greek: *sym-* (together) + *bio* (life)

living dependently; referring to a relationship where two organisms live in a dependent state

Human bodies have a **symbiotic** relationship with the bacteria that break down food in their stomachs.

The **symbiotic** relationship between the sisters was so strong that when one died, the other soon followed.

NOTE: Symbiotic relationships can be either biological or social. If they are social, *symbiotic* can be a negative word.

▶ *Related Word*

symbiosis (noun)   (sĭm′bē-ō′sĭs)   Manta rays live in *symbiosis* with remora fish, which eat parasites from the rays' skin while feeding on their leftover food.

Manta rays live in *symbiosis* with remora fish.

mal-

22. **malady** (noun)   măl′ə-dē

From Latin: *mal-* (badly) + *habēre* (to keep) (*Mal habitus* meant "ill-kept, in bad condition.")

disease; bad condition

The common cold is a **malady** that affects everyone at one time or another.

Pollution is an environmental **malady** that presents worldwide problems.

23. **malevolent** (adjective)   mə-lĕv′ə-lənt

From Latin: *mal-* (bad) + *volens* (wishing)

ill-willed; evil; filled with hate

Stepmothers, witches, and wolves often appear as **malevolent** characters in fairy tales.

▶ *Related Word*

malevolence (noun)   The *malevolence* of the Nazis resulted in the deaths of over 12 million Europeans.

24. **malpractice** (noun)   măl-prăk′tĭs

From Latin: *mal-* (bad) + *practice*

failure of a licensed professional to give proper services

After the physician left a surgical instrument in her abdomen, the woman accused him of **malpractice.**

A client accused the lawyer of **malpractice** when she missed the client's court date.

To commit *malpractice,* one must be licensed or regulated by the government. Lawyers, accountants, attorneys, actuaries, dentists, physicians, nurses, psychologists, and chiropractors are examples of professionals who can be sued for *malpractice*. In contrast, nonprofessionals can only be accused of negligence.

Exercises

Part 2

■ Definitions

Match each word in the left-hand column with a definition from the right-hand column. Use each choice only once.

1. malady __j__

2. malpractice __a__

3. benign __d__

4. apathy __f__

a. failure to give proper services

b. capable of being broken down by natural processes

c. political confusion

d. not containing cancer cells

5. symbiotic ___l___   e. study of living tissue

6. biopsy ___e___   f. lack of feeling

7. anarchy ___c___   g. helpful

8. benefactor ___i___   h. keeping an identity secret

9. biodegradable ___b___   i. donor

10. beneficial ___g___   j. illness

                                                            k. evil

                                                            l. living dependently

■ *Meanings*

Match each word element to its meaning. Use each choice only once.

1. bene- ___d___   a. life

2. mal- ___c___   b. without

3. bio-, bio ___a___   c. bad

4. a-, an- ___b___   d. good

■ *Words in Context*

Complete each sentence with the word that fits best. Use each choice only once.

a. anarchy	e. beneficial	i. symbiotic
b. anonymous	f. benign	j. malady
c. apathy	g. biodegradable	k. malevolent
d. benefactor	h. biopsy	l. malpractice

1. Learning that my mother's tumor was ___f, benign___ made us all happy.

2. Depending upon each other for survival, peanut plants have a(n) ___i, symbiotic___ relationship with the nitrogen-fixing bacteria that live on their roots.

3. Because the victim wanted to remain ___b, anonymous___, the TV producers hid her face and electronically changed her voice.

4. The pathologist examined tissue from the **h, biopsy**_____ for cancer.

5. A vaccine now protects children from the **j, malady**_____ of chicken pox.

6. Many people try to use **g, biodegradable**_____ containers that will not cause harm to rivers and streams.

7. Patients rarely accuse a careful physician of **l, malpractice**_____.

8. Owning a pet can be **e, beneficial**_____ to the mental health of a lonely person.

9. In many action-thriller movies **k, malevolent**_____ criminals want to destroy the world.

10. The **d, benefactor**_____ Andrew Carnegie funded 2,500 public libraries worldwide.

■ *Using Related Words*

Complete each sentence by using a word from the group of related words above it. Use each choice only once.

1. apathy, apathetic

Many Americans complain about the political **apathy**_____ of citizens who do not vote. But eighty-three-year-old Myun Ja Chang, a recent U.S. citizen born in Korea, attends a voter workshop to prepare for exercising her rights. In contrast to the often **apathetic**_____ attitude of native-born citizens, she believes strongly in the power of citizen choice.

2. symbiotic, symbiosis

The tiny Miami blue butterfly ranks now as the world's rarest species. With only eight adults left, the Florida Wildlife Conservatory Commission has declared it an endangered species. When a caterpillar, the butterfly lives in **symbiosis**_____ with ants. In this **symbiotic**_____ relationship, ants take care of the caterpillar; in return, the caterpillar's body gives off a sweet substance that the ants eat.

3. malevolence, malevolent

If you slice into a tomato, are you a **malevolent**_____

person? Do we show **malevolence**_____ when we forget to water plants? Malcolm Wilkins, an English botanist, claims that plants have feelings and that when they are hurt they produce crackling noises inaudible to the human ear.

4. anarchy, anarchists, anarchic

In a famous case, Nicola Sacco and Bartolomeo Vanzetti, who were

anarchists_____, were found guilty of murder. Their supporters charged that the two men were convicted because of their

anarchic_____ beliefs that all forms of government oppress people. They felt that **anarchy**_____ is, therefore, desirable. Even though evidence surfaced that other people had committed the murder, the men were executed in 1927.

5. anonymous, anonymity

To protect freedom of the press, reporters have often assured their

sources that they will be **anonymous**_____. One famous

source who has kept his (or her) **anonymity**_____ for more than three decades is "Deep Throat," who gave information to reporters on the Watergate scandal in the early 1970s.

■ *Reading the Headlines*

This exercise presents four headlines that might appear in newspapers. Read each headline and then answer the questions that follow. (Remember that small words, such as *is, are, a,* and *the,* are often left out of newspaper headlines.)

CAMPAIGN TO USE BENEFICIAL BIODEGRADABLE MATERIALS IS MET WITH APATHY

1. Are the materials helpful? __yes__

2. Is the campaign being greeted with enthusiasm? __no__

SYMBIOTIC RELATIONSHIP BETWEEN BENEFACTOR AND COLLEGE PRESIDENT CALLED BENIGN

3. Do the benefactor and the president depend on each other?

__yes__

4. Does the benefactor receive money? __no__

5. Is the relationship called harmful? __no__

BIOPSY RESULTS IN MALPRACTICE SUIT AS PATIENT ACCUSES PHYSICIAN OF MALEVOLENTLY IGNORING HIS MALADY

6. Was a tissue sample taken? __yes__

7. Does the patient think the physician meant to do harm? __yes__

8. Was the patient sick? __yes__

ANARCHY ERUPTS IN STREETS AFTER ANONYMOUS TERRORIST GROUP BOMBS GOVERNMENT BUILDINGS

9. Are the streets calm? __no__

10. Is the identity of the terrorist group known? __no__

Chapter Exercises

■ *Practicing Strategies: New Words from Word Elements*

See how your knowledge of word elements can help you understand new words. Complete each sentence with the word that fits best. Use each choice only once. You may need to capitalize some words.

a. anesthetic	e. audition	i. malaria
b. antipathy	f. benevolent	j. malodorous
c. atonal	g. biohazard	k. peddler
d. audiometer	h. centipede	l. spectacles

1. A(n) **d, audiometer** _____ measures one's ability to hear.

2. At a(n) **e, audition** _____, people listen to you in order to determine if you should be hired for a performance.

3. People once thought that bad air caused the disease of **i, malaria** _____.

4. Something **j, malodorous** _____ has a bad smell.

5. **b, Antipathy** _____ describes feelings "against" others, or hatred.

6. A(n) **g, biohazard** _____ is a living thing that can cause harm.

7. A(n) **h, centipede** _____ is an insect said to have one hundred feet.

8. Since it lacked harmony and a strong melody, we found the **c, atonal** _____ music hard to listen to.

9. People wear **l, spectacles** _____ so they can look and see better.

10. A(n) **k, peddler** _____ travels on foot selling things.

■ *Practicing Strategies: Combining Context Clues and Word Elements*

Combining the strategies of context clues and word elements is a good way to figure out the meaning of unknown words. In the following sentences, each italicized word contains a word element that you have studied in this chapter. Using the meaning of the word element and the context of the sentence, make an intelligent guess about the meaning of the italicized word. Your instructor may ask you to check the meaning in your dictionary when you have finished.

1. We thought the *pediform* sculpture was rather strange.

   Pediform means **in the form of a foot** _____.

2. A virus is the *pathogen* of polio.

   Pathogen means **something that causes a disease** _____.

3. A *maladroit* person often drops items and bumps into things.

   Maladroit means **clumsy**_____.

4. They played an *audiobook* when they took a car trip.

   Audiobook means **a book one listens to**_____.

5. No bacteria can infect a patient in an *aseptic* operating room.

   Aseptic means **extremely clean; sterilized; without germs**___.

■ *Practicing Strategies: Using the Dictionary*

Read the following definition. Then answer the questions below it.

> **pearl**[1] (pûrl) *n.* **1.** A smooth, lustrous, variously colored deposit, chiefly calcium carbonate, formed around a grain of sand or other foreign matter in the shells of certain mollusks and valued as a gem.   **2.** Mother-of-pearl; nacre.   **3.** One that is prized for beauty or value.   **4.** *Printing* A type size measuring approximately five points.   **5.** A yellowish white. ❖ *v.* **pearled, pearl•ing, pearls** —*tr.*   **1.** To decorate or cover with or as if with pearls.   **2.** To make into the shape or color of pearls. —*intr.*   **1.** To dive or fish for pearls or pearl-bearing mollusks.   **2.** To form beads resembling pearls. [ME *perle* < OFr. < Lat. **pernula*, dim. of *perna*, ham, seashell.]

1. List all the parts of speech for pearl. **noun, transitive verb,**

   intransitive verb_____

2. What is the definition number and part of speech of the definition that best fits this sentence, "This famous stamp is the *pearl* of my

   collection"? **3, noun**_____

3. What is the definition number and part of speech of the definition that best fits this sentence: "The color of that dress is *pearl*"?

   5, as a noun_____

4. What is the definition number and part of speech of the definition most

   used in printing? **4, noun**_____

5. In which language did *pearl* originate? **Latin**_____

■ *Companion Words*

Complete each sentence with the word that fits best. Choose your answers from the words below. You may use each word more than once.

Choices: of, toward, about, with, by, to, for

1. Unfortunately, the runner showed only apathy **toward, for** the race.

2. The heart patient falsely accused the cardiologist **of** malpractice.

3. Spinach is beneficial **to** one's health.

4. The pedigree **of** the prizewinning dog showed many famous ancestors.

5. The pathology **of** lung cancer often involves behavior such as smoking.

6. Because of the poverty of his childhood, the famous athlete felt empathy **for, toward** poor young people.

■ *Writing with Your Words*

This exercise will give you practice in writing effective sentences that use the vocabulary words. Each sentence is started for you. Complete it with an interesting phrase that also indicates the meaning of the italicized word.

1. I'd like to remain *anonymous* when _____

   _____.

2. My *malevolent* boss _____

   _____.

3. *Biodegradable* materials _____

   _____.

4. My dog's *pedigree* _____

   _____.

5. The lecture was *inaudible*, so _____

_____.

6. To me, one *auspicious* sign is _____

_____.

7. The *anarchic* crowd _____

_____.

8. The rapper was *conspicuous* because _____

_____.

9. I become *introspective* when _____

_____.

10. The stray cat was *pathetic* because _____

_____.

■ *Making Connections*

These questions will help you relate the words you have learned in this chapter to your own life. Answer each question by writing a paragraph or more on a separate sheet of paper.

1. Describe the most memorable malady you have ever had.
2. What kind of person could you show empathy for? Why?
3. On which issue do you think the public is too apathetic? Why?

Passage

The Disease That Science Eliminated

It started with a fever and developed into a rash. Soon, sores appeared all over the body. Many sufferers died from damage to their hearts, livers, and lungs. This was smallpox, the most destructive disease in human history. Here is the story of its defeat.

Today, when so many diseases can be prevented or cured, it may be difficult for us to feel **empathy** for the people that smallpox attacked. There was no cure, and one in four who got the disease died. Those who survived were forever marked, for **(1)** smallpox left **conspicuous** scars called "pocks." Smallpox was also highly contagious; everything a sick person had touched could be infectious. Often, sick people were "quarantined," or separated, from healthy ones. **(2)** This meant that **pathetically** ill people were sometimes left alone to die.

(3) Smallpox struck people of all classes, including those with royal **pedigrees.** Two princes died of it in 1700 and 1711, ruining the alliances that depended upon their marriages. It killed King Louis XV of France in 1774.

In the 1600s and 1700s, smallpox changed history in the Americas by wiping out much of the Native American population. Since the disease had been newly introduced by Europeans, Native Americans had little resistance to it. When first exposed, they died in great numbers. In at least one shameful incident, a smallpox epidemic was started deliberately when **(4) malevolent** Jeffrey Amherst, an English soldier, sent infected blankets to Native Americans.

The defeat of this deadly disease is one of medical science's great triumphs. The first steps were taken in China over 1,000 years ago, when **anonymous** physicians protected people by giving them the disease deliberately. To do this, material from the pox sore of an infected person was introduced into a healthy person. If this procedure was done carefully, **(5)** the receiver usually developed a **benign** version of the **malady,** but would then be protected from smallpox for life. By 1700, this practice had spread throughout Asia and the Middle East. It was brought from Turkey to England in the early 1700s. Although the method protected many people, it was not always safe, for some developed severe smallpox and died.

Then, in 1796, Edward Jenner, an English doctor, made an important discovery. Jenner had noticed that milkmaids never seemed to get smallpox. He reasoned that through their contact with cows, they got a related but relatively **benign** disease, called "cowpox," which protected them from smallpox. To test this theory, on May 14, 1796, Jenner took a small sample of a cowpox sore from the finger of Sarah Nelmes, a milkmaid, and applied it to a sore on eight-year-old James Phipps. James developed a very slight infection—and never contracted smallpox. Because cowpox came from cows, which were named *vacca* in Latin, Jenner called this procedure a "vaccination."

As Jenner treated more people, **(6)** he became certain of the **beneficial** effects of vaccination. He was eager to publish his findings, but **(7)** the Royal Society **impeded** his efforts by rejecting his paper. Finally, to **expedite** publication, Jenner printed the results himself.

Even after the publication of Jenner's findings, **(8)** public reaction remained **apathetic,** especially in large cities. In a three-month search of the London area, Jenner located no volunteers for vaccination. Although the method was soon endorsed by physicians and used often in the English countryside, Londoners did not commonly undergo vaccination until almost fifty years later. **(9)** In fact, an **audit** of the "Bills of Mortality," or record of deaths in London, shows smallpox to be a common cause of death until the 1840s.

Resistance to vaccination lasted even longer in France and Germany, where opponents accused physicians of **malpractice** for deliberately introducing disease into a healthy person. Ministers objected to doctors interfering with "God's will" by preventing disease. However, others in these countries trusted Jenner's method. The French emperor Napoleon had his entire army vaccinated in 1805.

In the Americas, rapid adoption of vaccination was an important factor in the population growth of the New World. People in both English and Spanish colonies made wide use of the method.

Jenner lived to see honors and awards, as well as attacks and betrayals. Through it all, he remained dedicated to the cause of vaccination. He worked so hard on its behalf that he had no time to earn money practicing medicine. Although he died a poor man, this **benefactor** left a great gift to the world.

A century after Jenner's death, smallpox vaccination was practiced almost universally, and fewer and fewer people contracted the disease. In the second half of the twentieth century, the number of cases decreased every year, **(10)** an **auspicious** sign for world health. The last case was reported in 1977.

Today, all that remains of the smallpox virus are two small samples—one in the United States and one in Russia. The samples are being kept alive in case they are needed for scientific study or to produce new vaccine if that should ever be needed. Otherwise, this once-deadly killer of mankind has vanished from the earth.

■ *Exercise*

Each numbered sentence below corresponds to a sentence in the Passage. Fill in the letter of the choice that makes this sentence mean the same thing as the corresponding sentence in the Passage.

1. Smallpox left ____**d**____ scars.
   a. harmless   b. sick   c. huge   d. noticeable

2. This meant that ____**c**____ ill people were sometimes left alone.
   a. entirely   b. slightly   c. pitifully   d. mercifully

3. Smallpox struck those with royal ____**b**____.
   a. wealth   b. ancestries   c. powers   d. dependence

4. __d__ Jeffrey Amherst sent infected blankets to Native Americans.
   a. Careless   b. Ill   c. Thoughtful   d. Evil

5. The receiver usually developed a benign form of the __c__.
   a. treatment   b. sample   c. illness   d. problem

6. Jenner became certain of the __a__ effects of vaccination.
   a. helpful   b. sad   c. fast   d. noticeable

7. The Royal Society __a__ his efforts.
   a. blocked   b. speeded   c. inspected   d. ignored

8. Public reaction remained __b__.
   a. enthusiastic   b. uninterested   c. skeptical   d. shocked

9. A(n) __a__ of the "Bills of Mortality" shows smallpox to be a common cause of death.
   a. examination   b. publication   c. official record   d. accusation

10. This was a __d__ sign for world health.
    a. reasonable   b. bad   c. noticeable   d. favorable

■ Discussion Questions

1. Why was the word *vaccination* taken from a word meaning "cow"?

2. What were some of the ways that smallpox changed history?

3. Given Jenner's life story, would you have wanted to be him? Why or why not?

◀ ENGLISH IDIOMS

Food

Perhaps because of the importance of food, many widely used English idioms contain references to cooking and things we eat. A sensitive, difficult issue is called a *hot potato*. Ideas that are not fully thought out are often called *half-baked*. When we are in difficulty, we are *in hot water*.

People who feel strong and energetic are *feeling their oats*. However, when we are disgusted with something, we are *fed up* with it, and when we lose our tempers, we *boil over*.

Other expressions refer to the birds we eat. To ruin or destroy one's hopes or plans is to *cook one's goose*. *Duck soup* refers to something easily done, and "That test was duck soup" means it was easy.

Idioms also refer to fruits and vegetables. To *go bananas* and to *go nuts* both mean to go crazy. One's *salad days* refer to the days of one's youth.

To *take with a grain of salt* means not to take seriously. To *cry over spilt milk* means to complain about something that can no longer be prevented.

The butter of the yak, a relative of the ox, had great value to the people of Tibet. When they wanted to please someone, they presented tubs of the butter as a present. Today, to *butter up* means to flatter.

Word Elements: Speech and Writing

College students and professionals speak and write every day. Not surprisingly, English has many words to describe communication. The first part of this chapter contains three elements related to speech; the second part gives two elements for writing. Part 2 also presents three pairs of words that people often confuse in speech and writing and helps you learn to use these confusing words correctly.

Chapter Strategy: Word Elements: Speech and Writing

Chapter Words:

Part 1

dict	contradict	*voc, vok*	advocate
	dictator		invoke
	edict		revoke
log, loq, -logy	colloquial		vociferous
	ecology		
	loquacious		
	monologue		
	prologue		

Part 2

-gram, -graph,	demographic	*Confusable Words*	affect
-graphy,	epigram		effect
graph	graphic		conscience
scrib, script	inscription		conscious
	manuscript		imply
	transcribe		infer

Quiz Yourself

To check your knowledge of some chapter words before you begin to study, identify these statements as true or false. Answers are on page 411.

To **contradict** is to agree.	True	False
A **vociferous** person is noisy.	True	False
A **monologue** is spoken by one person.	True	False
Demographic trends refer to animals.	True	False

You will learn the answers as you study this chapter.

Did You Know?

Shortening English

English speakers seem to like short words. The most widely used English words all have four or fewer letters. Listed from number one to ten, they are *the, of, and, a, to, in, is, you, that,* and *it.*

In fact, when an English word is used frequently, it is often shortened, or *clipped.* Many people now refer to *television* as *TV,* and *telephone* as *phone.* Most students use the word *exam* to refer to an *examination. Fax,* as in *fax machine,* has been shortened from *facsimile.*

Some words were clipped over fifty years ago, so long ago that people may not remember the original words. The word for a common malady, the *flu,* was clipped from *influenza.* A *bus* was once called an *autobus,* and signs for *autobuses* can still be seen in Scotland. The word *caravan* has been replaced by *van.*

Some clippings date back even further. In the 1500s, Italian comedies featured a foolish character named *Pantaloon* who wore an unfashionable, loose-fitting garment to cover his legs. This piece of clothing became known as *pantaloons,* a word shortened to *pants* in the 1800s. For centuries, when people parted, they said, "God be with you" to each other. Four hundred years ago, this was shortened to "good-bye."

A relatively modern way to shorten expressions is to form an *acronym,* a series of words that are replaced by their initial letters. *Laser* stands for *l*ight *a*mplification by *s*imulated *e*mission of *r*adiation. *Radar* was created from the initials of *r*adio *d*etection *a*nd *r*anging.

In business, an IPO is an *i*nitial *p*ublic *o*ffering of stock. *BASIC* is a computer acronym for *b*eginner's *a*ll-purpose *s*ymbolic *i*nstruction *c*ode. In sports, a *scuba* diver uses a *s*elf-*c*ontained *u*nderwater *b*reathing *a*pparatus. If an athlete sprains a muscle, "*rice*," meaning *r*est, *i*ce, *c*ompression, and *e*levation, is often prescribed.

Acronyms have also been devised for lifestyles. *Dinks* are *d*ouble *i*ncomes, *n*o *k*ids—that is, childless couples who both work outside the home. The U.S. census now counts the number of *POSSLQ*s, or unmarried *p*ersons of the *o*pposite *s*ex *s*haring *l*iving *q*uarters. Even political views have acronyms. People who favor reforms, until they are personally affected, are referred to as *nimby*s, or *n*ot *i*n *m*y *b*ack *y*ard.

DENNIS the MENACE

"YOU USE TOO MANY BIG WORDS. CAN'T YOU TALK SMALLER?"

Learning Strategy

Word Elements: Speech and Writing

Human beings are skilled communicators. Not surprisingly, English has many word elements that are related to communication in oral and written form. Part 1 of this chapter concentrates on speech, and Part 2 addresses writing.

Element	Meaning	Origin	Function	Chapter Words
Part 1				
dict	speak	Latin	root	contradict, dictator, edict
log, loq, -logy	word; speak; study of	Greek; Latin	root; suffix	colloquial, ecology, loquacious, monologue, prologue
voc, vok	voice; call	Latin	root	advocate, invoke, revoke, vociferate
Part 2				
-gram, -graph, -graphy, graph	write	Latin; Greek	suffix; root	demographic, epigram, graphic
scrib, script	write	Latin	root	inscription, manuscript, transcribe

Word Elements

Part 1

The word roots for Part 1 are explained below in more detail.

dict (speak)
   This root appears in several common words. *Dictation* is something **spoken** by one person and copied down by another. *Diction* is the clearness and quality of one's **speech.**

log, loq, -logy (word; speak; study of)
   The roots *log* and *loq* mean word or speak. To be *eloquent* is to **speak** well. We record our words in a *log*. However, the suffix *-logy* means "study of." You may have taken courses in *biology* (the **study of** living things), *psychology* (the **study of** the mind), or *anthropology* (the **study of** human beings).

voc, vok (voice; call)
   A record that contains the human **voice** speaking or singing is called a *vocal* recording. *Vocabulary,* meaning "things spoken by the **voice,**" or "words," also comes from *voc*. You will not confuse this root with the others if you remember to associate it with the word *voice*.

Words to Learn

Part 1

dict

1. **contradict** (verb)   kŏn′trə-dĭkt′

   From Latin: *contra-* (against) + *dict* (speak)

   to say or put forth the opposite of something

   > In court, the defendant **contradicted** the statement he had given police.

   > It is not wise to **contradict** your boss in front of coworkers.

   ▶ *Related Words*
   contradiction (noun)   The *contradictions* between the reports of the two eyewitnesses puzzled us.

   contradictory (adjective)   The children's *contradictory* stories made us suspect that neither was telling the truth.

   Oxymorons are *contradictions* of language, or statements in which one word seems to *contradict* another. Examples are *definite maybe, sweet sorrow, exact estimate, jumbo shrimp, killing with kindness, dull shine, whole half, awfully good, devout atheist,* and *plastic silverware.*

   ---

2. **dictator** (noun)   dĭk′tā-tər

   From Latin: *dict* (speak) (A dictator is a ruler who speaks with power; whatever the ruler says is done.)

   a ruler with total authority

   > Former **dictator** Saddam Hussein killed thousands of Iraqis.

   ▶ *Related Words*
   dictatorial (adjective)   (dĭk′tə-tôr′ē-əl)   The chairperson's *dictatorial* style alienated committee members.

   dictatorship (noun)   Often there is no freedom of speech or press in a *dictatorship.*

3. **edict** (noun)   ē′dĭkt′

   From Latin: *e-* (out) + *dict* (speak)

   an order or decree

   > On September 26, 1996, the Taliban issued an **edict** forbidding females from working or going to school.

In 1998, the White House published an **edict** requiring that government regulations be written in plain English.

Edicts can have long-lasting effects. On May 4, 1493, Pope Alexander VI issued an edict dividing the "New World," or the Americas, between Spain and Portugal. Today these countries rule not one square inch of land in the Americas. However, their legacy is seen in the many countries whose inhabitants speak Spanish, and in Brazil, where Portuguese is spoken.

---

log, loq, -logy

4. **colloquial** (adjective)   kə-lō′kwē-əl

From Latin: *com-* (together) + *loq* (speak) (When we "speak together" with friends, our speech is colloquial.)

informal conversation or expression

> E-mails to friends typically use a **colloquial** style.

▶ *Related Word*
colloquialism (noun)   The word "hey" is a *colloquialism* for "hello."

5. **ecology** (noun)   ĭ-kŏl′ə-jē

From Greek: *oikos* (house) + *-logy* (study of) (Ecology is concerned with the environment, the "home" or "house" in which we all live.)

the relationship of living things and their environment

> Fire plays a key role in the **ecology** of many forests.

> After a study showed the harmful effects of cutting down trees on the **ecology** of animal life, Szechuan, China, put controls on logging.

> Although trees are sparse in both systems, the **ecology** of the desert is different from that of the plains.

▶ *Related Words*
ecological (adjective)   (ĕk′ə-lŏj′ĭ-kəl)   Acid rain has ruined the *ecological* balance of many lakes and ponds.

ecologist (noun)   *Ecologists* have shown that bats play a key role in many environments.

The science of *ecology* is increasingly needed to protect plant and animal life. The rain forests of the world are being cleared to obtain lumber and provide farmland. *Ecologists* have demonstrated how this leads to the extinction of forest animals and plants. Plants that have great value to medicine may be lost forever. Human life is affected because the leaves of rain forest trees release oxygen into the air. Some nations are making progress on these issues. In 1998, Suriname, in South America, announced that a valuable rain forest covering 12 percent of its land would be declared a nature reserve.

_____

6. **loquacious** (adjective)   lō-kwā′shəs

From Greek: *loq-* (speak)

very talkative

> The **loquacious** beautician talked nonstop throughout my haircut.
>
> The TV talk show host had to cut off the **loquacious** actor by calling for a commercial.

▶ *Related Word*
  loquaciousness (noun)   None of us appreciated the woman's *loquaciousness* during the movie.

7. **monologue** (noun)   mŏn′ə-lôg′

From Greek: *monos* (one) + *log* (speak)

a speech or performance by one person

> To start his show, TV host Jay Leno gives a clever **monologue.**
>
> In Hamlet's **monologue** "To be or not to be," Shakespeare examines the mind of a person who cannot make a decision.

8. **prologue** (noun)   prō′lôg′

From Greek: *pro-* (before) + *log* (speak)

the introduction to a literary or artistic work

> In the **prologue** to the movie *Titanic,* there is a search for the sunken ship.
>
> In a **prologue** that sets the stage for *Romeo and Juliet,* Shakespeare calls the lovers "star-crossed."

an introductory event

> The South's withdrawal from the Union was the **prologue** to the Civil War.
>
> The 1929 stock market crash became the **prologue** to the Great Depression.

▶ *Common Phrase*
  prologue to

voc, vok

9. **advocate** (verb) ăd′və-kāt′; (noun) ăd′və-kĭt

   From Latin: *ad-* (toward) + *voc* (to voice, call)

   to urge publicly; to recommend (verb)

   > Animal rights activists **advocate** a vegetarian diet.

   a person who publicly urges a cause (noun)

   > **Advocates** of gun control want stricter laws for carrying weapons.

   ▶ *Common Phrase*
     an advocate of (noun). She is *an advocate of* women's rights.

10. **invoke** (verb) ĭn-vōk′

    From Latin: *in-* (in) + *voc* (to call) (*Invocāre* means "to call upon.")

    to call in assistance; to call upon

    > Martin Luther King's "I Have a Dream" speech powerfully **invoked** the core values of the United States.

    > The social worker **invoked** the aid of the police to remove the child from the abusive home.

    ▶ *Related Word*
      invocation (noun) (ĭn′və-kā′shən) The rabbi gave an *invocation*. (*Invocation* means "prayer.")

    The Fifth Amendment to the U.S. Constitution states that those accused of a crime cannot be forced to testify against themselves. Thus, when asked a question whose answer may injure their case or make them appear guilty, accused people may "*invoke* the Fifth Amendment" and refuse to answer.

    ---

11. **revoke** (verb) rĭ-vōk′

    From Latin: *re-* (back) + *vok* (to call)

    to cancel or withdraw

    > Olympic Games officials **revoke** the medals of athletes who test positive for illegal drugs.

► *Related Word*

revocation (noun)   (rĕv′ə-kā′shən)   A pilot who sleeps on a flight may face the *revocation* of his license.

12. **vociferous** (adjective)   vō-sĭf′ər-əs

From Latin: *voc* (voice) + *ferre* (carry)

crying out noisily; speaking loudly

The **vociferous** audience shouted for more songs.

At a city hearing, **vociferous** neighborhood residents forcefully protested the replacement of low-cost housing with expensive condominiums.

Exercises

Part 1

■ Definitions

Match each word in the left-hand column with a definition from the right-hand column. Use each choice only once.

1. contradict ___l___
2. advocate ___j___
3. vociferous ___k___
4. revoke ___a___
5. prologue ___i___
6. edict ___d___
7. monologue ___h___
8. loquacious ___c___
9. dictator ___f___
10. invoke ___g___

a. to cancel
b. informal
c. very talkative
d. order; decree
e. the relationship of living things and their environment
f. ruler with total authority
g. to call in for assistance
h. speech by one person
i. introduction to book or play
j. to recommend
k. crying out noisily; speaking loudly
l. to say something opposite

■ *Meanings*

Match each word element to its definition. Use each choice only once.

1. dict _____**b**_____

2. log, loq, -logy _____**a**_____

3. voc, vok _____**c**_____

a. word; speak; study of

b. speak

c. voice; call

■ *Words in Context*

Complete each sentence with the word that fits best. Use each choice only once.

a. contradict   e. ecology   i. advocate
b. dictator   f. loquacious   j. invoke
c. edict   g. monologue   k. revoke
d. colloquial   h. prologue   l. vociferous

1. Noise from traffic can affect the **e, ecology** _____ of nearby forests by disturbing animals.

2. Because Sam was failing in school, his dad decided to **k, revoke** _____ the privilege of using the family car.

3. Standing alone on a stage, the actor delivered a powerful **g, monologue** _____.

4. In the 1700s, George I of England issued a(n) **c, edict** _____ that protected pigeons from harm.

5. I am a(n) **i, advocate** _____ of rights for children with disabilities.

6. The **f, loquacious** _____ woman talked on and on throughout our card game.

7. Clouds are usually a(n) **h, prologue** _____ to rain.

8. Students should use formal rather than **d, colloquial** English when they write term papers.

9. The **l, vociferous** man shouted slogans at the political rally.

10. The small, poor country tried to **j, invoke** the aid of its rich neighbor during the famine.

■ *Using Related Words*

Complete each sentence by using a word from the group of related words above it. You may need to capitalize a word when you write it in a sentence. Use each choice only once.

1. revoke, revocation

The Pulitzer Prize committee has been reviewing an award won in

1932, and may decide to **revoke** it! If put in place, the

revocation would take effect because winner Walter Duranty wrote about the Soviet Union, but ignored the policies of dictator Joseph Stalin that led to the deaths of millions of people in the Ukraine.

2. colloquial, colloquialisms

Farmers have invented many **colloquialisms** for weather.

"White Plague," a play on words on the disease known as the Black

Plague, is a **colloquial** expression for "hail," which causes much destruction of crops. Residents of Wisconsin and Michigan call rain that falls after March 31 "time release rain" because it is well timed for crop growth.

3. ecology, ecological, ecologists

Ecologists have warned that even a few degrees of global

warming would have a major effect on world **ecology**_____.
Melting ice would cause higher sea levels, and the wildlife that occupies shorelines and shallow water would have difficulty surviving. Areas that once supported crops might turn into deserts. As the earth warmed, the **ecological**_____ balance would be upset.

4. dictator, dictatorial, dictatorship

Joseph Stalin, **dictator**_____ of the Soviet Union from 1929 to 1953, ranks among history's cruelest leaders. Under him, the Soviet **dictatorship**_____ imprisoned millions of people in "gulags," or prison camps. His **dictatorial**_____ politics led to the deaths of his close allies as well as countless Soviet citizens.

5. contradicted, contradictory, contradiction

The great architect Frank Lloyd Wright is a study in **contradiction**_____. His masterful artistic achievements often were **contradicted**_____ by his disturbing private behavior. He left his family for the wife of a client. He left debts and unfulfilled contracts. Wright's example shows that public achievements and private behavior may be **contradictory**_____.

■ *True or False?*

Each of the following statements contains at least one word from this section. Read each statement and then indicate whether you think it is probably true or probably false. Your instructor may ask you to reword false statements to make them true.

__F__   1. A dictator allows much freedom.

__F__   2. Vociferous and loquacious people are quiet.

__F__   3. A monologue is given by several people.

<u>T</u>   4. A prologue would be put at the beginning of a book.

<u>F</u>   5. People who contradict themselves are consistent.

<u>T</u>   6. Most people would advocate revoking the licenses of drunk drivers.

<u>F</u>   7. When we invoke aid, we refuse it.

<u>F</u>   8. Ecologists want to destroy the environment.

<u>T</u>   9. We talk to friends using colloquial language.

<u>F</u>   10. An edict is never issued by the government.

Word Elements

Part 2

The second part of this chapter presents two word elements that relate to the concept of writing. Then three pairs of easily confused words, which college students often have trouble distinguishing, are introduced.

-gram, -graph, -graphy, graph (write)

This suffix has three spellings. It is spelled *-gram,* as in *telegram,* a **written** message sent by wires. (*Tele-* means "far.") The spelling *-graph* is used in *autograph,* a person's signature, or "self-**writing.**" (*Auto* means "self.") Finally, the suffix can be spelled *-graphy,* as in *photography* (literally, "**writing** in light"). *Graph* can also function as a base word.

Graffiti, that often illegal writing that appears in elevators, on overpasses and walls, and, of course, in bathrooms, has plagued us throughout history. The word *graffiti* comes, through Italian, from the word element *graph.* Archaeologists have discovered the name of Padihorpakhered, who, identifying himself as a powerful Egyptian priest, carved on the sandstone sides of a monument in Thebes 2,700 years ago. Thus, like *graffiti* writers of today, he assured himself notice.

Graffiti has a long history.

scrib, script (write)

> This root is found in many common words. A *script* is the **written** form of a television program, movie, or play. When small children make **written** marks, they often *scribble*. A *scribe* **writes** down the words of other people.

Words to Learn

Part 2

-gram, -graph, -graphy, graph

13. **demographic** (adjective) děm′ə-grăf′ĭk

    From Greek: *demos* (people) + *-graph* (write)

    referring to population characteristics

    > **Demographic** studies showed that in 2002, Hispanics had become the largest ethnic minority in the United States.

    > **Demographic** trends show a rise in the elderly population of the United States.

▶ *Related Words*

>   **demographics** (noun, plural)   U.S. *demographics* reveal that more people are choosing to remain single.
>
>   **demography** (noun)   (dĭ-mŏg′rə-fē)   The United States is working to update data on *demography* every year, rather than every ten years.
>
>   **demographer** (noun)   *Demographers* study the increases in lifespan of the U.S. population.

14. **epigram** (noun)   ĕp′ĭ-grăm′

From Greek: *epi-* (on) + *-gram* (write)

a short, clever saying, often in rhyme

>   Benjamin Franklin's **epigram** on loans is "He that goes a-borrowing, goes a-sorrowing."
>
>   One of playwright Oscar Wilde's famous **epigrams** is "I can resist anything but temptation."

15. **graphic** (adjective, noun)   grăf′ĭk

From Greek: *graph* (write) (*Graphe* meant "drawing, writing.")

referring to drawings or artistic writing (adjective)

>   Weather reports include **graphic** information.

described vividly or clearly (adjective)

>   **Graphic** scenes of sex or violence usually earn a film an "R" or "X" rating.
>
>   The eyewitness described the crime in **graphic** detail.

artistic design or drawing (noun)

>   The "swish" **graphic** has come to symbolize Nike.

scrib, script

16. **inscription** (noun)   ĭn-skrĭp′shən

From Latin: *in-* (in) + *script* (write)

carving or writing on a surface

>   The names of those who died in the Vietnam War are **inscribed** on a stone memorial in Washington, DC.
>
>   Antique dealers look for **inscriptions** on objects that identify their manufacturers and dates.

a signed message on a picture or in a book

> "Don't forget me, M. Goldberg" was the **inscription** the teacher wrote in her student's yearbook.

▶ *Related Word*

inscribe (verb)   (ĭn-skrīb′)   The winner's name is *inscribed* on the award.

> Atif, an excellent student who died in a car accident, is *inscribed* in professor Judy McDonald's memory. (In this sentence, *inscribe* is used in a nonphysical sense.)

17. **manuscript** (noun, adjective)   mǎn′yə-skrĭpt′

From Latin: *manu* (by hand) + *script* (write)

the original text of a book or article before publication (noun)

> Hoping to see his book in print, Lawrence sent his **manuscript** to several publishers.

> The original **manuscript** of *The Life and Times of Frederick Douglass* sold for several thousand dollars at a recent auction.

referring to writing done by hand, or printing (adjective)

> Beautiful medieval **manuscript** lettering took years to master.

> Children use **manuscript** writing until they learn cursive in the third grade.

The Library of Congress keeps the original *manuscript* of the Declaration of Independence and sometimes displays it. Like most texts, it was heavily edited. Written by Thomas Jefferson, it included eighty-six changes made by the Continental Congress.

---

18. **transcribe** (verb)   trǎn-skrīb′

From Latin: *trans-* (across) + *scrib* (write)

to make a complete written copy

> Medieval friars **transcribed** beautiful copies of manuscripts.

> Court reporters **transcribe** every word of a legal proceeding.

to copy something into another form

> The interview was **transcribed** into written form and posted on the Web site.

▶ *Related Words*

> **transcriber** (noun)   The *transcriber* turned the dictation into a letter.

> **transcription** (noun)   The musician made a *transcription* from the complex orchestral piece to a simpler piano composition. (A *transcription* is a change from one form to another.)

> **transcript** (noun)   We ordered a *transcript* of the TV interview. (A *transcript* is a written copy. It is also an official copy of a student's grades.)

Confusable Words

19. **affect** (verb)   ə-fĕkt′

to have an influence on; to change

> The moon **affects** ocean tides.

20. **effect** (noun)   ĭ-fĕkt′

a result

> The moon has an **effect** on ocean tides.

NOTE ON POSSIBLE CONFUSION: Try to remember that *affect* is usually a verb and *effect* is usually a noun, as in the following.

> The great teacher *affected* my life.

> The great teacher had an *effect* on my life.

▶ *Common Phrase*
effect on

Computers create dazzling special effects. But some effects use more humble tools, like food. Mixing water with milk made the rain more noticeable in the 1952 movie *Singing in the Rain*. The blood in the movie *Psycho* (1960) looks thick because the mixture contained Hershey's chocolate. And that awful sound we hear of bashing in heads in horror movies? It's a watermelon being hit by a hammer!

---

21. **conscience** (noun)   kŏn′shəns

sense of right and wrong; moral sense

> The child's guilty **conscience** made her return the candy bar she had stolen.

▶ *Related Word*
   conscientious (adjective) (kŏn′shē-ĕn′shəs)   Anna's good grades could largely be due to her *conscientious* note taking.

22. **conscious** (adjective)   kŏn′shəs

aware; awake

> We are not **conscious** when we sleep.
>
> Marsha was **conscious** of the tension in the room.

▶ *Common Phrase*
   conscious of

▶ *Related Word*
   consciousness (noun) The boy lost *consciousness* after the football accident.

NOTE ON POSSIBLE CONFUSION: Remember that *conscience* is a noun and *conscious* is an adjective, as in the following two sentences.

My *conscience* was bothering me.

I am *conscious* of my responsibility.

23. **imply** (verb)   ĭm-plī′

to suggest; to say something indirectly

> His tilted head and shy smile **implied** that he liked the pretty woman.

▶ *Related Word*
   implication (noun)   (ĭm′plĭ-kā′shən)   Professor Lois Daly feels that the TV series *Star Trek* has many religious *implications*.

24. **infer** (verb)   ĭn-fûr′

to conclude; to guess

> From his tilted head and shy smile, people **inferred** that he liked the pretty woman.

▶ *Related Words*
   inference (noun)   (ĭn′fər-əns)   The chemistry student drew an *inference* from the results of her experiment.
   inferential (adjective)   (ĭn′fə-rĕn′shəl)   This difficult problem requires *inferential* thinking.

James Joyce's book *Ulysses* was voted the most important book of the twentieth century by the prestigious Modern Library. About the same time, it was reported that many original copies of the book, given by Joyce to publishers and friends, had uncut pages. These pages, joined at the edges, would have needed to be separated to be read. This strongly *implies* that, indeed, the great masterpiece was not read. From the location of the uncut pages, we can *infer* that some people started the book, but read fewer than one hundred pages.

NOTE ON POSSIBLE CONFUSION: A speaker or writer *implies;* a listener or reader *infers*.

▶ *Common Phrase*
    draw an inference

Exercises

Part 2

■ *Definitions*

Match each word in the left-hand column with a definition from the right-hand column. Use each choice only once.

1. demographic ___k___

2. affect ___d___

3. inscription ___g___

4. infer ___i___

5. graphic ___l___

6. transcribe ___c___

7. conscious ___a___

8. imply ___e___

9. epigram ___f___

10. manuscript ___h___

a. aware

b. a sense of right and wrong

c. to make a complete written copy

d. to influence

e. to hint

f. short, witty saying

g. carving on a surface

h. text of a book before publication

i. to draw a conclusion

j. a result

k. referring to population statistics

l. referring to drawings or charts

■ *Words in Context*

Complete each sentence with the word that fits best. Use each choice only once.

a. demographic   e. manuscript   i. conscience
b. epigram   f. transcribe   j. conscious
c. graphic   g. affect   k. imply
d. inscription   h. effect   l. infer

1. "Little strokes fell great oaks" is an example of a(n) **b, epigram**.

2. I was not **j, conscious** that there was someone else in the room.

3. The executive asked her assistant to **f, transcribe** her dictation into written form.

4. The teenager had a guilty **i, conscience** after he lied to his parents.

5. I try not to let bad news **g, affect** my mood.

6. The description of the cold weather was so **c, graphic** that we began to shiver.

7. Anne of Cleves wrote this **d, inscription** in a book to Henry VIII: "When you look at this book, think of me."

8. We **l, infer** from the annoyed tone in your voice that you are angry with us.

9. The mayor was concerned about the **h, effect** of increasing the number of flights at the city airport.

10. The rare **e, manuscript** of the first edition of the book was on display at the library.

■ *Using Related Words*

Complete each sentence by using a word from the group of related words above it. You may need to capitalize a word when you write it in a sentence. Use each choice only once.

1. affect, effect

   Which has a greater **effect**_____ on a person, heredity or environment? In the 1800s and early 1900s, scientists believed that heredity had a far greater influence. Since then, environment has been

   shown to **affect**_____ people strongly. For example, in a study done by Skeels in the 1930s, when children placed in an orphanage were given loving attention, their IQs increased dramatically.

2. inscription, inscribed

   A seal, the personal symbol of an important individual, was once

   inscribed_____ into a ring. To sign a document, a circle of hot wax was dripped on it, and the ring was pressed into it so that the

   inscription_____ would show. The seal assured the reader that a letter was authentic.

3. demographics, demographic, demographers

   The report "**Demographic**_____ Trends in the Twentieth Century" reveals that the U.S. population multiplied four times between 1900

   and 2000. **Demographers**_____ also discovered that Florida's population grew more than that of any other state. Another trend in

   U.S. **demographics**_____ was that the percentage of minorities in the U.S. population had doubled.

4. consciences, conscientious

   Early Protestant settlers in America were said to have had a "Protestant

   work ethic." According to this ethic, their **consciences**_____ would bother them if they did not work hard enough. Thus, these people were

   often **conscientious**_____ workers.

5. infer, imply

When a plane crashes, the Federal Aviation Administration tries to

infer _____ the cause. An accident may be due to human or mechanical failure, and loss of life can be great. However, statistics

imply _____ that you are still safer riding in a plane than driving a car.

■ *True or False?*

Each of the following statements contains one or more words from this section. Read each sentence carefully and then indicate whether you think it is probably true or probably false. Your instructor may ask you to reword false statements to make them true.

T   1. If someone made a transcription of a manuscript, it would be copied.

T   2. Demographic trends have an effect on the population.

T   3. An inscription may be written.

T   4. To be conscious is to be aware.

F   5. Smiles imply sadness.

T   6. A person without a conscience is dangerous.

F   7. An epigram is long.

F   8. A graphic description is not very vivid.

T   9. Illness affects our health.

T   10. We infer feelings from the expressions on people's faces.

Chapter Exercises

■ *Practicing Strategies: New Words from Word Elements*

See how your knowledge of word elements can help you understand new words. Complete each sentence with the word that seems to fit best. Use each choice only once.

a. biography   e. hologram   i. revocalize
b. cardiogram   f. interlocution   j. script
c. dialogue   g. pictograph   k. sociology
d. dermatology   h. prescription   l. travelogue

1. A book written about someone's life is a(n) **a, biography** .

2. The written text for a play is a(n) **j, script** .

3. The study of skin, or "derma" is **d, dermatology** .

4. Since *cardio* means "heart," the picture of heartbeats is called a(n) **b, cardiogram** .

5. The study of society is called **k, sociology** .

6. When we "voice something again," we **i, revocalize** it.

7. A(n) **h, prescription** is something that must be written out before you can get medicine. (*Pre-* means "before.")

8. In a(n) **c, dialogue** , two people have a conversation.

9. A spoken account of a trip might be called a(n) **l, travelogue** .

10. Cavemen used **g, pictograph** writing based on pictures.

■ *Practicing Strategies: Combining Context Clues and Word Elements*

Combining the strategies of context clues and word elements is a good way to figure out the meaning of unknown words. In the following sentences, each italicized word contains a word element that you have studied in this chapter. Using the meaning of the word element and the context of the sentence, make an intelligent guess about the meaning of the italicized word. Your instructor may ask you to check the meaning in your dictionary when you have finished.

1. The *entomologist* specialized in ants, bees, and wasps.

   Entomologist means **scientist who studies insects** .

2. Delivering a *eulogy* in his brother's honor, Winston said many wonderful things about him.

   Eulogy means **speech, especially for someone who has died** .

3. A *scribe* once helped unschooled people who could not express themselves in writing.

   Scribe means **a person who writes things for people** .

4. At the *colloquium*, many people gave talks about the economy.

   Colloquium means **conference; meeting at which people come together to talk** .

5. Three people took part in the *interlocution*.

   Interlocution means **conversation; talk** .

■ *Companion Words*

Complete each sentence with the word that fits best. Choose your answers from the words below. You may use each word more than once.

Choices: of, on, from, to, draw, for

1. High winds are a prologue **to** a hurricane.

2. Gloomy days can have an effect **on** people's moods

3. After the revocation **of** civil liberties, people fled the country.

4. I am an advocate **of, for** equal pay for equal work.

5. We can **draw** an inference from evidence.

6. A mother is often conscious **of** her baby's every movement.

■ *Writing with Your Words*

This exercise will give you practice in writing effective sentences that use the vocabulary words. Each sentence is started for you. Complete it with an interesting phrase that also indicates the meaning of the italicized word.

1. I am a *vociferous* opponent of _____

_____.

2. My favorite *colloquial* expression is _____

_____.

3. The most *loquacious* person I know _____

_____.

4. The rare *manuscript* _____

_____.

5. I would *invoke* someone's aid if _____

_____.

6. People *imply* that others are stupid when _____

_____.

7. The awful *edict* _____

_____.

8. The witty *epigram* _____

_____.

9. The *demographic* makeup of the school _____

_____.

10. The *dictator* _____

_____.

■ *Making Connections*

These questions will help you relate the words you have learned in this chapter to your own life. Answer each question by writing a paragraph or more on a separate sheet of paper.

1. Describe something you have worked at conscientiously. Describe both what you did and the results of your work.

2. Under what conditions should a parent revoke a child's privileges? Be specific in your answers.

3. Think of something meaningful you might inscribe in a book that is a gift. Whom would you give it to, what would you say, and why?

Passage

Beautiful and Bright: The Life of Hedy Lamarr

*In the 1940s, Hedy Lamarr was called the most beautiful woman
in Hollywood. Today, she is remembered not only for her looks and movie
roles but also for inventing a system that revolutionized weaponry and cell
phone communication. Born in 1913, she was truly a woman ahead of her
time.*

Hedy Krisler was born into a wealthy family in Vienna, Austria.
Although she had the benefits of money, she had very little formal
education. Enchanted by movies, the sixteen-year-old Hedy appeared in
one that was quite **graphic.** People were shocked by a girl revealing her
body, and the film was banned in several countries, including the United
States.

Hedy's parents, perhaps worried about their wild child, pressured
her into marrying at the age of seventeen. They chose a wealthy weapons
manufacturer. As a young "trophy" wife, she accompanied him everywhere. **(1)** Unfortunately, he was **dictatorial** and never allowed her to be
alone. As a result, Hedy attended many meetings on the technical aspects
of manufacturing weapons. There she listened and learned.

Among the people she met was Adolf Hitler. Listening to the violent
dictator of Germany, **(2)** Hedy became **conscious** of his evil aims. She
heard enough to **infer** that he was plotting the destruction of the Jews,
Gypsies, and several other groups. **(3)** By 1936, **edicts** limiting the rights
of Jews and others had already been issued, and Hedy must have realized
that **(4)** this was but the **prologue** to an incredible level of hatred and violence. This especially alarmed her, for she was Jewish.

She decided she must escape from her husband. He had assigned a
maid to watch her day and night, and **(5)** Hedy knew she could not **contradict** his orders. So she gave the maid a sleeping potion, slipped out the
second-floor window, and took a train to London.

There, she met Louis B. Mayer, head of MGM studios. He agreed to
put her in movies, as long as she wouldn't appear in shocking films. On a
boat to the United States, Mayer renamed her "Hedy Lamarr," in honor of
a silent film star.

Lamarr was immediately put in films and her looks—if not her act-
ing—received rave reviews. But she was aware of the trouble Hitler was
brewing in Europe. Her **conscience** must have been heavy, when she
thought of the family she had left behind. In 1940, she met George
Antheil, a musician, at a party. **(6)** Both were **vociferously** anti-Nazi. This
unlikely pair agreed to work on a torpedo guidance system. Legend has it
that the idea was first written on a cocktail napkin, and that Lamarr wrote
her phone number on Antheil's windshield in lipstick.

The problem they tackled was that the flight of **(7)** U.S. torpedoes
could be **affected** by jammed radio frequencies. Since radios guided torpedoes, the torpedoes would miss their targets if the radio frequencies
were disabled. Lamarr and Antheil invented a "secret communication system" that allowed the guidance system to rapidly "hop" across radio frequencies. Antheil used his musical experience for invention; the system

used holes in a scroll like those of a player piano. Lamarr contributed the weaponry knowledge she had learned in Austria.

The pair approached the National Inventors' Council for help in obtaining a patent. **(8)** They **invoked** the aid of the chair, Charles F. Kettering. Of the several hundred thousand inventions offered to the society, theirs became one of the few to be granted a patent.

Almost immediately, the government declared the invention to be secret, "classified" information. Although this **implied** it was valuable, the invention remained unused in World War II. Antheil thought that it appeared amateurish because it was based on a player piano system. Lamarr asked to be put on an important committee, but instead, she was asked to sell her kisses for war bonds, like other Hollywood stars. Here **(9)** she proved herself such an effective **advocate** that she sold $7 million worth of bonds in one night!

After twenty years, the patent expired. Meanwhile, Lamarr had appeared in several minor movies, and had had a bumpy personal life. She was to have six unsuccessful marriages. As she stated, "Any girl can be glamorous—all you have to do is stand still and be stupid."

Soon after the patent had expired, a variation of Lamarr's system, called "spread spectrum," was used to guide weapons in Cuba. In 1985, the U.S. government declassified the information. Since then, the **effects** of Lamarr's idea have been seen in cellular phones, pagers, wireless Internet systems, and GPS guidance systems. All these things would be much more expensive and difficult to use were it not for her invention.

Lamarr never made a cent from her patent. Toward the end of her life, however, she received several honors as an inventor. The Canadian company that developed the technology gave her part ownership in its business. At long last, she and her partner started to receive recognition. Lamarr died on January 19, 2000, at age 86. **(10)** Today she is **inscribed** in our memory as a glamorous star, a brilliant inventor, and a dedicated patriot. As Lamarr said, "Films have a certain place in a certain time period. Technology is forever."

■ *Exercise*

Each numbered sentence below corresponds to a sentence in the Passage. Fill in the letter of the choice that makes the sentence mean the same thing as its corresponding sentence in the Passage.

1. Unfortunately, he was ____ *a* ____.
   a. authoritarian   b. cruel   c. absentminded   d. embarrassing

2. Hedy became ____ *c* ____ of his evil aims.
   a. fearful   b. anticipatory   c. aware   d. helpful

3. __d__ limiting the rights of people had been issued.
   a. Proposals   b. Introductions   c. Writings   d. Orders

4. This was the __d__ to hatred and violence.
   a. plotting   b. final point   c. taking back   d. introduction

5. Hedy knew she could not say something __c__.
   a. to agree   b. similar   c. opposite   d. informal

6. Both were __d__ anti-Nazi.
   a. totally   b. quietly   c. descriptively   d. loudly

7. The flight of U.S. torpedoes could be __b__ by jammed radio frequencies.
   a. resulted   b. changed   c. destroyed   d. saved

8. They __d__ the aid of the president.
   a. wanted   b. rejected   c. hinted at   d. called in

9. She was such an effective __a__ that she raised $7 million.
   a. supporter   b. beauty   c. woman   d. inventor

10. Today she is __c__ in our memories as a star, an inventor, and a patriot.
    a. aided   b. forgotten   c. written   d. hoped

■ *Discussion Questions*

1. What clues suggest that Lamarr was an intelligent person?

2. What do you think of Lamarr's U.S. patriotism?

3. How do you think her status as a female movie star affected the acceptance of Lamarr's invention?

◆ENGLISH IDIOMS

Speech and Writing

Many English idioms contain concepts of speech and writing. To *talk back* means to answer rudely. To *talk down to* is to speak to somebody as if he or she were stupid. However, to *talk up* something means to make it appear to be good. When we *talk big,* we boast, or brag, making something appear better than it actually is. When we *talk over* a problem, we discuss that problem for quite a while. To *talk* people *out of* something is to persuade them not to do it. A person might *talk a friend out of* quitting college.

When we *talk through our hats,* we don't know the facts but make unsupported or untrue statements anyway. When a person *sweet talks* someone else, he falsely flatters that person. On the other hand, when he *talks turkey* he speaks the truth frankly, or *tells it like it is.*

Writing also plays a part in our idioms. To do something *to the letter* is to do it exactly. When we say *"It's nothing to write home about,"* we mean we are not enthusiastic about something.

To see the *handwriting on the wall* is to realize that disaster is coming. In the Bible, Belshazzar, king of Babylon, saw a hand appear at a feast and write on the wall a cryptic message that only the Jewish prophet Daniel could understand. The message predicted the destruction of Belshazzar's kingdom.

REVIEW

Chapters 9–12

■ *Passage for Word Review*

Complete each blank in the Passage with the word or phrase that makes the best sense. The choices include words from the vocabulary lists along with related words. Use each choice only once.

WHY MY STEPFATHER WAS COURT-MARTIALED

a. affect	e. conspicuous	i. given carte blanche
b. audit	f. destitute	j. incredulous
c. beneficial	g. deviation	k. malevolent
d. centigrade	h. effect	l. verify

Background: This is a memorial tribute to the author's stepfather, Milton Markman. A few hours after this story was told to the author's vocabulary class, the elderly Mr. Markman collapsed unexpectedly and died.

In 1941, when my stepfather was drafted into the U.S. Army, he had no interest or experience in cooking. Therefore, he was

(1) <u>j, incredulous</u> when he was told that, on a written test, he had displayed a talent for preparing food. Army officials offered him a six-week course in becoming a chef. My stepfather accepted because he was sure he would be able to eat lots of leftovers.

As things turned out, he received good grades in cooking school. He

became head chef of an army kitchen and was **(2)** <u>i, given carte blanche</u> to run things as he wanted. All went well until he had to deal with spinach.

Because spinach contains many vitamins that are **(3)** <u>c, beneficial</u> to human health, the army supplied it several times per week. Unfortunately, the soldiers simply refused to eat it. Even seeing spinach on their plates put them in a bad mood. After many hours spent cooking spinach, my stepfather realized that, at the end of the meal, he was throwing all of it away. To save time and effort, he decided simply to dispose of the hated vegetable before it was cooked.

Unfortunately, one day a visiting army officer, passing through the

camp, noticed a large, **(4)** <u>e, conspicuous</u> pile of raw spinach in

the garbage. Another officer was sent out to **(5)** <u>l, verify</u>

that the first officer had seen everything correctly. Then an army

accountant made an official **(6)** **b, audit** _____ of the amount that was missing from the raw spinach supply. At the end of this investigation, the army accused my stepfather of destroying government property.

At his court-martial my stepfather told the army officers that his

intentions had not been **(7)** **k, malevolent** _____. Instead, he was simply trying to save the army the trouble of cooking the unwanted vegetable. Nevertheless, the army officers found him guilty and deducted five dollars from his pay for the next three months. Because he did not have much money, this loss of pay was enough to leave him

(8) **f, destitute** _____ for quite a while.

After the trial, however, one officer talked to my stepfather privately

and told him that cooking spinach would **(9)** **a, affect** _____ the way that the army thought about the vegetable. Raw spinach was government property, but cooked spinach was considered garbage. In other words, if the spinach was cooked, it could be thrown out.

From then on, my stepfather cooked all the spinach and then immediately put it into a garbage can. By following this procedure without any

(10) **g, deviation** _____, he kept everyone happy. The government did not have its property thrown out, and the soldiers did not have spinach on their plates.

■ *Reviewing Words in Context*

Complete each sentence with the word or term that fits best.

AN ETHIOPIAN'S JOURNEY TO THE UNITED STATES

a. ambivalence	e. conscious	i. destitute	m. incredulous
b. benefactors	f. creed	j. edict	n. introspect
c. beneficial	g. decades	k. empathy	o. malady
d. bilingual	h. defiant	l. expedite	p. nonchalant

Background: Semir, a student in the author's class, tells the story of his family's journey from Ethiopia to Saudi Arabia and the United States.

1. Ethiopia, my home, is not like the United States. It is an underdeveloped

country, with many **i, destitute** _____ people who live in poverty.

2. For three **g, decades**_____, almost thirty years, there was civil war in my homeland.

3. A(n) **j, edict**_____ ordered all young men into the army; to avoid this, my father escaped to Saudi Arabia.

4. As a teenager, my mother must have been **h, defiant**_____ to some authority, for she spent some time in prison.

5. My aunt was **e, conscious**_____ that my mother was in danger when she left prison, so she worked to get her out of Ethiopia.

6. My aunt tried hard to **l, expedite**_____ her departure. My mother went to Saudi Arabia and married my father.

7. I was raised in Saudi Arabia and so I was **d, bilingual**_____, since I spoke Tigrinya and Arabic.

8. Originally, my mother was a Christian, but she now follows the Muslim **f, creed**_____.

9. When we came to the United States, I was surprised and delighted by the **k, empathy**_____ that other Ethiopian immigrants felt for us.

10. We had many **b, benefactors**_____ who gave us things to make our lives easier.

11. Watching TV shows like *Sesame Street* was **c, beneficial**_____ to my English.

12. People are often **m, incredulous**_____ when I tell them that I spent only two weeks in English as a Second Language classes in high school!

13. In more thoughtful moods, I **n, introspect**_____ about my life in the United States.

14. Although people are richer here, I feel some **a, ambivalence**_____ about all of the freedom in the United States and the lifestyles of the people.

15. At times, people in the United States seem **p, nonchalant**_____ about family life; but in Ethiopia people care deeply about family ties.

■ *Reviewing Learning Strategies*

New Words from Word Elements   Below are some words you have not studied that are formed from Greek or Latin word elements. Using your knowledge of these elements, write in the letter of the word that best completes each sentence. Use each choice only once. You may have to capitalize some words.

a. accredited   e. dictaphone   i. scribble
b. audiologist   f. graphemes   j. telepathy
c. biometrics   g. microphobia   k. uniped
d. binary   h. malediction   l. verdict

1. A fear of germs and microbes is <u>g, microphobia</u>.

2. Sensing or feeling from far away is <u>j, telepathy</u> because *tele-* means "far."

3. A(n) <u>k, uniped</u> is an animal that walks on one foot.

4. A(n) <u>b, audiologist</u> is a specialist in the study of measuring hearing.

5. The written word f-a-n has three <u>f, graphemes</u>.

6. A(n) <u>h, malediction</u> is "bad speech," or a curse.

7. A jury is said to "speak the truth" when it gives a(n) <u>l, verdict</u>.

8. Something <u>d, binary</u> consists of two parts.

9. <u>c, Biometrics</u> is the branch of science that takes statistical data, or measurements, on living things.

10. We can believe in the skill of a doctor or dentist who is <u>a, accredited</u>.

Answers to Quizzes

Chapter 1

Quiz Yourself
Page 8   altruistic—false; novice—false; frugal—true; intrepid—true

Page 13   1. noun, transitive verb, intransitive verb   2. 2, as a noun   3. Old French

Chapter 2

Quiz Yourself
Page 40   chaotic—false; thrive—true; supplant—true; cartel—false

Page 42   1. The Bruins were losing, 3-1, but, to the Rangers' surprise, the Bruins ended up winning the ice hockey game, 4-3.   2. Ohio, not Penn, was expected to win. The game was tied at the end, so it went into overtime. Penn won.   3. The Bulls had been playing away from their home town and had been losing games. They won this game, which was also away from home, by a lot.

Page 43   1. b   2. a   3. c

Page 43   1. b   2. a

Page 44   1. face   2. annoyance; problem

Page 44   1. replaced   2. agreement

Chapter 3

Quiz Yourself
Page 72   boisterous—true; harassed—false; flaunt—false; chagrined—true

Page 74   1. having indented curves   2. severe   3. a heavy knitted cloth

Page 75   1. (really) shocked   2. energetic   3. doubting

Page 85   1. c   2. e   3. d   4. a   5. f   6. b

Chapter 4

Quiz Yourself

Page 102   pinnacle—true; accolade—true; adulation—false; mammoth—false

Page 103   1. c 2. a 3. d 4. e 5. b

Page 104   1. a person who is outgoing toward others and seeks their company
2. hatred 3. horrible, terrible, worthy of hatred

Page 105   1. careful 2. resist, tolerate, bear 3. required

Page 116   1. poor 2. has died 3. dumb 4. painful 5. lied

Part 2   Introduction

Page 139   Reaction—prefix "re-"; root "act"; suffix "-ion"
Unlikely—prefix "un-"; root "like"; suffix "-ly"
Exchanges—prefix "ex-"; root "change"; suffix "s"
Reviewing—prefix "re-"; root "view"; suffix "-ing"
Invisibly—prefix "in"; root "visible"; suffix "-ly"

Chapter 5

Quiz Yourself

Page 142   interminable—false; impartial—true; exploit—true; equilibrium—true

Page 143   1. d 2. a 3. c

Pages 144–145   remarry—marry again; insecure—not secure; equidistant—equal in distance

Pages 145–146   revive—to live again; incredulous—not believing

Page 158   1. b 2. c 3. d 4. f 5. e 6. a

Chapter 6

Quiz Yourself

Page 178   vivacious—false; congenital—true; maverick—false; psychosomatic—false

Page 179   1. b 2. e 3. d 4. c 5. a

Page 185   1. a 2. b 3. e 4. c 5. f 6. d

Chapter 7

Quiz Yourself
Page 211   jettison—true;   staunch—false;   status quo—false;   perverse—false

Page 228   1. c   2. h   3. f   4. b   5. g   6. a   7. e   8. d

Chapter 8

Quiz Yourself
Page 245   contemporaries—false;   cliché—false;   discord—true;   zenith—false

Page 262   1. a   2. c   3. d   4. e   5. b   6. f

Chapter 9

Quiz Yourself
Page 281   metric—false;   integrity—false;   ambiguous—false;   dilemma—true

Page 283   a. two   b. three   c. four   d. five   e. six   f. seven

Chapter 10

Quiz Yourself
Page 315   veracity—true;   defiant—false;   claustrophobic—true;   star-crossed—false

Page 316   catty—mean, vicious gossip;   birdbrain—stupid or foolish person;   lionize—idolize, worship;   dinosaur—out of date, old;   can of worms—having lots of problems;   puppy love—childish, youthful love;   hogwash—nonsense, silly, worthless talk

Page 322   1. a   2. d   3. c   4. b

Chapter 11

Quiz Yourself
Page 345   pathetic—false;   malady—true;   benign—false;   expedite—false

Page 346   1. a   2. b   3. d   4. c

Chapter 12

Quiz Yourself
Page 376   contradict—false;   vociferous—true;   monologue—true;   demographic—false

Index of Words, Word Elements, and Idioms

Word elements are printed in italics.

Subject Index